Now You See It
and Other Essays on Design
Michael Bierut

Princeton Architectural Press
New York

Published by
Princeton Architectural Press
A McEvoy Group company
202 Warren Street, Hudson, New York 12534

Visit our website at www.papress.com.

Editor: Sara Stemen

Special thanks to: Janet Behning, Nolan Boomer,
Nicola Brower, Abby Bussel, Barbara Darko, Benjamin
English, Jan Cigliano Hartman, Lia Hunt, Valerie Kamen,
Simone Kaplan-Senchak, Jennifer Lippert, Sara McKay,
Eliana Miller, Rob Shaeffer, Sara Stemen, Paul Wagner,
and Joseph Weston of Princeton Architectural Press —
Kevin C. Lippert, publisher

Library of Congress Cataloging-in-Publication Data
Names: Bierut, Michael, author.
Title: Now you see it and other essays on design/
Michael Bierut.
Description: First edition. | New York : Princeton
Architectural Press, 2017.| Includes bibliographical
references and index.
Identifiers: LCCN 2017020824 | ISBN 9781616896249
(hardback)
Subjects: LCSH: Commercial art—United States. | Graphic
arts—United States. | BISAC: DESIGN / Graphic Arts /
General. | DESIGN / Essays.
Classification: LCC NC998.5.A1 B45 2017 | DDC 741.6—dc23
LC record available at https://lccn.loc.gov/2017020824

CONTENTS

**And suddenly, with the terrible clarity
of a man too long deceived,
Leamas understood the whole ghastly trick.**

John le Carré
The Spy Who Came in from the Cold
1963

PREFACE

I may have become a graphic designer because I was a frustrated writer. I liked the paintings in the Cleveland Museum of Art, but I liked the posters in the gift shop even more. Somehow, the combination of words and images seemed exciting and purposeful. The paintings waited quietly upstairs in the gallery; the posters mixed it up with the crowds on the street. Words made art come alive. Combining words and pictures gave form to ideas.

Some of my earliest creative efforts were homemade publications, handmade knockoffs of favorite magazines like *Mad* or *Cracked*. It helped that my father was a salesman for a company that sold printing equipment. One day he took one of my self-authored one-off comic books to work and returned with a box full of copies. Xerox machines were still a rarity, and the mimeographic copier at my local library was expensive (a quarter a page) and produced blurry reproductions on faintly greasy paper. My dad's print run was a miracle: crisp and authoritative, not to mention great-smelling. The power of mass production conferred its own authority. Many years later I read an interview with one of my heroes, the artist Ed Ruscha, who described funding his own publishing efforts:

Cornelia Butler and Margit Rowell, *Cotton Puffs, Q-Tips, Smoke and Mirrors: The Drawings of Ed Ruscha* (New York: Whitney Museum of Art, 2004).

"It is almost worth the money to have the thrill of seeing four hundred exactly identical books stacked in front of you." I still get that thrill every time.

I was once asked if it was important for a graphic designer to know how to draw. I answered that I'd prefer one who knew how to read. Typography is the fundamental starting point for our work. Letterforms together become words, then sentences, then paragraphs, all in the service of communicating ideas. When you design a logotype, the name of the client is usually nonnegotiable. And often the name has the design within it. The right sequence of letters can almost design themselves. On the other hand, an unlucky grouping may look wrong no matter what you do. Graphic designers working with text serve as casting directors when they pick a typeface. What kind of characters do you want to speak these lines?

Perhaps because of this intimate connection between graphic design and language, reading and writing have had a different relationship to graphic design than to other design disciplines. Writers are inevitably participants — active or unwitting — in the graphic design process. And every reader on earth, whether the text is an eight-hundred-page book or a four-letter exit sign, is undergoing an experience orchestrated by a (usually invisible) graphic designer. Words are at once the designer's raw materials and reason for being, simultaneously a means to an end and the end itself. I am suspicious of any graphic designer who is not an enthusiastic reader.

When I began writing about graphic design, it was with all the self-consciousness that only a lifelong manipulator of letterforms could bring to the task. I was not very good at the beginning, and even now it is a painful process. In my professional life as a graphic designer, I have been supported by an army of enablers. When I sit down to write, I am entirely on my own. But I have been lucky to have had good editors and collaborators, including Steven Heller, Chee Pearlman, Rick Poynor, Bill Drenttel, and Jessica Helfand. I've also been grateful for (and recommend) advice from seasoned writers like William Zinsser (on the importance of having something to say), Anne Lamott (on how to face a terrifying blank page), and (of course) E. B. White (on omitting needless words, something I still hate to do). There are few things I get to do all by myself. Writing is one of them. That's what makes it so nerve-racking and so gratifying.

The oldest piece in this book is almost thirty years old. In 1989 graphic design was still territory that was largely unexplored by writers and critics. The profession's trade magazines were beautifully illustrated but mostly stuck to laudatory profiles. The first substantial history of the field, Philip Meggs's *History of Graphic Design*, was barely five years old. And the notion that things like logos and posters and typefaces might be written about in a way that would make them interesting to a general audience would have seemed naive, if not downright laughable.

Today anyone with a software program with a pull-down font menu and a coffee shop with free wireless has the capacity to create and publish things that would have astonished my nine-year-old comic-book-drawing self. Contact with the means of production has made people more interested in the mechanics of graphic design. As a result, there is more written about graphic design every day — from long, thoughtful essays to 140-character bursts — than I ever would have dreamed possible. This attention to the ways that messages are shaped has the potential to make each of us a more critical consumer of mass communication. Each of us is a publisher. Each of us is a critic. Each of us lives in a world that's inundated with misinformation, half-truths, and fake news, so much of it beautifully packaged and beguilingly delivered. Thinking hard about the forms that ideas take may be the most important kind of thinking of all.

To Dorothy, Liz, Drew, and Martha

From Drawing Board to Desktop

In 1972, when I was a sophomore in high school in suburban Cleveland, Ohio, I was asked to do a poster for our drama club's production of *Arsenic and Old Lace*. I found a nice, big piece of cardboard, did the most elaborate piece of hand lettering I could manage with a couple of black felt-tipped pens, and turned it in to the play's director. That was on a Friday. When I arrived for class on Monday morning, my poster was hanging in every hallway, in every stairwell, and on every bulletin board in the school. Among my peers I was considered a good artist and was used to getting compliments for my work, but the miracle of mass production took things to a different level altogether. More people saw my poster than would actually see the play. It was at that moment that I decided to become a graphic designer. My dream was to design album covers for rock bands.

I majored in graphic design at the University of Cincinnati's College of Design, Architecture, and Art. Most of my classmates were like me: good high-school artists who had discovered that it might be possible to do art for a living. The tools we used were more sophisticated than felt-tipped pens, but for the most part my studio classes wouldn't have looked unfamiliar to a student at the École des Beaux-

Originally appeared as "Drawing Board to the Desktop: A Designer's Path," *New York Times*, February 7, 2009.

Arts one hundred years earlier. My fiancée was getting a business degree, and for her classes she had to work with computers. This involved long hours of entering data on keypunch cards, which she would carry to the university's mainframe computer for processing. Hours later she would get a big sheaf of accordion-folded printouts in return. I remember tagging along on some of these tedious late-night expeditions and being grateful that I was going into design. Thank God: I'd never have to worry about those boring computers. My T square and I were inseparable.

I started my career in New York working as an assistant designer for Massimo Vignelli, the designer of the Bloomingdale's logo and the classic geometric New York subway map. If you worked in a design studio in 1980, you were surrounded by colored paper, rubber cement, X-ACTO knives, and cans of aerosol spray glue. Our work was done by hand, whether it was a symbol, an annual report, a book design, or a poster. It was messy and occasionally smelly. What we did was a craft, like making a perfect pineapple upside-down cake. Even for an experienced designer, doing simple things demanded methodical, even surgical, procedures. If a client wanted a revision, it generally took overnight. If the client was in a different time zone, it might take days. Mistakes were time-consuming, costly, and occasionally even dangerous: every designer my age has at least one scar as a souvenir of a long-ago late-night slipup with an X-ACTO knife. Being a good designer was one thing. Attaining the physical mastery it took to execute a complex design was something else altogether.

And, like every design studio those days, we sat in the middle of a complex ecosystem of other businesses: typesetters, retouchers, paper makers, printers. All of these were based squarely in the physical world, whether it was molten lead, rumbling airbrush compressors, or enormous, greasy Heidelberg presses. As I got better at my job, I spent less time with my T square and my wooden drawing board and more time in meetings with clients. Still, I was proud that when a deadline was threatening I could jump in and knock out a flawless pasteup as fast as any kid in the office. Like a chef, I brought my knives with me.

One day some carpenters came in our open-plan studio and started framing up some walls. Behind those walls we were about to start on a top-secret project for a top-secret client. The client was IBM, and the project was the packaging for the introduction of their line of brand-new personal computers. Like everyone else in the office, I assumed that these machines were just fancy hybrids of typewriters and calculators. We did all the artwork for the packaging with rubber cement, colored paper, and paint. We had no idea, but we were looking at the beginning of the end, and the end came quick.

Nearly forty years later, I'm a partner in the New York office of an international design consultancy, Pentagram. We do everything from logos to websites, exhibitions and architecture, products and posters. There are about eighty designers in our office on Fifth Avenue. Every single one of them spends the better part of every day in front of a big monitor. Not one has a drawing board. Design work that would have taken me a week in 1980 can now be done on a personal computer in less than an hour. Cutting and pasting, when necessary, is a special task performed in the basement, often by interns. I get the impression that this kind of work, to which I once applied myself with the pride and intensity of a master chef, is now regarded as a chore akin to dishwashing. Design school graduates are now more likely to have spent their high-school years manipulating software programs instead of drawing on bristol board. They want to get out of the basement and up to the computers, where the real action is.

The technology we have at our disposal is dazzling, and our efficiency is such that clients have come to expect fast solutions and near-instantaneous revisions and updates. We are proud to deliver them. Still, I wonder if we haven't lost something in the process: the deliberation that comes with a slower pace, the attention to detail required when mistakes can't be undone with the click of a mouse. Younger designers hearing me talk this way react as though I'm getting sentimental about the days we all used to churn our own butter.

Not wanting to be dismissed as a Luddite, I keep quiet about these things. Still, I keep one tool at my desk that dates from the good old days: my T square. I use it to scratch my back.

Learning to Draw with Jon Gnagy

Originally published in *AIGA Journal 7*, no. 3, 1989.

In the early 1960s, St. Theresa's, my grade school alma mater in Garfield Heights, Ohio, had no art program. The official reason was that the diocese's spartan budgets precluded activities deemed "nonessential." I suspected the severe and terrifying Ursuline nuns that ran the place probably felt uncomfortable teaching subjects without clear right and wrong answers. Yes, a few more hours of catechism every week would do our immortal souls more good. Besides, the chaos of paint, paper, and paste was more typical of the moral slackness and outright nihilism St. Theresa's associated with public school kids, who got to wear whatever they wanted to school and probably had alcoholic parents to boot.

My only clue that I had nascent art ability came from my first-grade teacher, a popular "lay instructor" named Mrs. Kinola. She was impressed with some drawings I had done of classroom objects as part of a spelling exercise and sent them home to my parents with a note on the order of "Mike looks like he might be a real artist!"

But what did this mean? As far as I knew, there were no artists in Garfield Heights. Most of the adults

I knew were either housewives or men who did things involving large machines.

Like many of my friends, I liked to get up early on Saturday mornings, say five thirty or so. The shows on before the cartoons had an eerily tragic aspect. Even then I could sense that those time slots were some sort of neglected holding cells for unwanted programs.

That's where I discovered Jon Gnagy. Although I had never seen an artist, I know immediately that Jon Gnagy was one. There he was on television, standing in front of an easel, wearing a coarse flannel shirt and sporting a goatee. This last detail seemed especially telling, as I had never seen a living person with facial hair in my life; beards were for people like Abraham Lincoln or Jesus. Jon Gnagy was, like them, definitely not of Garfield Heights.

On each episode of his show, *Learn to Draw with Jon Gnagy*, he would demonstrate, step by step, how to make a drawing. The viewer was meant to follow along at home. Electrified by my discovery of this potential mentor, I joined in enthusiastically. I still remember his authority, lack of condescension, and patience as he showed how a blank piece of paper could be methodically transformed into a still life, landscape, or portrait. I vowed to reorganize my schedule around this program.

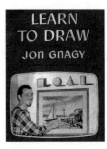

Jon Gnagy, *Learn to Draw with Jon Gnagy: America's Television Art Instructor* (New York: Arthur Brown and Bro., 1950).

After watching in rapture for several weeks, I began to make some realizations. First, the most striking quality of Gnagy's work was its realism, a characteristic all the more miraculous because the drawings were created (more or less) right before your eyes. Circles became ripe apples. Squares, cozy little farmhouses. But it sometimes happened too quickly to follow; the most dramatic transformations seemed to occur during the commercials.

Second, art appeared to require specialized tools. Gnagy referred regularly to special pencils and chalks, not to mention something called a "kneaded" eraser and a baffling item called a "paper stomp." I gamely played along at home with my No. 2 Mongol and shirt cardboards, but it soon became obvious that I was in over my head. The solution was a boxed kit advertised on each episode that contained all the necessary implements, as well as an instruction book. After much campaigning by me and, no doubt, much research by my parents, I got the official *Learn to Draw* kit for Christmas.

The tools it contained were wonderful, but the revelation was the instruction book. I carried my copy everywhere for two years, studying every detail with a fervor that would have impressed the nuns at St. Theresa's. With the book I was no longer bound to the television show, the schedule of which had gotten more and more irregular. Some weeks it wasn't on at all. No matter: I had the book. I attempted each drawing at least once (including the impossible *Harlequin Dane*, "the aristocrat of dogs.") My favorites, like *Whistle Stop* and *RFP America*, were repeated over and over until I knew them by heart, like a piano student with "Moonlight Sonata."

I recently discovered a copy of *Learn to Draw with Jon Gnagy* in a New York art supply store. Although it appeared to be a recently printed edition, it was completely — I guarantee, *completely* — unchanged from the book I had dog-eared so relentlessly back in Garfield Heights. As I turned the pages, I grew more and more dizzy with déjà vu; the effect each image had on me far exceeded anything the smell of madeleines would have had on Marcel Proust.

The seven drawings were particularly potent. Seeing *Covered Bridge*, for instance ("a scene that features depth by use of 'aerial perspective'"), I realized that single image constituted my total experience with that particular subject. In other words, although I could have sworn otherwise, I have never seen a covered bridge in real life. Other designers of a certain age have similar memories. "Did you have Jon Gnagy when you were little?" I will ask. A positive response invariably takes the form of a dreamy, unfocused look, and a murmured, "Oh, God, that drawing of the Great Dane."

The one thing that impresses me most about Jon Gnagy now, though, isn't an image or a drawing. It's a particular attitude about art, specifically the idea that it could be demystified. I expected Gnagy's book, some many years later, to be quaint and comical. Instead, it seems sincere and heartfelt. His goal was "to help you awaken that hidden talent so you may find happiness and genuine fun in the world around you through the hobby of drawing and painting."

Perhaps, in the end, Jon Gnagy drove me out of the world of fine art and into graphic design. I eventually became a good artist by high-school standards, which basically meant I could draw realistically. Gnagy knew all along that this is what we all secretly want to do, and so he taught drawing in terms of design: a circle that had to become a pumpkin was just another problem to be solved. And there was a secret to the process—nothing mysterious—and it was promised on page three of the instruction book: "ON THE NEXT PAGE IS THE SECRET OF REALISTIC DRAWING."

And sure enough, turn the page, and there it was: "SHADING IS THE SECRET OF REALISTIC DRAWING."

By the time I got to college, I could shade the hell out of anything, but realistic drawing was considered a pretty cheap commodity. What was valued in the fine arts department seemed to be self-expression, or individuality, or passion, or something mysterious like that. Graphic design, on the other hand, was taught in the tradition of Jon Gnagy: methodical, straightforward, and, to quote the man himself, "genuine fun." So I became a graphic designer. And to my fine-artist friends, especially the most eccentric and broodingly tormented, I ask, What's the mystery? It's all on page four.

This Is
My Process

First appeared in
Design Observer,
September 9, 2006.

For over twenty years, I've been writing proposals for projects. And almost every one of them has a passage somewhere that begins something like this: "This project will be divided in four phases: Orientation and Analysis, Conceptual Design, Design Development, and Implementation." All clients want this. Sometimes there are five phases, sometimes six. Sometimes they have different names. But it's always an attempt to answer a potential client's unavoidable question: Can you describe the process you use to create a design solution that's right for us?

The other day I was looking at a proposal for a project I finished a few months ago. The result, by my measure and by the client's, was successful. But guess what? The process I so reassuringly put forward at the outset had almost nothing to do with the way the project actually went. What would happen, I wonder, if I actually told the truth about what happens in a design process?

It might go something like this:

When I do a design project, I begin by listening carefully to you as you talk about your problem and read whatever background material I can find that relates to the issues you face. If you're lucky, I have also accidentally acquired some firsthand experience with your situation. Somewhere along the way an idea for the design pops into my head from out of the blue. I can't really explain that part; it's like magic. Sometimes it even happens before you have a chance to tell me that much about your problem! Now, if it's a good idea, I try to figure out some strategic justification for the solution so I can explain it to you without relying on good taste you may or may not have. Along the way, I may add some other ideas, either because you made me agree to do so at the outset, or because I'm not sure of the first idea. At any rate, in the earlier phases hopefully I will have gained your trust so that by this point you're inclined to take my advice. I don't have any clue how you'd go about proving that my advice is any good except that other people — at least the ones I've told you about — have taken my advice in the past and prospered. In other words, could you just sort of, you know... trust me?

I actually wrote this passage in frustration after repeatedly attempting to devise wording for a "universal" client proposal.

Now, an intelligent client might ask a number of reasonable questions: How can a bunch of random conversations yield the information you need to do your work? Shouldn't the strategic justification be in place before the design work begins? If you show me one solution, how will I know it's the only one that will work? On the other hand, if you show me a bunch of solutions, how will I know which one is best? What will happen if I don't like any of them? Finally, can you explain that magic part to me again?

Not only that, but my "honest" description of the process is an idealized one. Sometimes I have one great idea but can't convince the client it's great and I have to do more ideas. Sometimes this leads to a better idea. Sometimes it leads to a worse idea. Sometimes after I go back and explore other ideas we all come back to the original idea. Sometimes the client accepts an idea and then produces other people who haven't been involved up to that point who end up having opinions of their own. One way or another it always seems to get done, but never as originally promised.

Although I've managed to enjoy a relatively successful career as a designer, I've always had the vague sense that I was doing something wrong. A better designer would be able to able to manage the process properly, moving everyone along cheerfully from Phase One to Phase Two, right on schedule and right on budget. What was wrong with me?

You may have had the same feeling; it seems to be pretty common among the designers I know. Then, this past summer, I was lucky enough to participate in AIGA's

Since 2008 this
program has been
offered in partnership
with the Yale
University School
of Management.

Robert Austin and Lee
Devin, *Artful Making:
What Managers Need
to Know about
How Artists Work*
(Upper Saddle River, NJ:
Financial Times
Prentice Hall, 2003).

Business Perspectives for Creative Leaders program at Harvard Business School (which I highly recommend, by the way). Part of the assigned reading was a book that one of the instructors, Rob Austin, wrote with Lee Devin called *Artful Making: What Managers Need to Know about How Artists Work. Artful Making* has an interesting message: we may have been right all along.

What makes the book particularly interesting is the collaboration of the two coauthors. Austin is a Harvard Business School professor who has focused on information technology management; Devin is not a business school teacher but a professor of theater at Swarthmore College. At the outset, the writers acknowledge that the nature of work is changing in the twenty-first century, characterizing it as "a shift from an industrial economy to an information economy, from physical work to knowledge work." In trying to understand how this new kind of work can be managed, they propose a model based not on industrial production, but on the collaborative arts, specifically theater. Interestingly, the process of mounting a play is not that different from doing a design project. The iterative process, the role of improvisation, the adjustments that are made in response to audience feedback, all of these elements are a part of any design process. And, in a way, they've always been the ones that have been vaguely unnerving to me.

Evidently, this unease is common. The authors take pains to point out that they're not advocating a "loose" process or one that lacks rigor. "A theater company," Austin and Devin point out, "consistently delivers a valuable, innovative product under the pressure of a very firm deadline (opening night, eight o'clock curtain). The product, a play, executes again and again with great precision, incorporating significant innovations every time, but finishing within thirty seconds of the same length every time." They are careful to identify the defining characteristics of this kind of work: allowing solutions to emerge in a process of iteration, rather than trying to get everything right the first time; accepting the lack of control in the process and letting the improvisation engendered by uncertainty help drive the process; and creating a work environment that sets clear enough limits that people can play securely within them. They call this artful making: in short, "any activity that involves creating something entirely new." This includes not just the obvious "arty" things, but, for instance, "a successful response to an unexpected move

See also my favorite
book, Moss Hart's
Act One (New York:
Random House, 1959).

by a competitor" or "handling a sudden problem caused by a supplier."

Over nearly two hundred pages, Austin and Devin make a persuasive case — a vigorous argument, really — for a process that most designers would find familiar. I read the book, in fact, with a certain degree of smugness: we already know all this stuff, I kept thinking. More interesting to me was the tone that the authors take with their presumed reader, a kind of imaginary Old School Boss. Addicted to flow charts and timelines. Suspicious of ambiguity, unexpected outcomes, and, especially, artists. You know the type. That's who they're addressing when they say, almost consolingly, "We know our industrial age thought patterns intimately. We're comfortable with them. We love them because they are so successful for us..." Hey, who do they mean, "we"?

I was still feeling a little superior a few weeks later, attending one of Rob Austin's sessions at the AIGA HBS program. He was talking about his book and showing a slide that compared two processes. On the left was a diagram of the iterative, cyclical process used to develop software at a company that Austin admires, Trilogy. On the right was a sequential process, with arrows leading in turn from "Concept Generation" to "Product Planning" to "Product Engineering" to "Process Engineering" to "Production Process." This diagram was labeled "Clark and Fujimoto's Description of the Automaking Process."

I'll be damned if I've ever heard of Clark or Fujimoto, but the thing on the right looked eerily familiar. For good reason: I've used a version of it in hundreds of proposals over the years. I never really believed it was an accurate way to describe the process. I simply never had the confidence to describe the process in any other way. Like a lot of designers, I've considered my real process my little secret. With their work, Rob Austin and Lee Devin provide a new way not to think about what we do, but to help others understand it.

Kim B. Clark (president of Brigham Young University-Idaho and former dean of Harvard Business School) and Takahiro Fujimoto (professor of the Faculty of Economics at the University of Tokyo) are influential theorists in industrial technology and operations management.

Donal McLaughlin's Little Button

First appeared in
Design Observer,
July 25, 2007.
Originally appeared
in a different form in
Yale Alumni Magazine.

When Donal McLaughlin graduated from the Yale School
of Architecture in 1933, the centerpiece of his portfolio
was a design for an observatory in New York's Central Park,
a domed building — "one big circle," he remembered
much later — that would provide a window on the heavens.

His observatory was never built. But little did he
know then that his most famous design would be another
circular form, something you and countless people around
the world have seen millions of times over the past half
century: the emblem of the United Nations.

I had never heard of Donal McLaughlin when I got
a call from Mark Branch, executive editor of the *Yale Alumni
Magazine*, asking if I'd like to interview him for an upcoming
issue. I said yes, and a few weeks later, I found myself talking
to a designer with a career that had placed him at the center
of some of the major events of the twentieth century.

That career began inauspiciously. "It was the height
of the depression. Architects were not working anywhere,"
he told me. Luckily, an old friend in Washington got him a job
at the National Park Service. His park work led to positions
in the offices of industrial designers Walter Dorwin Teague
and Raymond Loewy, where he worked on exhibits for the

1939 New York World's Fair for Kodak and Chrysler. There he learned he was good at something: making complicated information understandable. A few months before Pearl Harbor, Washington called again.

"'Wild Bill' Donovan" — the storied head of the Office of Strategic Services, predecessor to the Central Intelligence Agency — "was looking for some designers to create a war room for FDR, using the kinds of advanced techniques we'd developed for the World's Fair. It was to be built underneath the White House." The subterranean war room was never built, but excited by the potential of the experience, McLaughlin left private practice, moved back to Washington, and joined the OSS's Presentation Branch as chief of their graphics division.

Throughout the war, McLaughlin's services were constantly in demand. His group designed films, displays, insignia, and diagrams, work he remains proud of to this day. "My time at Yale and my time at the OSS were really the great standout years of my life," he says now. "We weren't advertisers. We weren't trying to sell anything. Our whole message during the war was simply to take information and put it into forms that people could easily understand."

This was an era when the country's best designers were eager to put their talents in the service of their nation in a way that is, sadly, almost unimaginable today. McLaughlin's colleagues included a who's who of postwar American design: architect Eero Saarinen, stage designer Jo Mielziner, landscape designer Dan Kiley, and pioneering African American graphic designer Georg Olden. Nothing seems to have been out of bounds: toward the war's end, for instance, McLaughlin's team created not only the visual displays that were used to convict Nazi war criminals in the Nuremberg trials but the distinctive arrangement of the courtroom itself.

Around that same time, McLaughlin was given his most memorable assignment. The US State Department announced its intention to convene the United Nations Conference on International Organization in San Francisco in June 1945, and the OSS's Presentation Branch was asked to create displays, certificates, maps, guides for the delegates, and one seemingly modest thing. "It was my good fortune," McLaughlin told me, "to be assigned the problem of designing a lapel pin for conference identification." He went through dozens of designs, struggling with the challenge of accommodating a suitable image with the

Rumors persist that the fabled "war room" in fact exists, and no less than Ronald Reagan asked to see it on his first tour of the White House in January 1981. (Tom Dewe Mathews, "To the War Room!" *Guardian*, November 14, 2001.)

Emblem for the
United Nations, Donal
McLaughlin, 1945.

conference's name, date, and location, all in a one-and-one-sixteenth-inch-diameter circle. His solution was what McLaughlin describes as "an azimuthally equidistant projection showing all the countries in one circle," flanked by crossed olive branches. It appeared not only on the delegates' pins but was stamped in gold on the cover of the United Nations Charter. On June 26, the charter was signed by delegates of fifty nations, and the United Nations was established. Donal McLaughlin, without fully intending to, had designed its emblem.

Talking with McLaughlin, I found myself thinking of that little pin. At the time, it must have seemed like a little job, almost the kind of thing an ambitious designer would consider a nuisance. We've all done projects like that, often with teeth gritted. There's a lesson here: you never know what might happen to those little jobs.

After the war, McLaughlin returned to private practice in Washington. His long career has included many striking achievements, including the interior design of Tiffany and Co.'s flagship store on Manhattan's Fifty-Seventh Street, as well as designs for countless government agencies, public institutions, and small nonprofits; he has taught at Howard University and American University. But, after more than sixty years, that one project stands out for him. "It's like an old, warm friend," he says of the UN emblem. Then his mood darkens: "The fact that some in our current administration have treated it with contempt really bothers me." McLaughlin was an idealist then, and clearly he remains one today. "I still believe that the UN is really our only hope for world peace."

McLaughlin died on
September 27, 2009,
at the age of 102.

On July 26, 2007, McLaughlin celebrated his one hundredth birthday, his modesty and idealism still very much intact. "I dreamed once of being an architect and building in brick and stone," he remembered with a laugh. "And instead, the thing I'm best known for is a button." But what a button: an emblem that's been seen by millions of people on every continent in every corner of the globe. It's hard to imagine what greater legacy Donal McLaughlin could hope to leave behind.

Happy birthday, Donal McLaughlin.

In 1967, just after my tenth birthday, we moved from a cramped 1940s bungalow in an older Cleveland suburb to a brand-new house in up-and-coming Parma, Ohio.

First appeared in
Design Observer,
October 20, 2006.

I'm not sure why I know exactly how much it cost, but I do. Was the figure — $29,900 — a constant subject of whispered discussion between my mom and dad in the months leading up to the move? It must have been. Like most young couples, they were on the verge of getting in over their heads, and it must have been scary. What I do remember was a sense of endless promise. Our house was new. All the houses on the street were new. The streets themselves were new. I had been walking the earth for a full decade, but that fall I felt I was finally assuming my birthright as an American. I was moving into a brand-new house.

Until the postwar building boom, Parma was mostly farmland. In 1967 our street marked development's southernmost incursion; for as long as I lived there, uncharted wilderness began at the border of our backyard. It was fun to play in the woods, but better still were the vaguely illegal pleasures afforded by living in what would be, until my high-school years, one big construction site, with new houses always under construction and new neighbors always moving in. We entertained ourselves by stealing wood to build clubhouses, jumping into basement excavations, staging massive wars with two-by-fours and dirt clods, and — in one memorable incident — rolling a six-foot-diameter wooden cable spool down a hill, "just to see what would happen," as I later tearfully confessed to my parents. (What happened was it gained speed, escaped everyone's control, and smashed into a neighbor's Ford Fairlane.)

Our house was built on Sarasota Drive in 1967.

The term *snout house* was formalized by designer and sociologist Dolores Hayden in *A Field Guide to Sprawl* (New York: W. W. Norton, 2004).

In an expression of wishful thinking not atypical of northern Ohio, every street in our neighborhood was named after a town in Florida: Tamarac, Tamiami, Sarasota. The houses came in two models: ranch and split-level. We lived in a split-level. The house to our left was a ranch. The house to our right was another split-level. It was identical to ours. The house across the street was a split-level too, but with the floor plans reversed. Going in that house was always a disorienting, Bizarro World experience. Differentiating each house was its dominant architectural feature: the decorative element on the garage door. We had a star; our neighbors had moons, windows, abstract shapes. Picking this element must have been a moment of truth for the new homeowners, an opportunity to make a statement, but I don't remember anyone ever ascribing any significance to these insignia. Like the whole neighborhood, they just seemed to appear overnight.

Everyone on our street lived in what would later be called a snout house, that garage-centric building type so reviled today that certain municipalities have outlawed them. My mom didn't care much about urban planning principles; she liked being able to get the groceries from her car to the kitchen without braving the Cleveland winter. It just seemed modern, like the way our dinette area was three steps up from our wood-paneled den, the television fully watchable over the decorative wrought-iron railing. (During breakfast, at least: it was off at dinnertime.)

I lived in that house for the next eight years. Today that doesn't seem that long — as I write, I've been working on a single signage project nearly that long, I'm sorry to say — but by the time I left for college, that house had been my whole life. I concocted homemade gunpowder from a chemistry set in the basement, fought with my dad about haircuts on the stairs, read *Catcher in the Rye* on the floor of my bedroom, and listened to the *White Album* on the big stereo console in the living room. More than anything else, I remember that first time we walked through it in 1967. It never looked better than when it was completely new and completely empty.

It will be empty again soon enough. My brothers left for college three years after I did. Four years later my dad died of a heart attack in that paneled den on my thirtieth birthday. He had just finished cutting the grass; a golf game was on the television. My mom lived there alone for the next twenty years. Finally, this fall it became too much, and she moved to a condo near my brother Don.

Former senator John Edwards wrote a book, *Home: The Blueprints of Our Lives,* in which sixty Americans, including Isabel Allende, Mario Batali, John Mellencamp, and Maya Lin, talk about their childhood homes. There are pictures. I note with some relief that our house is hardly the most unpicturesque. Not surprisingly, Steven Spielberg's house in Scottsdale is quintessentially suburban; Jamie-Lynn Sigler, better-known as TV's mob heiress Meadow Soprano, hails from a snout house that is absolutely textbook. The idea of the humble beginning clearly has staying power in our national mythology.

In his introduction, Edwards describes home as "the place that helps to define how we see ourselves and how we choose to make our way in the world." I became a designer, and at first glance that house on Sarasota Drive doesn't seem to have many design lessons to impart. But somewhere behind that suburban facade is the way it was forty years ago: full of promise and unblemished by time, disappointment, or mortality. Maybe design is nothing more than a way to keep making everything new again.

John Edwards, *Home: The Blueprints of Our Lives* (New York: William Morrow, 2006).

The Figure/ Ground Relationship

First appeared in Design Observer, September 25, 2009.

Adapted from the foreword to Adrian Shaughnessy, *Graphic Design: A User's Manual* (London: Lawrence King, 2009).

The "just designing" quote is from Sara Martin, "The Peter Saville Principle," *Eye*, March 13, 2009.

In an interview with Adrian Shaughnessy, the legendary graphic designer Peter Saville once mentioned something valuable he learned ten years into his career: that there is so much more to design than "just designing."

Just *designing*? *Just* designing? As a design student graduating nearly thirty years ago, I would have been stunned to hear this. Designing was everything to me. I had just spent five years in design school. I had entered college as someone who could do a nice pencil drawing of a bowl of fruit. I spent the next sixty months moving shapes around on grids, manipulating squares of colored paper, resolving compositions, drawing letterforms, learning the difference between Helvetica and Univers and between Herbert Bayer and Herbert Matter, redrawing a logo a hundred times until it was perfect, calculating the column lengths of Garamond set 12/13 on a 35-pica measure, and — for this was the point of it all — learning the difference between good design and bad design. When I graduated, my goal was to work with all my heart to create the former and avoid — nay, obliterate from the face of the earth — the latter. And now I learn that not everything's about designing? What else is there?

But it's true. I spent five years transforming myself into a designer. But what had I been before? That's simple: I had been a regular person, like most other people in the world. And, as it turns out, it's those people who actually make it possible — or difficult, or impossible, depending — for designers to do their work. And Saville was right: most of that work isn't about designing.

This is the secret of success. If you want to be a designer, no matter how compelling your personal vision or how all-consuming your commitment, you need other people in order to practice your craft. Not all projects need clients, of course. But unless you're independently wealthy, you'll need to finance the production of your work. This means persuading people to hire you, whether it's bosses at first, or, once you're on your own, clients. And people always have a choice. They can hire you or they can hire someone else. How can you get them to hire you? A good question, and although it has nothing to do with actually doing design work, you'll need an answer for it if you ever intend to actually do any design work.

Once you're doing design work, you face another challenge: How do you get someone else to approve the work you've created and permit it to get out into the world? But, you might protest, certainly they'll recognize good design work when they see it. After all, you do, and your classmates did, and your teachers did. Ah, but that was in the rarefied world of design school. You are now back in the world of regular people. And regular people require patience, diplomacy, tact, bullshit, and very occasionally brute force to recognize good design, or, failing that, to trust that you can recognize it on their behalf. Again, this is hard work, and work that, strictly speaking, has nothing to do with designing.

Finally, once your work is approved, your challenge is to get it made. This may mean working with collaborators like writers, illustrators, photographers, type designers, printers, fabricators, manufacturers, and distributors. It also means working with people who may not care about design, but who care passionately about budgets and deadlines. Then the whole process starts again. In some ways it gets easier each time. In other ways it's always the same.

I remember a lesson from my first year of design school, a series of exercises that we did to learn about the figure/ground relationship, the relationship between the thing that's the subject of a visual composition and the area that surrounds it. For me, this is one of the most magical things about graphic design. It's the idea that the spaces between the letterforms are as important as the letters themselves, that the empty space in a layout isn't really empty at all but as filled with tension, potential, and excitement. I learned you ignore the white space at your peril.

In many ways, the lesson of success in design is the same, and it's a lesson that every great designer has learned one way or another. Designing is the most important thing, but it's not the only thing. All of the other things a designer does are important too, and you have to do them with intelligence, enthusiasm, dedication, and love. Together, those things create the background that makes the work meaningful, and, when you do them right, that makes the work good.

What's That Crashing Sound, or Eisenman in Cincinnati

In September 1975, I arrived at the University of Cincinnati to study graphic design at what was then called the College of Design, Architecture, and Art (DAA). I had decided to become a graphic designer without ever having met one; I had decided to study at DAA without ever having visited it. The day I moved into my dorm room was overcast and drizzly. A funny smell hanging in the air turned out to be the cooking of Ivory soap; Procter & Gamble's giant Ivorydale plant was just upwind of us.

Sometime later, thumbing through a guide to colleges — God knows why; it was too late to do anything about it — I discovered that I had chosen to spend five years in a place that many considered the ugliest college campus in America.

High in the hills of Clifton above downtown Cincinnati, the university had assembled by the mid-'70s a collection of buildings almost heartbreaking in their banality. There was some half-hearted collegiate gothic (Memorial Hall), third-rate colonial revival (McMillan), heavy-handed neoclassicism (Wilson Auditorium), and a remarkably unpoetic Louis Kahn knockoff, Crosley Tower. I myself lived in a ghastly, nine-year-old, twenty-seven-

First appeared in Design Observer, October 12, 2006.

Many exciting videos of the implosion of my freshman-year dorm can be found online, but my favorite is "Sander Hall implosion: When the walls of 27-story University of Cincinnati dormitory came tumblin' down" at https://youtu.be/Euuoof1TN-U.

story glass tower called Sander Hall that was both airless and soulless and that would be imploded, in the style of Pruitt-Igoe, shortly after my tenth reunion.

The design school complex was more of the same. The older part dated from the late '50s: a pair of connected Suburban Modern buildings, Alms (1953) and DAA (1958), were approached via a footbridge that would shortly be overshadowed by Corbu's at Carpenter Center. Connecting to them from the east was Wolfson, DAA's brand-new homage to Paul Rudolph, a grim exercise in brutalism that, like many things in Cincinnati, had arrived ten years too late. All three buildings sat at odd angles to one another that seemed as careless as everything else on campus.

In was in this ensemble that I would spend most of my waking hours for the next five years. The design school, then as now, housed an admirable range of disciplines: architecture, planning, industrial design, fashion design, interior design, and graphic design. I was impressed and somewhat intimidated by the students in the other fields. The industrial designers seemed to be guys from Kentucky who liked to draw cars and were pleased to discover you could major in this in college; they were also good at using power tools. The fashion designers were beautiful TaB-addicted Miss Indianas who, even en charrette at two in the morning, looked ready to don tiaras, hop on floats, and deploy blinding smiles. And so on.

The architects, naturally, dwelt at the top of the pecking order. It is ever thus. But there was a delicious irony in this, for their position entitled them to a dubious honor: the occupation of the newly built Wolfson Building. This was desirable only in theory, as the new addition turned out to be soul-crushingly Orwellian. Meanwhile, the quarter-century-old DAA building, where we designers lived, was careworn and cheery by comparison. The architects were trapped in concrete boxes. We designers were surrounded by big banks of dirty windows looking out on Burnet Woods, battered full-height movable walls covered in graffiti, and an endless supply of industrial four-legged metal stools in various states of deterioration.

It was one of these stools that caught our attention late one bleary night. Finding a good one was always a challenge. Years of hard use had rendered many of them wobbly and worse. Several were unusable and, one might conclude upon examination, actually dangerous. I forget who said it first: "You know, we should just put this thing out of its misery before it hurts someone." Nor do I remember who said what followed: "Yeah, we should just drop it down the Wolfson stairwell."

So it came to be that a half dozen of us were stationed along the multiple landings of the Wolfson stairwell, the windowless six-story volume that was the fulcrum between the shambles of the DAA Building and its harsh addition. A volunteer carried the doomed stool up to the top floor. The others stood to view the event from various angles and, thoughtfully, to make sure no strangers chose that moment to come along and stick their heads over the handrail. I was in my fourth year. It was two in the morning. The stool was suspended over the void. Countdown and release. Utter silence as each of us glimpsed the silvery blur falling downward past our landing. And then, an explosive, earsplitting crash, far louder than any of us would have predicted, one that seemed to reverberate off the concrete walls for minutes. It was physically transporting. It was better than sex. None of us spoke as we carried the mangled piece of metal, nearly twisted beyond recognition, out to the dumpster by the Wolfson loading dock and tenderly set it to rest. We were still a little shaken from the experience.

We would reprise this event only one or two more times: it was too thrilling to make a regular event out of it, plus there was a finite supply of stools. But how pleasing it was to bring violent life to the design school complex! How great it was to find a use for the battered furniture of DAA, and, better still, the sterile, panopticon-like stairwell of the gruesome Wolfson building! And: How great was that crashing sound?

Less than a year after my graduation, as if by some prearranged signal, the University of Cincinnati undertook the first of a series of planning projects under DAA Dean Jay Chatterjee that would completely transform the campus. Hargreaves and Associates devised a pedestrian-driven master plan, Chatterjee instituted what is now referred to bluntly as the Signature Architect Program, and the University of Cincinnati at last acquired some decent buildings by architects who liked their signatures writ large and unmistakable. Alumnus Michael Graves contributed a robust engineering building; Harry Cobb, the elegant College Conservatory of Music; Frank Gehry, the rather charming Vontz Center for Molecular Studies; and Thom Mayne, the university's remarkable new recreation center.

Aronoff Center for Design and Art, Cincinnati, Ohio, Eisenman Architects, 1996.

But the centerpiece is Peter Eisenman's transformation of the DAA complex, the Aronoff Center for Design and Art, housing the renamed School of Design, Architecture, Art, and Planning (DAAP). "What is that thing?" was the headline of a story on the building in the March 2000 issue of the university alumni magazine, and indeed the Aronoff Center is by far the campus's most provocative newcomer. It was baffling to many: that same issue of the UC magazine took pains to debunk a litany of rumors that included "There are no square rooms," "Everyone will get lost," "Too much space is wasted," "The building cost too much," and "One corridor goes nowhere." (Regarding this last, the magazine helpfully points out that it's actually a staircase at Eisenman's Wexner Center in Columbus that goes nowhere, but, hey, everyone makes that mistake!) It's telling that the (false) rumors together paint what one suspects is a more vivid (and accurate) portrait of the building than would a dry recitation of the (true) facts.

Paul Goldberger, "Saluting a Building by a Man Who Stirs Things Up," *New York Times*, October 14, 1996. Goldberger compared the Aronoff Center favorably to Paul Rudolph's Art and Architecture Building at Yale and Le Corbusier's Carpenter Center at Harvard.

Me, I loved the building the minute I saw a picture of it. Even after working for fifteen years in New York, I still felt vaguely provincial: this building changed that. Form follows function? If your desired function is to get a story above the fold on the front page of the arts section of the *New York Times*, Eisenman's building had assumed the ideal form. So I was honored to be asked to design a book on the Aronoff Center timed to its grand opening. Along with a fellow alum, Asya Palatova, I sorted through dozens of plans and hundreds of images and worked my way through essays by Sarah Whiting, Kurt Forster, Silvia Kolbowski, and Jeffrey Kipnis, who, among others, had been asked to explain this building. It was reassuring in this sometimes baffling thicket of words to discover an aphorism by Frank Gehry: "The best thing about Peter's buildings is the insane spaces he ends up with. That's why he is an important architect. All that other stuff, the philosophy and all, is just bullshit as far as I'm concerned." I too loved the spaces, but I can't say I understood them. Until I visited the Aronoff Center for the first time on the day it officially opened.

Cynthia Davidson, editor, *Eleven Authors in Search of a Building* (New York: Monacelli, 1997).

I entered the building through its non-entrance, got lost in one of its corridors that only *seemed* to go nowhere, and finally found my way back into the original DAA building. Like the Alms and Wolfson buildings, the old DAA was largely unaltered by the addition. However, the

Now You See It

three old buildings had, in effect, provided the blueprint for the transformation; it was the extrapolation of their seemingly random spatial relationships that had dictated the geometry of the building that now joined them. I crossed from DAA to Alms and back to Wolfson and finally into the new addition.

That's when it hit me: Eisenman had done exactly what we had done in that stairwell twenty years before. Through some impossible feat of topology, he had simply taken the existing building complex, dropped it straight through its own bleak heart, and smashed it. Then he took the gloriously twisted result and built it, full size, right where it landed. And there it stands, to this very day.

I can't say it made sense to drop those old metal stools back when I was a college junior. I can't say that Eisenman's spaces make sense. I don't know why we did it, and I don't know why he did it. All I can say for sure is that sometimes something just feels right. And all these years later, I can still hear that crashing sound.

Cheap Music and Commercial Art

8

First appeared in a somewhat different form in Design Observer, February 16, 2007.

If I'm asked to name my creative inspirations, my list includes the usual suspects: Picasso, Rauschenberg, and Cezanne. Aalto, Saarinen, and Eames. Holland, Dozier, and Holland.

Wait, who?

I am referring to, of course, one of the greatest songwriting teams in history: Brian Holland, Lamont Dozier, and Eddie Holland Jr.

Lamont Dozier and Brian Holland were the composers. Eddie Holland was the lyricist. Together, they wrote "Heat Wave," "Nowhere to Run," and "Jimmy Mack" for Martha Reeves and the Vandellas. "Can I Get a Witness" and "How Sweet It Is (to Be Loved by You)" for Marvin Gaye. "Mickey's Monkey" for the Miracles, "(I'm a) Roadrunner" for Junior Walker & the All-Stars, and "This Old Heart of Mine (Is Weak for You)" for the Isley Brothers. "Baby, I Need Your Loving," "I Can't Help Myself (Sugar Pie, Honey Bunch)," "It's the Same Old Song," "Reach Out (I'll Be There)," "Standing in the Shadows of Love," and "Bernadette" for the Four Tops. And, of course, "Where Did Our Love Go," "Baby Love," "Stop! In the Name of Love," "I Hear a Symphony," "You Can't Hurry Love," "You Keep Me Hangin' On," and "Reflections" for the Supremes.

This incredible run included twenty-five top ten singles — including five consecutive number ones for the Supremes — between 1963 and 1967. Yes, all that, in only four years.

What passes for pop music today is tepid gruel. Consider, instead, the real thing. Can you hear it? That great two-chord vamp that begins "Heat Wave." The lovely fermata that follows "I just want to stop..." in the bridge for "How Sweet It Is." The tense, echoing guitar figure that introduces "You Keep Me Hangin' On." The guttural shout from Levi Stubbs that precedes the chorus of "Reach Out (I'll Be There)." And that beautiful, "Oooh...ooh" that floats, suspended over the handclaps, in "Baby Love."

Brian Holland, Lamont Dozier, and Eddie Holland had nine-to-five jobs: writing songs for Motown Records. They didn't think they were making art at the time. "I remember saying back at Motown, man, I would love to write classic songs, like a 'White Christmas,'" Brian Holland told an interviewer. It was no coincidence that Motown was headquartered in the home of Ford, Chrysler, and General Motors. The goal was cranking out product. "Early on, Brian and Lamont were already writing together, and they were very prolific at writing melodies and producing tracks," remembered Eddie Holland. "It was the lyric writing which slowed them down. So I suggested that I join the team as a lyricist, so that their production output would be much higher." Increasing production output: that was the name of the Detroit game.

Brian Holland is quoted in Dale Kawashima, "Legendary Trio Holland-Dozier-Holland Talk about Their Motown Hits, and New Projects," Songwriter Universe, 2005.

But what delicacy and genius the writers brought to the process. What amazes me most is the way they managed to create a different sound for each artist. Martha Reeves was the happy party girl. The Supremes were always bittersweet, repeating words like incantations. And, my favorites, the agonized, obsessively paranoid Four Tops. It was a remarkable kind of quasi-industrial creative process that could produce "Reach Out" (which Dave Marsh called "a terrifying melodrama" and Phil Spector called "black Dylan") or that most disturbingly obsessive love song of all, "Bernadette," which conjures up a world so dark, so fraught with agonizing self-doubt, that it's hard to believe it's only three minutes long.

Dave Marsh with John Swenson, editors, The Rolling Stone Record Guide (New York: Random House, 1979).

The production facility at Motown in its glory days was formidable. H-D-H's fellow songwriters included Smokey Robinson, who wrote not only for the Miracles but Mary Wells ("My Guy"), Marvin Gaye ("Ain't That

Peculiar"), and Norman Whitfield, who created the dark, towering sound of the late Temptations ("Cloud Nine," "Ball of Confusion," "Papa Was a Rollin' Stone"). The writers would deliver finished (or even half-finished) songs to the best studio band in history, the Funk Brothers, grounded by the best bass player in history, James Jamerson. (If you doubt these superlatives, check out *Standing in the Shadows of Motown*, the 2002 documentary that brought these unheralded superstars some long-deserved recognition.)

As Noël Coward wrote in an entirely different era, "Extraordinary how potent cheap music is." Sometimes our most artless, workmanlike efforts surprise us with their staying power. Years ago, when someone like a cab driver would ask me what I did for a living, I'd say, "commercial artist." Everyone has a computer now — hell, everyone's a graphic designer — so there's no longer any need to look for a more understandable synonym.

But I have to admit, I always liked the forthright sound of Commercial Artist. I believe that's what Brian Holland, Lamont Dozier, and Eddie Holland were. And if I could toss off a single poster one one-hundredth as good as "Bernadette," I'd retire a very happy designer.

Noël Coward, *Private Lives*, 1930.

Style:
An
Inventory

Style as learning

It is your first big assignment in design school. You know, or think you know, about problem solving. You know, or think you know, about communication. You know about composition, about white space, about kerning. But this is not enough. With all those issues addressed, there are still decisions to be made, decisions that seem perfectly, maddeningly arbitrary. What typeface? What color? Not what does it say or how does it work, but what does it look like? These decisions, arbitrary though they are, have an oversized impact. How do you decide? Do you copy something you like? (Is that plagiarism?) Do you do something that no one else has ever done? (Is that even possible?) The blank piece of paper is overwhelming. You make your choices, and you look at the results. This is your first lesson in the power of style.

Style as destiny

Style was never discussed when I was a student. There was a vague sense that genuine style emerged unconsciously in its own time, like breasts or facial hair. Trying too hard would derail the process and result in something less than authentic. What a wonderful promise: within each of us is a

First appeared in Design Observer, November 29, 2012.

Written for the 2013 School of Visual Arts *Senior Library*.

unique voice that will reveal itself, but only through patience and practice. Use the force, Luke. Do or do not. There is no try.

Style as compulsion
Where does style come from? Put more broadly, why do people do what they do? Nature or nurture? Free will or intention? How much of our particular version of the design process is hardwired directly into our basic brain functions? The designer can't help it.

Style as ideology
It is unnerving to some that certain design decisions, particularly those related to style, are motivated subconsciously. "I don't know; I just like it that way" doesn't always work for teachers, bosses, clients, and judges of design competitions. Thus we have the postrationalizations of the style deniers. Ideology is the superego to style's id.

Style as habit
At the outset of his political career, Barack Obama decided to wear nothing but dull blue, black, and gray suits so he could focus his attention on more important things. Here is William James in 1877: "The more of the details of our daily life we can hand over to the effortless custody of automatism, the more our higher powers of mind will be set free for their own proper work."

William James, *Habit* (Ann Arbor: University of Michigan, 1890).

Style as uniform
Gustave Flaubert: "Dress like a bourgeois, think like a revolutionary."

The attribution of the Flaubert quote is somewhat apocryphal. It is also associated with Charles Baudelaire, among others.

Style as epithet
Stefan Sagmeister originated the easy-to-remember equation "Style = Fart." He later said he no longer believed this, acknowledging that appropriate use of style could aid communication.

Style as crutch
Every great designer has a default mode that provides a solution when original thinking, for whatever reason, is impossible. This default mode, deployed with regularity, becomes associated with that designer's unique personal style. Do not fear your default mode, but do not seek it, either. Simply know that there's a safety net if you need it. Knowing that makes you less likely to need it.

Style as assimilation

We are taught to value originality, to assume that the first goal of every design solution is differentiation. If you think that standing out in a crowd is a universal goal, take a look around. You will see few people sporting hula skirts or top hats. Instead, everyone is trying to fit in. Some design challenges have the same requirement. If you're creating packaging for spaghetti sauce, you can make it jump out from the shelf by making it look like a bottle of shampoo. But people in the pasta aisle aren't looking for shampoo. They're looking for spaghetti sauce. And what makes spaghetti sauce look like spaghetti sauce is the aggregation of a hundred small stylistic cues that need to be understood and mastered. Once you know how to fit in, you can decide what it will take to break out.

Style as nemesis

Paul Rand almost never talked about or even acknowledged living graphic designers: his heroes tended to be European, usually obscure, and preferably dead. But in *Design Form and Chaos*, he described the styles of some of his contemporaries, and one can almost imagine him spitting out the adjectives between clenched teeth: "squiggles, pixels, doodles; corny woodcuts on moody browns and russets; indecipherable, zany typography; peach, pea green, and lavender; tiny color photos surrounded by acres of white space." On the other hand, I remember being introduced to Rand's work as a first-year design student in 1975 and thinking it looked naive and old-fashioned.

Paul Rand, *Design Form and Chaos* (New Haven: Yale University Press, 1993).

Style as straitjacket

Philip Glass: "I know you're all worried about finding your voice. Actually you're going to find your voice. By the time you're thirty, you'll find it. But that's not the problem. The problem is getting rid of it."

Philip Glass interviewed by Zachary Woolfe, "Remixing Philip Glass," *New York Times Magazine*, October 5, 2012.

Style as rebellion

How to break out. If you're right-handed, draw with your left hand. Determine the most sensible, practical thing to do, and then do the exact opposite. Pick a color at random. Force yourself to use the typeface you hate the most. Take on a problem that you've never faced before. Overturn the game board and make up new rules based on where the pieces fall.

Oscar Wilde, *The Picture of Dorian Gray*, 1890.

Style as substance

Oscar Wilde: "It is only shallow people who do not judge by appearances."

Style as groupthink

Everyone's doing it — why can't I? It's difficult to resist the zeitgeist, particularly if it doesn't even feel like the zeitgeist, but simply the way things are supposed to look these days.

Style as time stamp

[Year] called, they want their [dated graphic trope] back.

Style as denial

I don't like to think I have an identifiable style, says the designer with the identifiable style. A way of working can become so comfortable that small differences can seem exaggerated. With surprising regularity, a designer is blind to the fact that it all looks alike, that the same patterns are being repeated over and over. The entire field of psychiatry exists to address this problem in daily life. At what point do you need professional help?

Style as trademark

You can identify an Emily Dickinson poem by the punctuation alone. There is an entire profession called "forensic linguistics"; its specialists can authenticate a Shakespeare sonnet or derive a criminal profile from a ransom note. What evidence are you leaving behind?

Style as narcissism

Or, falling in love with your own handwriting.

Style as disguise

Planner Andrés Duany has said that the comforting style of New Urbanism — front porches, picket fences — is nothing more than the nostalgia-imbued Trojan horse in which the radical planning ideas — no cars, tiny yards — are delivered. Mary Poppins: "A spoonful of sugar helps the medicine go down."

Style as professionalism

Eero Saarinen's motto was "The style for the job." His design for the TWA Terminal was as different from his General Motors Technical Center was as different from his US Embassy in London as air travel is from automotive engineering is from international diplomacy. Purists viewed him with suspicion, but he was enormously successful and made the cover of *TIME* magazine. After his early death, his work seemed to date badly. Today, everyone loves the TWA Terminal.

Style as prostitution
The oldest profession(alism). Who would the client like me to be today? "I'm a whore," Philip Johnson liked to admit, preempting any criticism.

Johnson is quoted in *The Charlottesville Tapes: Transcript of the Conference at the University of Virginia School of Architecture* (New York: Rizzoli, 1985).

Style as homage
The gala invitation done in the mode of the event's honoree. At a party for architecture dean Jay Chatterjee, famously fond of bow ties, attendees were asked to wear bow ties.

Style as impersonation
It can be surprisingly satisfying to attempt to channel the voice of John Baskerville, or William Morris, or Alvin Lustig, or Robert Brownjohn. Satisfying and, to some, dangerously addictive. Like a painting student copying an old master at the Musée des Beaux Arts, Hunter S. Thompson once typed out the entire text of *The Great Gatsby* by F. Scott Fitzgerald. He said he wanted to find out what it felt like to write a masterpiece.

Style as indulgence
Even at its emptiest, style can be a source of great pleasure. I work in a building that was constructed one hundred years ago as a bank. In the basement, side by side, are two vaults. Each vault has a massive door manufactured by the Remington & Sterling Company, made of brass and steel, with a gleaming mechanism visible behind glass. Each door is covered with elaborate, hand-engraved filigree, graceful and exuberant, purely decorative, and destined to be — literally — locked away from public view, for the decoration is all on the inside. But that's not the amazing thing. The amazing thing is that the doors have slightly different patterns. One is based on oak leaves. The other is based on maple leaves. It's as if some craftsperson said, back in 1912: These two doors for the job at 204 Fifth Avenue, are they right next to each other? I'd better make sure they're different. The vault doors would work just fine without any decoration at all, of course. That makes the gift even more special.

Thirteen Ways of Looking at a Typeface

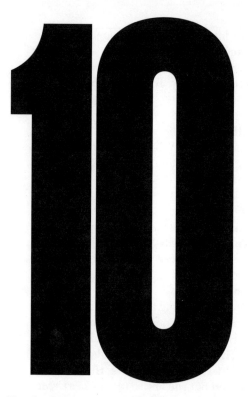

First appeared in
Design Observer,
May 12, 2007.

The title is an homage
to one of my favorite
poets, Wallace Stevens.

For the first ten years of my career, I worked for Massimo Vignelli, a designer who is legendary for using a very limited number of typefaces. Between 1980 and 1990, most of my projects were set in five fonts: Helvetica (naturally), Futura, Garamond #3, Century Expanded, and, of course, Bodoni.

For Massimo, this was an ideological choice, an ethical imperative. "In the new computer age," he once wrote, "the proliferation of typefaces and type manipulations represents a new level of visual pollution threatening our culture. Out of thousands of typefaces, all we need are a few basic ones, and trash the rest." For me, it became a time-saving device. Why spend hours choosing among Bembo, Sabon, and Garamond #3 every time you needed a Venetian Roman? For most people — my mom, for instance — these were distinctions without differences. Why not just commit to Garamond #3 and never think about it again? My Catholic school education must have well prepared me for this kind of moral clarity. I accepted it gratefully.

Then, after a decade, I left my first job. Suddenly I could use any typeface I wanted, and I went nuts. On one of my first projects, I used thirty-seven different fonts on sixteen pages. My wife, who had attended Catholic school herself, found this all too familiar. She remembered classmates who had switched to public school after eight years under the nuns: freed at last from demure plaid uniforms, they wore the shortest skirts they could find. "Jesus," she said, looking at one of my multiple font demolition derbies. "You've become a real slut, haven't you?"

It was true. Liberated from monogamy, I became typographically promiscuous. I have since, I think, learned to modulate my behavior — like any substance abuser, I learned that binges are time-consuming, costly, and ultimately counterproductive — but I've never gone back to five-typeface sobriety. Those thousands of typefaces are still out there, but my recovery has required that I become more discriminating and come up with some answers to this seemingly simple question: Why choose a particular typeface? Here are thirteen reasons.

1. Because it works.
Some typefaces are just perfect for certain things. I've specified exotic fonts for identity programs that work beautifully in headlines and even in text, but sooner or later you have to set that really tiny type at the bottom of the business reply card. This is what Franklin Gothic is for. Careful, though: some typefaces work too well. Frutiger has been used so much for signage programs in hospitals and airports that seeing it now makes me feel that I'm about to get diagnosed with a brain tumor or miss the 7:00 to O'Hare.

Eurostile, Aldo Novarese, 1962.

2. Because you like its history.
I've heard of several projects where the designer found a font that was created the same year the client's organization was founded. This must give the recommendation an aura of manifest destiny that is positively irresistible. I haven't had that luck yet but still try to find the same kind of evocative alignment. For instance, I was never a fan of Aldo Novarese's Eurostile, but I came to love it while working on a monograph on Eero Saarinen: they both share an expressiveness peculiar to the postwar optimism of the 1950s.

ITC Tiffany, Edward Benguiat, 1974.

3. Because you like its name.
Once I saw a project in a student portfolio that undertook the dubious challenge of redesigning the Tiffany & Co. identity. I particularly disliked the font that was used, and I politely asked what it was. "Oh," came the enthusiastic

response, "that's the best part! It's called Tiffany!" On the other hand, Bruce Mau designed *Spectacle*, the book he created with David Rockwell, using the typeface Rockwell. I thought this was funny.

4. Because of who designed it.

Once I was working on a project where the client group included some very strong-minded architects. I picked Cheltenham, an idiosyncratic typeface that was not only well suited to the project's requirements, but was one of the few I know that was designed by an architect, Bertram Goodhue. Recently, I designed a publications program for a girls' school. I used a typeface that was designed by a woman and named after another, Zuzana Licko's Mrs. Eaves. In both cases, my clients knew that the public would be completely unaware of the story behind the font selection, but took some comfort in it nonetheless. I did too.

Cheltenham, Bertram Grosvenor Goodhue and Ingalls Kimball, 1896.

5. Because it was there.

Sometimes a typeface is already living on the premises when you show up, and it just seems mean to evict it. "We use Baskerville and Univers 65 on all our materials, but feel free to make an alternate suggestion." Really? Why bother? It's like one of those shows where the amateur chef is given a turnip, a bag of flour, a leg of lamb, and some maple syrup and told to make a dish out of it. Sometimes it's something you've never used before, which makes it even more fun.

6. Because they made you.

And sometimes it's something you've never used before, for good reason. "We use ITC Eras on all our materials." "Can I make an alternate suggestion?" "No." This is when blind embossing comes in handy.

7. Because it reminds you of something.

Whenever I want to make words look straightforward, conversational, and smart, I frequently consider Futura, upper- and lowercase. Why? Not because Paul Renner was straightforward, conversational, and smart, although he might have been. No, it's because forty-five years ago, Helmut Krone decided to use Futura in Doyle Dane Bernbach's advertising for Volkswagen, and they still use it today. One warning, however: what reminds you of something may remind someone else of something else.

8. Because it's beautiful.

Cyrus Highsmith's Novia is now commercially available. He originally designed it for the headlines in *Martha Stewart Weddings*. Resistance is futile, at least mine is.

Novia, Cyrus Highsmith, 2007.

9. Because it's ugly.

Years ago, I was asked to redesign the logo for *New York* magazine. Milton Glaser had based the original logo on Bookman Swash Italic, a typeface I found unimaginably dated and ugly. But Glaser's logo had replaced an earlier one by Peter Palazzo that was based on Caslon Italic. I proposed we return to Caslon, and distinctly remember saying, "Bookman Swash Italic is always going to look ugly." The other day, I saw something in the office that really caught my eye. It was set in Bookman Swash Italic, and it looked great. Ugly, but great.

10. Because it's boring.

Tibor Kalman was fascinated with boring typefaces. "No, this one is too clever, this one is too interesting," he kept saying when showed him the fonts I was proposing for his monograph. Anything but a boring typeface, he felt, got in the way of the ideas. We settled on Trade Gothic.

11. Because it's special.

In design, as in fashion, nothing beats bespoke tailoring. I've commissioned custom typefaces from Jonathan Hoefler and Tobias Frere-Jones, Joe Finocchiaro, Matthew Carter, and Chester Jenkins. It is the ultimate indulgence, but well worth the extra effort. Is this proliferation? I say bring it on.

12. Because you believe in it.

Sometimes I think that Massimo Vignelli may be using too many typefaces, not too few. A true fundamentalist requires a monotheistic worldview: one world, one typeface. The designers at Experimental Jetset have made the case for Helvetica. My partner Abbott Miller had a period of life he calls "The Scala Years" when he used that typeface almost exclusively. When the time is right, I might make that kind of commitment myself.

John L. Walters, "Reputations: J. Abbott Miller," *Eye*, Autumn 2002.

13. Because you can't not.

When I published my first book of essays, I wanted it to feel like a real book for readers — it had no pictures — so I asked Abbott to design it. He suggested we set each one of the seventy-nine pieces in a different typeface. I loved this idea, but wasn't sure how far he'd want to go with it. "What about the one called 'I Hate ITC Garamond?'" I asked him. "Would we set it in ITC Garamond?" He looked at me as if I was crazy. "Of course," he said.

The book is beautiful, by the way, and not the least bit slutty.

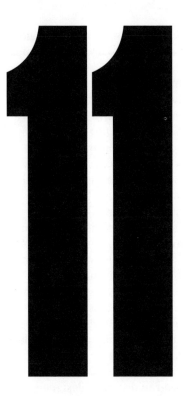

11

Invasion of the Neutered Sprites

My first paying job as a graphic designer — strictly speaking, as a commercial artist — was doing the illustrations for a filmstrip, one of those slideshows timed to a recorded soundtrack that was popular in mid-twentieth-century classrooms. It was intended to introduce an inner-city youth employment program to potential participants. It was 1975, the summer I graduated from high school. My work was directed by a charismatic black guy whom I worshipped and whom I now picture as Idris Elba. Nearly thirty-five years later, I can remember only two things about that project. First, the soundtrack he had picked was the very hip (to me) "Maiden Voyage" by Herbie Hancock. Second, and more importantly, I had a lot of trouble figuring out how to draw the characters that would represent the participants in this program, whose poses would be used to illustrate the step-by-step requirements of enrollment and successful completion.

My first attempts were ambitious: eyes, noses, hairdos, clothing. Idris was patient. "Listen, you've got to simplify these. I don't want people distracted by these hats and stuff." I tried again. "Better, but can you make it so you can't tell whether they're black or white?" Okay, one more

First appeared in
Design Observer,
April 21, 2009.

Generic healthcare icon,
artist and date unknown.

Otto Neurath,
*Modern Man in the
Making* (New York:
Alfred A. Knopf, 1939).

Roger Cook and Don
Shanosky, *Symbol
Signs: The Development
of Passenger/Pedestrian
Oriented Symbols for
Use in Transportation-
Related Facilities*
(Washington, DC: US
Department of
Transportation, 1974).

time. "Look, Mike, I don't want people even to know whether these are men or women. They just have to look like...people, you know?" I tried another drawing. Idris was getting antsy. "Right, but these are too stiff looking. Can you make them look a little happier?" Finally I reduced the figures down to their essence: eyeless balls representing heads, atop curvy stars, with the four points representing fingerless, toeless arms and legs. "That's it!" said my first client.

Without really knowing what I was doing, for my first paying job, I had contributed to a plague: the profusion of sexless, blankly cheerful little people that I have come to call Neutered Sprites. They're everywhere. Behold!

Representing the archetypical homo sapiens isn't easy. Leonardo da Vinci's Vitruvian Man, from around 1490, was the artist's attempt to map a kind of universal humanity, but it's anything but: white, muscled, and long-haired, he looks too much like Owen Wilson to serve as a placeholder for most of the world's population, or at least for me. Over 350 years later, Le Corbusier's Modulor comes a lot closer. But it's still undeniably, even militantly, masculine, a strident standard bearer for the modernist utopia.

The quest for a completely neutral approach to human representation led other midcentury designers to pure geometry. Trained as sociologist and political economist, Otto Neurath created a language of symbols called Isotype to convey complex statistical ideas in a simple visual way. There's no mistaking the gender of Neurath's square-shouldered, round-headed figures: he frankly calls them "man symbols," fitting the title of his masterwork, *Modern Man in the Making.* But they are undoubtedly landmarks and clearly progenitors to the now-ubiquitous bathroom symbols formalized by Roger Cook and Don Shanosky in 1974 as part of the AIGA-led US Department of Transportation Symbol Signs program.

The design world, however, clearly had a need for a less rigid, "friendlier" way of representing people. Hence, starting in the late '50s, the rise of the Neutered Sprites. I suspect that many of those who draw these have a vague image in their minds of the dancing figures in Henri Matisse's collages. These have all the characteristics for which one seeks in vain in Corbu and Neurath. They are nimble, lively, happy. They are not obviously young or old, black or white, male or female. And one last thing, which is the best of all. Drawing the human figure, as anyone who has taken a life-drawing class can testify, is difficult. Neutered

Sprites are — or at least they appear to be — really easy to draw. I remember realizing that with great relief back on that very first job. The little bastards just came pouring out of my felt-tipped pen, one after another. "Hey," I thought to myself, "this isn't going to take that long after all."

The traditional habitat of the Sprites today, of course, is Nonprofitland. Finding them isn't hard. Look for logos for organizations dedicated to community building, or health supporting, or any kind of relentlessly positive thinking. There you will find these little figures by the dozens, prancing around, holding hands, embracing their families, and generally celebrating the universal themes of wellness, happiness, and goodness.

Unfortunately, they have come to have the opposite effect on me. They make me sour and depressed, not least because of my dim memories of having personally contributed to their proliferation. So, I hereby take a sacred pledge: with da Vinci, Corbu, and Otto Neurath as my witnesses, I swear I will never create another Neutered Sprite. I invite you to join me. Together, we can defeat this epidemic!

Fear
of
Color

Written as an
introduction to Eddie
Opara and John
Cantwell, *Color Works:
An Essential Guide to
Understanding and
Applying Color Design
Principles* (New York:
Rockport, 2013).

First appeared as
"Chromatophobia"
in Design Observer,
February 13, 2013.

The first step, they say, is admitting you have a problem.

A long time ago, when I used to do a lot of freelancing, I got a call from a friend of mine who had just gotten a job at a well-known cosmetics company. She had an assignment for me. Her company was famous for using a color wheel — a specially printed diagram with dozens of colors arranged in concentric circles — at their department store counters. The time had come, as it did periodically, to update the colors. Various experts had been consulted, all the requested changes had been tabulated, and all that remained was for someone to designate specifications for the colors that were changing. This task was seen as more or less clerical, and kind of a pain in the ass. "We know exactly what we want," my friend told me, "but no one here has time to do it." She asked if I would do it and said they would pay me $2,500.

Now, this sort of thing didn't exactly seem like graphic design to me — there was no typography involved, for one thing — but $2,500 was a stupendous amount of money for me at the time, probably the most I had ever been offered for a single project. I said yes. I was told I could buy whatever supplies I needed, so I bought every color specification guide I could find, even splurging on exotic imports from Germany and Japan. Finally, one day after work, I sat down at our kitchen table, with my pages of notes on the revisions on one side, my multiple specification guides on the other, and the color wheel in the middle. We even happened to own a matte-black Richard Sapper–designed Artemide Tizio lamp, which coincidentally was the exact model that was used at the cosmetic counters where the color wheel would be displayed. I trained it on the task at hand and got down to work.

Or, at least, I tried to work. Instead, I found myself staring helplessly at the mess before me, clueless as to how to begin. There were just so many chips, so many samples, so many ambiguous notes from the client: this color was supposed to "pop" more, this one was supposed to be "warmer but more neutral," and so forth. It was overwhelming. And in the middle of it all sat the color wheel. For the first time I wondered: What was it really for? How did it help women choose and apply their makeup? Why were so many colors necessary? How could anyone tell that colors looked out of date? Did these colors really look the same to other people as they did to me? And how did they look to me, anyway?

I sat for hours, disconsolately shuffling color chips around, getting more and more confused and despondent. Finally, my wife, Dorothy, who had been trying to ignore my heaving sighs, came over. "Can you tell me again what this is all about?" she asked. Dorothy is not a designer and has never taken a single class in art or design, so I explained carefully. To my surprise, she responded with enthusiasm: yes, of course she knew this particular color wheel — all of her friends did. In fact, she herself thought that it was out of date and had thought so for some time. I was amazed. Really? She nodded. "Now, what exactly are you supposed to be doing?" I showed her the particulars of my assignment and by way of example indicated a particularly vexing instruction from the client: "They say they want this one to be more like a soft..." (I had to refer to my notes at this point) "...celadon."

I had looked up celadon in the dictionary ("a pale yellow-grayish green") but it wasn't much help. Yellow, and gray, and green: really? That's three colors, goddammit! I showed Dorothy the chips I was considering, and she snorted in derision. "You think those are celadon? Let me see what else you have." She leaned over my shoulder and picked out a few options. "These look nice," she said. She was right. They did look nice. She asked if she could sit down and pick out some more. And some more after that. It was fun for her, and she was good at it. Eventually she designed the whole wheel, and for the next five years or so, women at cosmetic counters across America chose their makeup based on colors that my wife Dorothy picked out at our kitchen table.

That is when I began to realize that I had a case of chromatophobia, fear of color. From my earliest days as a designer I loved black and white. Such authority, such decisiveness. To this day, any collection of my favorite personal projects — posters, book covers, packaging — marks me as a follower of Henry Ford, another enthusiast for wheels who famously told buyers of his Model T that they could have whatever color they wanted as long as it was black. Every now and then, I dip my toe in the vast rainbow-hued sea. It usually comes up with no more than a little bit of red and an even littler bit of yellow. I admire people who can use color with authority. To me, they seem to be able to swim like fishes.

They say any fear can be surmounted, and I hope one day to begin to conquer mine. Until then, it's back to the comfort of my nice, dry towel, well away from the water's edge — suitably striped, of course, in my two favorite colors: black and white.

Flat, Simple, and Funny: The World of Charley Harper

A few years ago, we bought a little house at the southernmost tip of the Jersey Shore in a town called Cape May Point. It has a winter population of less than 250, which swells to over 4,500 when people like us come down for the summer.

First appeared in Design Observer, August 16, 2007.

Cape May Point is boring. There are no restaurants or mail delivery. There are only three businesses: the Cape May General Store, the lighthouse at Cape May Point State Park (admission $6 adults, $2 kids), and the biggest: the gift shop at the Cape May Bird Observatory.

I visited the gift shop a few years ago when we first started going down there. It was crowded, which it always is: sitting at the intersection of the East Coast's two main migratory corridors, Cape May is a legendary destination for bird watchers, host of the annual World Series of Birding. To my local disgrace, I'm not even an amateur birdwatcher. So the gift shop's multiple editions of esoteric guidebooks and the artillery-like telescopic equipment were of only passing interest. Imagine my surprise, though, when in the corner I spotted a find of my own — a design book, of all things, by a relatively obscure designer: Charley Harper.

The first time I heard his name may have been when one of my professors at the University of Cincinnati was asked to name his favorite designers. It was a list you'd expect: Paul Rand, Bradbury Thompson, Milton Glaser, Josef Müller-Brockmann, Armin Hofmann, and...Charley Harper. Wait a minute. I remember my surprise: a designer could be named Charley?

Charley Harper was a local hero, unknown for years outside southern Ohio and small circles of birders and nature buffs. Born in West Virginia in 1922, he grew up on a farm, and in many ways he stayed a farm boy all his life, from his studies at the Art Academy of Cincinnati to his brief stint (New York didn't take) at the Art Students League: modest, self-deprecating, funny. He opened a studio in Cincinnati after World War II, and his illustrations from those days are quintessential examples of American postwar commercial art.

Charley Harper, "Charley Harper Interviews Charley Harper," *Beguiled by the Wild: The Art of Charley Harper* (Gaithersburg, MD: Flower Valley, 1994)

Arthur Lougee, art director of *Ford Times*, the house magazine of the car company, was an influential patron, and commissioned Harper's earliest nature paintings, including many of birds. His illustrations in the widely circulated *Giant Golden Book of Biology* and *The Animal Kingdom* for the Golden Press consolidated his reputation as a wildlife artist — with a difference. "Wildlife art has traditionally been painted superrealistically," he once said. "But I've chosen to do it differently because I think flat, simple, and funny." As a result, Harper has been called "the only wildlife artist who has never been compared to Audubon and never will be." He called his style minimal realism. "Instead of trying to put everything in when I paint, I try to leave everything out. I distill reality, thereby enhancing identity. I never count the feathers in the wings — I just count the wings."

He gravitated to limited-edition silkscreens, and his style became ever more refined. As his work increased in rigor and precision, its debt to modernism became more pronounced, as did its connection to the output of designers like Rand and Hofmann, as well as Edward McKnight Kauffer and Erik Nitsche. Yet he never lost his sense of humor, as demonstrated by the wince-inducing puns used to title his paintings ("Family Owlbum," "Frog Eat Frog," "Howlloween," to name a few). His success permitted him to become more selective in his commissions, working almost exclusively for clients who shared his passions, such as the National Park Service and the Cornell University Lab of Ornithology.

Now You See It

In his ninth decade came a curious coda to a long career: overnight celebrity. Fashion and interior designer Todd Oldham, a childhood fan of *The Giant Golden Book of Biology*, rediscovered Harper — with a vengeance, it appears — and began collaborating with him on fabrics and home furnishings. It was an unlikely combination — the winner of the 1991 Perry Ellis Award for New Fashion Talent and an eighty-plus-year-old West Virginia farm boy — and it led to some unlikely results, including an Oldham-designed exhibition at Cincinnati's Contemporary Arts Center, the declaration of "Charley Harper Day" in Cincinnati on December 8, 2006, and, strangest of all, a monograph that might appropriately be called elephantine.

Pfwhooooooooooo,
Charley Harper, 1975.

Charley Harper: An Illustrated Life dwarfs comparable tomes on Rand, Thompson, Müller-Brockmann — indeed, any other graphic design book you've ever seen, and even most art books. At 421 pages, with a trim size of 19.4 × 13.4 × 2.4 inches and a net weight of 12 pounds (Bruce Mau's *Life Style* is a svelte 4.5), it caused consternation in my house even before it arrived. "Did you spend $150 on an advance order from Amazon?" my wife inquired, examining our monthly Amex bill. "Who in the hell is Charley Harper?" When the book arrived, however, we were both impressed: it's beautifully produced, a clear labor of love for designer-author Oldham. But as a tribute, it struck me as somewhat ill-fitting, just too over-the-top and lavish for a humble, soft-spoken designer who claimed to be unable to draw a straight line without a ruler or a circle without a compass. *Beguiled by the Wild*, Harper's 1994 collection, weighs one-fourth as much, costs $100 less, and makes nearly as good an introduction.

Todd Oldham,
*Charley Harper:
An Illustrated Life*
(Los Angeles:
AMMO, 2007).

Still, we are lucky to have both, for we no longer have the man. Charley Harper died on June 10 of this year. He was eighty-four. *Minimal Realism*, a memorial exhibition dedicated to the life and work of Charley Harper and his beloved wife of fifty years, Edie, opened the following year at the Cincinnati Art Museum.

The It
Factor

First appeared in
Design Observer,
January 16, 2007.

David Galbraith,
"I just saw a Zune, and
guess what? It's a piece
of shit," blog entry,
November 26, 2006.

*Imagine your son waking up on Christmas morning and
rushing to open his presents in breathless anticipation of getting
a shiny new iPod, only to find out he's got a Zune, which is like
coming second in chess.*

When I read this comment on Microsoft's hapless
music player on a blog by David Galbraith, I had a moment
of déjà vu. More than twenty years ago, I heard an author
describing an identical experience, except he was talking
about a little boy who was hoping for a real baseball bat;
his clueless parents got him a perfectly good non–Louisville
Slugger instead.

You know it when you see it. There's the iPod, and
there are all those other MP3 players; there's the Louisville
Slugger, and there are all those other baseball bats. As
you've probably heard, Steve Jobs unveiled a long-awaited
product last week; he intends to reduce the competition to
nothing more than all those other phones.

What makes something the real thing? It's more
than functionality, popularity, or beauty. The name of
the author who told the Louisville Slugger story was Owen
Edwards, and he had just written a book that gave the
phenomenon a name: *quintessence.*

It was 1983. "This is a book about things," Edwards and his coauthor Betty Cornfeld wrote in the introduction to *Quintessence: The Quality of Having It*, "things that offer more to us than we specifically ask of them and to which we respond more strongly than is easily explained. What the various things in this book have in common — whether candy or cars, cigarettes or shoes, baseball bats or blimps — is the quality of quintessence. In a wide variety of ways, they each exhibit a rare and mysterious capacity to be just exactly what they ought to be."

Betty Cornfeld and Owen Edwards, *Quintessence: The Quality of Having It* (New York: Three Rivers, 1983).

Edwards and Cornfeld try to unlock that puzzle, invoking along the way — among others — Marcel Proust, Immanuel Kant, Blaise Pascal, and John Ruskin (quoted on "the mysterious sense of accountable life in things themselves"). They take pains to point out that they're not interested in identifying the best: "'Best' is a judgment based on statistics, not taste or instinct; and in a world of constant technological innovation and furious competition, being the best of anything is usually a short term occupation." In some ways, long before David A. Aaker began publishing books on the subject, and barely ever using the word themselves, they created in *Quintessence* the best treatise ever written on what it means to be a great brand.

David A. Aaker has published over a dozen books on marketing and branding, including the classic *Managing Brand Equity* (New York: Free Press, 1991).

The structure of the book is simple. It consists of a series of tributes, each with a photograph, each either a single page or a two-page spread, to the things that Edwards and Cornfeld felt supported their thesis. The list is wildly diverse. The Stetson Hat. The Ace Comb. Wedgwood Plain White Bone China. The Spalding Rubber Ball. Ivory Soap. The Harley-Davidson ElectraGlide. Campbell's Tomato Soup ("a must for every cupboard and every bomb shelter"). Some of the items are luxurious (the Steinway Piano, the Mont Blanc Diplomat Pen, the Cartier Santos), but most are inexpensive (Oreo Cookies, the Zippo Lighter, the Timex Mercury 20521). Although many are name brands, a few are generic or homemade (the martini, the brown paper bag, the peanut butter and jelly sandwich).

If you doubt the critical acuity of Edwards and Cornfeld, consider that of the sixty-plus items they selected for *Quintessence*, in my opinion only a few would fail to make the cut nearly twenty-five years later. The Polaroid SX-70 camera, for instance, hasn't stood the test of time, and in most people's minds Frederick's of Hollywood Lingerie was long superseded by Victoria's Secret. But it says a lot that the single object in the book that looks truly dated is the one

Dike Blair, "Autoemotive Design: An Interview with J Mays, Head of Ford Motor Company Design," Thing.net, undated.

that was discontinued and then revived: the VW Beetle. Tellingly, New Beetle creator J Mays described his design approach in terms you sense the *Quintessence* authors would applaud: "There's a conscious effort on our part to try to take the next step forward while retaining the essence of the original idea."

Predictably, many of the products are familiar from our childhood; kids seem to have a nearly infallible sense of what makes something the real thing. "A rule of thumb often useful in determining whether something is quintessential," wrote Edwards and Cornfeld, "is whether it resembles a child's drawing of the thing." This childlike sensibility holds true today. Mays said the New Beetle's circular shape had much in common with Walt Disney's drawing of Mickey Mouse; David Galbraith goes to far as to label the Zune "unsafe for children," imagining that any child unlucky to get one will be fated to get "the shit kicked out of him at school by mocking friends chanting 'Zuny Zuny Zuny.'"

Oreo cookie patent drawing (detail), William A. Turnier, 1952.

I for one recall my unease at visiting a neighbor's house where the staples were not Oreos ("The quintessentiality of the Oreo is mysteriously and precariously balanced") and Coca-Cola ("Nothing works like Coke does. Not even water"), but rather Hydrox Cookies and RC Cola. No matter that Hydrox were invented before Oreos; no matter that I secretly thought they tasted better: there was just something profoundly disturbing about a family that would so obliviously distance itself from the American mainstream. If I'd learned these people were sacrificing live goats every Friday night on their basement bumper pool table, I wouldn't have been all that surprised.

Looking at the book today, one is struck by its sincerity. In 1983, indulging in poetic connoisseurship over something like M&M's ("little lapidary bits of confection, in their rather sober brown bag") seemed daring and even a bit transgressive. Writing in the *New York Times*, Christopher Lehmann-Haupt called the book "informative, pungent and witty"; the cover alone, with its lovely juxtaposition of cheap candy, cocktails, and luxury goods, seemed to promise a new way of thinking about everyday

The description of M&M's World is from a New York City tourism site: www.nyc.com/arts__attractions/mms_world.1089580.

life. Of course, today one isn't permitted to discover the charms of M&M's on one's own. Why bother when a bombastic 25,000-square-foot "retail experience" has been erected on Times Square to subject visitors to a "three story sensory immersion into the world of M&M's"?

Now You See It

Quintessence was a single drop in an ocean, the ripples from which, twenty-odd years later, have metastasized into a never-ending tsunami.

But the original still stands up to scrutiny, not just as a book of essays, but as an example of the very thing it sought to describe. In the making of *Quintessence*, Edwards and Cornfeld collaborated with John C Jay, then a wunderkind art director at Bloomingdale's, later an executive creative director at Wieden + Kennedy. His layouts look a little dated (the headlines are Bodoni — quintessential — but the text is, um, Avant Garde Book) Nonetheless, the pages are still clean, powerful, and confident. Ketchup bottles, sneakers, and Hershey's Kisses, all boldly rendered in Dan Kozan's black-and-white photographs, have never looked more iconic.

If you can get your hands on the first edition, grab it. The book was reissued in 2001, and in a redesigned form, with pretty color pictures, different typeface choices, and new layouts. It looks a little more modern, perhaps. But in an unspeakable bit of irony, it lacks somehow that quality that, according to Edwards and Cornfeld, "can no more be stalked and captured than can true love." In short, it simply is no longer quintessential.

Helmut Krone, Period.

First appeared in Design Observer, August 23, 2006.

Clive Challis, *Helmut Krone. The Book. Graphic Design and Art Direction (Concept, Form and Meaning) after Advertising's Creative Revolution* (Cambridge: Cambridge Enchorial, 2006).

A strange gulf exists today between the worlds of design and advertising. That makes it easy to forget that one of the greatest designers that ever lived was an advertising art director: Doyle Dane Bernbach's Helmut Krone.

Long before *branding* became a buzzword, Krone intuitively understood how graphic design could define an institution's personality. "The page," he once said, "ought to be a package for the product. It should look like the product, smell like the product....Every company, every product, needs its own package." Without ever designing a logo — often without even using a logo — he created corporate images that endure to this day. How many companies can be said to own a typeface the way that Volkswagen does Futura Bold? They have Helmut Krone to thank for that.

Finally, nearly ten years after his death, the man received the treatment he deserves: a beautifully designed, relentlessly researched, and gracefully written volume by Clive Challis, *Helmut Krone. The Book. Graphic Design and Art Direction (Concept, Form and Meaning) after Advertising's Creative Revolution.* The title is long, but Challis backs up every word in the book's 268 lavishly illustrated pages.

It leaves me with no doubt that something I once suspected is, in fact, true: Helmut Krone is God.

I sense that bit of hero worship would be scoffed at by many of those who knew Krone personally, which I never did. Another admirer, George Lois, once called him "a complex kraut" with a "dour, Buster Keaton face," "a fidgety perfectionist who worked with deadly Teutonic patience." And indeed, some of his simplest, clearest, most effortless-looking work was the product of brutal sweat.

Take, for instance, the tangled route to the legendary ad for VW that came to emblematize an entire decade's worth of creative advertising. According to Challis's book, Krone's original headline was "Wilkommen." The client rejected it — rightly so — and pulled "Think small" from the last line of Julian Koenig's copy. Could that be the headline? "He hated it with a passion. With a passion!" remembered his then-colleague Lois, who was at DDB working on VW's van account. "I suppose," Krone asked (and you can sense the exasperation), "you want me to make the car small?" After some back-and-forth (Krone also tried making the headline itself small), the final layout was painstakingly created. Said Koenig: "A little car up in the upper left corner at a little angle — which was the peculiar genius of Helmut."

Advertisement for Volkswagen, Julian Koenig (copywriter) and Helmut Krone (art director) for Doyle Dane Bernbach, 1959.

It is hard to imagine today the impact that this kind of advertising had in the early '60s, when most cars still had big fins and most ads for them featured polo ponies and people in evening wear sipping champagne. The understatement, the conversational tone of voice, the utter lack of glamour all foretold a revolution in the making. Yet, typically, Krone's revolutionary art direction was plunked securely on an absolutely conventional, even boring, layout, then called "old JWT No. 1" after the lumbering Madison Avenue standby J. Walter Thompson: two-thirds image above, centered headline, three columns of body copy below. No one knew like Krone did the power of taking the ordinary and making a subtle, transformative alteration. "There's a German word for it," he once said. "*Umgekehrt* — turned around slightly." Krone built his reputation on thousands of such slight turns.

Challis's book is filled with this kind of detail. Born in 1925 to immigrant parents in Yorkville, Manhattan's German enclave, Krone attended the High School for Industrial Art, where he hoped to become a product designer. But exposure to the work of the city's hottest young designer, Paul Rand, and one of the country's most acclaimed ones, Lester Beall, convinced the eighteen-year-old Krone that his future might lie with print. He followed naval service in World War II with postwar classes with Alexey Brodovitch and a stint at *Esquire*. Then, at the age of twenty-nine, he joined the best ad agency in town, Doyle Dane Bernbach, then a veritable murderers' row of art directors, all championed by the groundbreaking genius Bill Bernbach. With the exception of a few years in the early '70s, he would spend his entire career there.

Krone was addicted to "zigging when everyone else was zagging." His ads for Avis followed the triumph of VW, but neatly turned the JWT No. 1 formula on its head: little picture, big body copy, set in a fastidiously modified version of Eric Gill's Perpetua Bold. "No one was using it," Krone said. "I liked the fact that it was so unautomotive. Rather it was bookish, literate." Krone wanted people to read the copy. Perpetua still figures in Avis's promotional material forty years later. Like with VW's Futura, Krone made a choice, stuck with it, and made it stick.

And, in Avis's case, without resorting to something he hated: a logo. "I've spent my whole life fighting logos," he said when he was inducted into the Art Directors Club Hall of Fame. "Logos say 'I am an ad. Turn the page.'" It was amazing how often he succeeded in vanquishing them, or better still, replacing them with something better. His famous series of "famous faces" for Polaroid, for instance, bore no corporate signature but rather a silhouetted image of someone experiencing that then-magical product in use. Toward the end of his book, Challis devotes a spread to counting off Krone's breakthroughs. Ads with no headlines. Headlines as captions. Photographs as logo. Typeface as brand. No headlines or copy. No product, just a sea of white. The shock of the new, delivered in sharp, precise little doses.

An attempt to start his own agency in the early '70s didn't work; Krone seemed to enjoy the friction of straining not only against conventional advertising but against the conventions of an established workplace. His work in the years following his return to DDB continued to startle. I remember one of my design professors bringing in one of Krone's poetic magazine ads for the Audi Fox for us to admire: clearly, it was influenced by fashion advertising, but how daring to transpose that suggestive language to the world of cars. The same magazines would sometimes

Advertisement for Avis, Paula Green (copywriter) and Helmut Krone (art director) for Doyle Dane Bernbach, 1962.

also feature Krone's ads for Porsche. I was studying under Swiss-trained teachers, but Helvetica was never like this.

"I wanted to make the entire page like the car, which is strictly Braun," he later told *U&lc*. "I'm not into Swiss design. But I decided, for this, I have to be. So I brushed up on it...I used Swiss design principles, but because of its exuberance I called it American Swiss."

That combination of discipline and joy, of casual ease (to "brush up" on something we were spending five years studying!) and Teutonic precision: this is what makes Helmut Krone special. The most surprising discovery unearthed by Challis is his claim that Krone introduced into current practice a custom that, like so many other of his breakthroughs, we now take for granted: the use of a full stop, or period, after a headline. That period — "Think small." — was the hallmark of DDB's celebrated forthrightness. And more: "Putting a full point in a headline was an act of sedition," writes Challis. "It broke the pace and invited inspection — maybe even circumspection — of the statement. Of course this is exactly why Krone used one: he had statements to make which he wanted to be examined."

Let there be no doubt: these statements are still worth examining. And, with this book as a resounding full stop to an amazing body of work, Helmut Krone, indisputably, gets the last word.

Advertisement for Porsche, Tom Yobbagy (copywriter) and Helmut Krone (art director) for Doyle Dane Bernbach, 1979.

Pitch
Perfect

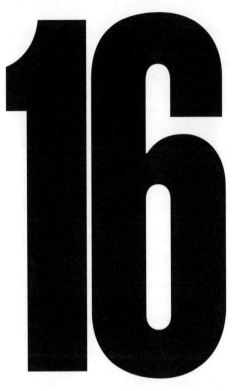

First appeared in
Design Observer,
September 30, 2008.

One of my first bosses taught me an important lesson.

Good designers are a dime a dozen, he said. Coming up with a great design solution is the easy part. The hard part, he said, is getting the client to accept the solution. "But if the work is good, don't the clients know it when they see it?" I asked.

My boss just looked at me silently for a long time. And then, with gentleness and no small amount of pity, he reached out and patted me on the head: poor kid.

He was right, of course. In any creative activity where clients are involved, you have to make the sale twice. Before you get to the customer, you have to sell the client.

And that's what I love most about the AMC series *Mad Men*, which starts its second season later this month. It gets so many things right about its subject, the advertising business, but it absolutely nails one thing: the art behind the art of the pitch.

As its fans know well, *Mad Men* is the brainchild of Matthew Weiner, who, on the strength of its unproduced, written-on-spec pilot episode, got hired as a writer and executive producer for *The Sopranos*. Production on his pet project didn't start until the HBO show had run its course.

On the surface, *Mad Men*, a drama set at Sterling Cooper, a fictional New York advertising agency in the early 1960s, wouldn't seem to have much in common with the iconic North Jersey mob epic. But, like Tony Soprano, creative director Don Draper operates in a world that is almost comically foreign to us: with its nonstop smoking, drinking, and sexual harassment — not to mention the use of plastic dry-cleaning bags as children's toys — it truly seems to be set in, well, another century.

Yet beyond the anachronisms and the astonishingly casual sexism, racism, and general bad behavior, the draw is the universality of the human stories caught in the period settings. In *The Sopranos*, the mob business was there to punctuate the inner conflicts of the characters. And where *The Sopranos* had whackings, *Mad Men* has client presentations.

In the very first episode, "Smoke Gets in Your Eyes," Don Draper, played by the amazing Jon Hamm, gets to demonstrate why he's considered one of the best creative directors in town by salvaging a meeting with unhappy clients from Lucky Strike, who are about to walk out.

Don Draper: Gentlemen, before you leave, can I just say something?

Agency head Roger Sterling: I don't know, Don. Can you?

Don [to the clients]: The Federal Trade Commission and Reader's Digest *have done you a favor. They've let you know that any ad that brings up the concept of cigarettes and health together...well, it's just going to make people think of cancer.*

[Client] Lee Sr. [sarcastically]: Yes, and we are grateful to them.

Don: But what Lee Jr. said is right. You can't make those health claims. Neither can your competitors.

Lee Sr.: So...we got a lotta people not sayin' anything that sells cigarettes.

Don: Not exactly. This is the greatest advertising opportunity since the invention of cereal. We have six identical companies making six identical products. We can say anything we want. [Pointing to Lee Jr.] How do you make your cigarettes?

[Client] Lee Jr.: I don't know.

Lee Sr.: Shame on you. We breed insect-repellent tobacco seeds. Plant 'em in the North Carolina sunshine. Grow it, cut it, cure it, toast it —

Don: There you go. [He writes "It's Toasted" on the blackboard.]

From "Smoke Gets in Your Eyes," Season 1, Episode 1, written by Matthew Weiner.

Lee Jr.: But everybody else's tobacco is toasted.

Don: No. Everybody else's tobacco is poisonous. Lucky Strike's is toasted.

Sterling [triumphant]: Well, gentlemen, I don't think I have to tell you what you just witnessed here.

Lee Jr. [hesitant]: I think you do.

Don: Advertising is based on one thing: happiness. And you know what happiness is? Happiness is the smell of a new car. It's freedom from fear. It's a billboard on the side of the road that screams with reassurance: whatever you're doing, it's okay. You...are...okay.

Lee Sr.: "It's toasted." I get it.

Of course, "It's toasted" actually was Lucky Strike's slogan in the late '50s: the show generally stops at nothing in its pursuit of verisimilitude and has been justly praised for getting every period detail right. (In the third episode, when the creative team is shown sniping at a Doyle Dane Bernbach Volkswagen ad, the dialogue establishes that "Lemon" was the second in a series that began the previous year with "Think Small." That's accuracy!) The model for Don Draper the adman in this case is Rosser Reeves, the Ted Bates copywriter who invented the idea of the Unique Selling Proposition. The key to Don Draper the character, however, is that speech about happiness. It's an illusion that he's as desperate to sell to himself as anyone else.

Alex Witchel, "Mad Men Has Its Moment," *New York Times*, June 22, 2008.

It's been observed, correctly, that the creative output of Sterling Cooper, which is barely ever shown being developed, more or less stinks. As George Lois told the *New York Times*: "When I hear '*Mad Men*,' it's the most irritating thing in the world to me. When you think of the '60s, you think about people like me who changed the advertising and design worlds. The creative revolution was the name of the game. This show gives you the impression it was all three-martini lunches." But Don Draper doesn't work at DDB or Papert, Koenig, Lois. Sterling Cooper is an old-school agency, and in 1960 big establishment agencies ran on smooth presentations, fastidious account handling,

See page 74.

and, actually, three-martini lunches. (Find a used copy of Jerry Della Femina's *From Those Wonderful Folks Who Gave You Pearl Harbor* if you have any doubt.)

There is one outright creative triumph in the series, and it's from the hands of secretary-turned-fledgling-copywriter Peggy Olson, played by the brilliant Elisabeth Moss. Peggy's first day at Sterling Cooper is our introduction to the show, and her story, along with Don's,

Now You See It

provides a connective thread throughout the first season. In what is seen as a surprising turn of events, humble Peggy comes up with an idea for Belle Jolie Cosmetics: each ad shows a single tube of lipstick, a portrait of a couple, and the headline Mark Your Man. For Sterling Cooper, this is as good as it gets. In another of the best scenes from the series, an account guy presents it to a grumpy-looking client (while Peggy waits nervously outside) and gets a response that will sound numbingly familiar to most creative people.

From "Babylon," Season 1, Episode 6, written by Andre and Maria Jacquemetton.

Client: I only see one lipstick in your drawing. Women want colors. Lots and lots of colors.

Jr. Client: "Mark Your Man." It's pretty cute.

Client: Oh, you like this? Well, maybe we should cut down to five shades, or one.

[Account exec] Ken Cosgrove: I'm not telling you to listen to anyone, but this is a very fresh approach.

Don: It's okay, Kenny. I don't think there's much else to do here but call it a day. [Rises and extends his hand.] Gentlemen, thank you for your time.

Client [baffled]: Is that all?

Don: You're a nonbeliever. Why should we waste time on kabuki?

Client: I don't know what that means.

Don: It means that you've already tried your plan, and you're number four. You've enlisted my expertise and you've rejected it to go on the way you've been going. I'm not interested in that. You can understand.

Client: I don't think your three months or however many thousands of dollars entitles you to refocus the core of our business —

Don: Listen. I'm not here to tell you about Jesus. You already know about Jesus. He either lives in your heart or He doesn't. [Cut to Don's colleagues, who look alarmed. Don bears down with his argument. He never raises his voice.] Every woman wants choices. But in the end, none wants to be one of a hundred in a box. She's unique. She makes the choices and she's chosen him. She wants to tell the world, he's mine. He belongs to me, not you. She marks her man with her lips. He is her possession. You've given every girl that wears your lipstick the gift of total ownership.

[Pause. The client looks at Don, then at the ads, then at Don again.]

Client [quietly]: Sit down.

Don: No. [evenly] Not until I know I'm not wasting my time.

Client [conceding]: Sit down.

Jesus God in heaven! Not until I know I'm not wasting my time! From the minute Don launched his this-meeting-is-over bluff, I was on the edge of my seat, and my lovely wife, Dorothy, will tell you that I literally clapped my hands at that line. For me, this sequence is as close to pornography as I ever get to see on basic cable.

The climax of the season's final episode, "The Wheel," is a competitive pitch for, of all things, a naming assignment. Kodak has invented a high-tech new device to project slides, and two bland-looking suits show up to see if Sterling Cooper has come up with something to call it. Then begins one of the most emotional scenes I've ever seen on television, delivered by an actor portraying a man so consumed with self-doubt and self-deceit that we wonder if he himself understands what he's selling.

From "The Wheel," Season 1, Episode 13, written by Matthew Weiner and Robin Veith.

Don: Well, technology is a glittering lure. But there is the rare occasion when the public can be engaged on a level beyond flash, if they have a sentimental bond with the product. My first job, I was in house, at a fur company. This old pro copywriter, Greek, named Teddy. And Teddy told me the most important idea in advertising is "new." It creates an itch. You simply put your product in there as a kind of calamine lotion. But he also talked about a deeper bond with the product: nostalgia. It's delicate. But potent.

He asks for the lights out, turns on the projector, and begins showing slides. Whirr. Click. I remember that sound myself!

Teddy told me that in Greek, nostalgia literally means "the pain of an old wound." It's a twinge in your heart, far more powerful than memory alone.

Don shows slides of his wife, his children, picnics, celebrations, family moments.

This device isn't a spaceship. It's a time machine. It goes backwards. Forwards. It takes us to a place where we ache to go again. It's not called the Wheel. It's called the Carousel. It lets us travel the way a child travels, around and around, and back home again, to a place where we know we are loved.

The slide reads, "Kodak introduces Carousel." The lights come up. One of the agency guys is weeping and rushes out of the room. The would-be clients look stunned.

[New business guy] Duck Phillips: Good luck at your next meeting.

Although the pitches are the high points for me, the world of *Mad Men* is rich and complex. There are wives,

Now You See It

mistresses, neighbors, colleagues, competitors, clients, and kids, all caught in a complicated, entirely believable web of relationships. Like a lot of people, I tuned into *Mad Men* a year ago out of professional curiosity and was immediately intrigued by the incredible production design but ultimately got hooked on the human stories.

The first season ends on Thanksgiving Eve, 1960. The characters stand at the threshold of a decade where everything is going to change in ways they can't imagine. The song over the last episode's final credits is Bob Dylan's 1963 "Don't Think Twice, It's All Right." One assumes the anachronism, and the irony, are both very much intentional.

Jerry Della Femina and the Cult of Advertising Personality

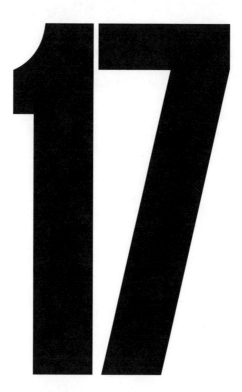

First appeared in Design Observer, July 25, 2010.

Charles Sopkin, "What a Tough Young Kid with Fegataccio Can Do on Madison Avenue," *New York Times Magazine*, January 26, 1969.

On Sunday, January 28, 1969, the readers of the *New York Times Magazine* met, most of them for the first time, a young man who was already a legend in certain circles around midtown Manhattan. "Lolling in a chair was the new creative supervisor of Ted Bates & Co. advertising agency, one Jerry Della Femina, 30 years old, a $50,000-a-year marvel out of Brooklyn, hired to bring a bit of sparkle to the Bates image." The writer, Charles Sopkin, described a brainstorming session for a new client, a "Japanese electronics company" called Panasonic. It was Della Femina's first day on the job, and he was surrounded by account executives, art directors, and copywriters awaiting his direction. Finally he cleared his throat. "I've got it! How about this for a headline: 'From Those Wonderful Folks Who Gave You Pearl Harbor.'"

The wunderkind's irreverence caused predictable consternation among his new straight-laced colleagues. There was "stupefied silence" and "one account executive dropped his pipe." And amongst the readers of the *Times* no doubt other pipes were dropped as well. With the Japanese attack barely twenty-five years old and World War II vets heading many households, the wisecrack must have shocked as many as it amused.

But one way or another, the message was delivered: there was a new kid in town. And that's just how Jerry Della Femina wanted it.

Out of that *Times* profile sprang a book with the same title as the proposed ad campaign (which, of course, never ran). *From Those Wonderful Folks Who Gave You Pearl Harbor: Front-Line Dispatches from the Advertising War* was published the following year.

In the staid world of advertising, Jerry Della Femina was something new: the self-created personality. The ad world had always had its share of vivid characters. David Ogilvy, one of the two fathers of the 1960s creative revolution, was known for wearing a full-length black cape with scarlet lining to work and donning a kilt for formal affairs, but Ogilvy was from Scotland and ran his own agency. More typical was Bill Bernbach, Ogilvy's American counterpart: soft-spoken, conservative in dress and manner. Overall, the advertising business was dominated by the genteel issue of the American establishment like Della Femina's one-time boss, the remote and legendary Ted Bates, a product of Phillips Andover and Yale (class of '24).

Jerry Della Femina, on the other hand, was a nobody, a tough kid from an Italian family who grew up on Avenue U in the Gravesend section of Brooklyn. He muscled his way into his first job by sending weeks of samples signed only with his initials before presenting himself triumphantly at the agency's door, announcing, "I'm J.D.F." He immediately went to work creating not just ads but his own image. "Even at the tender age of 26," reported his future amanuensis, Sopkin, "he understood with the startling clarity of a child from the street that the advertising industry is made up of gossips. He also perceived that many people in advertising lead lives of quiet desperation and that any deviation from the norm of behavior would be bound to attract attention." He kept it up as he jumped from job to job, building a reputation for attention-getting headlines to go with the attention-seeking personality. He wrote "What's the Ugliest Part of Your Body?" for a women's product called Pretty Feet; the Charlie Brown-as-embarrassed-pitcher-themed "Your Fly Is Open" for Talon zippers; and, memorably, a trade ad for McGraw-Hill with the banner "Before Hitler Could Kill Six Million Jews, He Had to Burn Six Million Books."

By the time Della Femina published *From Those Wonderful Folks*, he was the hottest guy in the hottest business in town, running his own start-up agency and

Jerry Della Femina and Charles Sopkin, editor, *From Those Wonderful Folks Who Gave You Pearl Harbor: Front-Line Dispatches from the Advertising War* (New York: Simon & Schuster, 1970).

obviously loving it. Charles Sopkin had picked Della Femina for the original *Times* profile because he was the only potential subject who didn't care if he was quoted by name. So the book is naturally All Jerry, All the Time: it reads as if he'd been locked in a room with a box of blank audio tapes and a case of Chivas and told to come out only when the first was full and the second was empty. Sopkin edited the tape-recorded results (lightly, it seems) into thirteen chapters' worth of stream-of-consciousness observations on the advertising business circa 1970, which is as fun to read today as it was then. Despite the endless references to extinct agencies and long-forgotten accounts, Della Femina's literary voice — a cross between Holden Caulfield and P. T. Barnum — is fresh, compelling, and entertaining.

Today we're invited to read Della Femina's memoir as a "key text for *Mad Men*," to quote the blurb from *GQ* prominently displayed on the book's newly redesigned cover. The most obvious connection between Della Femina's '60s and the '60s of *Mad Men* is the most titillating one: the uninhibited attitude toward sex and booze. "The whole place was filled with young guys who suddenly discovered that somebody was going to pay them a lot of money for the rest of their lives for doing this thing called advertising," Della Femina says of his first job, "and all of us got caught up in the insanity of it and went crazy. A whole group of people slowly went out of their skulls."

There are strip poker games. ("Nothing serious, just for a few laughs.") Copywriters drag their desks to stairwells to get a better view into the windows of adjacent apartment buildings. (Accused of belonging to an "organized gang of Peeping Toms," one of Della Femina's colleagues protests that he never belonged to anything organized.) And at the end of the day, "we haul out the booze, get a bucket of ice, and whoever wants a drink takes one." (In an interview on NPR, Della Femina recounted a typical lunch from those days: "As we were looking at our menu, the second martini — and then before the food arrived, the third martini would arrive. At that point then we would have two bottles of wine to go with our food. And then invariably someone would say, you know, I don't think I'm going to have dessert, I think I'll have a double scotch instead.")

But actually, all these wild hijinks, amusing as they are, are secondary to the real story that Della Femina wants to tell: a deadly serious tale of class warfare, with him and his cohorts taking down a moribund WASPy

Jerry Della Femina interviewed by Scott Simon, "Scotch for Dessert: An Adman's Spirited Memoir," *NPR Books*, July 24, 2010.

institution from within, bringing, in Sopkin's words, "chaos out of order." Della Femina begins his book with these words: "Most people think advertising is Tony Randall. In fact, they think this business is made up of 90,000 Tony Randalls. Guys all very suave, all very Tony Randall. They've been fed the idea of Hollywood that an advertising man is a slick, sharp guy. The people know zip about advertising." Today, it's hard to imagine anyone suaver, slicker, or sharper in advertising than creative director Don Draper, *Mad Men*'s profoundly repressed central character. Della Femina's goal is to debunk this slick image. He is the anti–Don Draper.

As a creative director — and as a pitchman — Don Draper, ironically enough, appears to have been modeled on Rosser Reeves, who was the right-hand man to none other than Della Femina's nemesis, Ted Bates. In *From Those Wonderful Folks*, Bates's agency represents all that Della Femina finds contemptible about the establishment advertising world, with its craven, glad-handing account executives and mind-numbing, insulting, repetitive commercials. Della Femina instead identifies with the new wave of copywriters and art directors who are bringing fresh air to Madison Avenue: Jews, Italians, and Greeks from the outer boroughs with real blood in their veins and dynamite in their portfolios.

The best parts of his book, and the parts that will ring the most true to creative people working today, are his accounts of the ad making process and his battles with timid agency superiors and fearful clients to get the work accepted. In the television world of *Mad Men*, this creative new wave has barely yet made an impact. The main roles of Smitty and Kurt, a young copy and art team hired by Draper from Doyle Dane Bernbach ("I sense the hand of Julian Koenig," says Draper while reviewing their portfolio), had been to introduce the office to marijuana. And poor Sal Romano, the dapper Italian American art director who was Sterling Cooper's one concession to ethnicity, crashed and burned in the third season when his long-closeted homosexuality was exposed.

The biggest creative success story in progress on *Mad Men* — and perhaps the series's true protagonist — is secretary-turned-copywriter Peggy Olson. You won't find her source material in Jerry Della Femina's book but in a more recent memoir, *A Big Life (in Advertising)* by Mary Wells Lawrence. Like Peggy, "Bunny" Wells started as a

Mary Wells Lawrence, *A Big Life (in Advertising)* (New York: Alfred A. Knopf, 2002).

rare female in a male-dominated business. She ended up becoming the youngest person ever to join the Copywriters Hall of Fame and was by 1969 reportedly the highest-paid person in advertising. Like Della Femina, she cultivated her image as carefully as any high-profile advertising campaign.

It is the critical role of this cult of personality that is the real lesson of *From Those Wonderful Folks Who Gave You Pearl Harbor*. It's of no little significance that Della Femina describes his book as "dispatches from the advertising war" in his subtitle. He — and Mary Wells, and George Lois, and the other standard-bearers of the creative revolution — imagined themselves in daily battle with the products of northeastern boarding schools and the Ivy League. Outrage was their weapon, and chutzpah (or, in Della Femina's case, *fegataccio*) provided their armor. As cultural critic Thomas Frank was to observe much later in his fascinating book *The Conquest of Cool: Business Culture, Counterculture, and the Rise of Hip Consumerism*, "If Della Femina was the zeitgeist barometer he clearly believed himself to be, by the end of the 1960s, the American adman was not a touchy defender of consumer excess but a jaded scoffer contemptuous of the institutions of consumer society, scornful of the imbecile products by which it worked, and corrosively skeptical of the ways in which the establishment agencies foisted them on the public."

Thomas Frank, *The Conquest of Cool: Business Culture, Counterculture, and the Rise of Hip Consumerism* (Chicago: University of Chicago Press, 1998).

True. But what Frank misses — and, I reluctantly admit, what the creators of *Mad Men* have been largely missing in the show's first three seasons — is the sense of exuberance and joy — perhaps reckless, perhaps misguided — that infuses every page of Della Femina's book. In 1970 he was confident that talent and guts would be sufficient to overthrow the establishment order, or at least to provide himself with a perch within it. And his confidence was well placed: today he leads an enviable life as a publisher and restaurateur, with a newly relevant forty-year-old book to his credit.

In that light, the end of the *New York Times* article that started it all ends with an especially arresting prediction. "The WASPs blew it," declares Della Femina. "They sat around and said, 'This is it, and we don't have to work for it.' My group will eventually blow it, too. We'll sit around with our funny clothes, and we'll get old and fat and start sliding. And then the next revolution is going to take place. The hot writer is going to be Pedro Jimenez, and the hot art director is going to be George Washington Smith. What a crazy scene

Now You See It

that's going to be!" Reading this today, it took me a second
to realize he was talking about agency creative departments
dominated by Hispanics and African Americans.

The new season of *Mad Men* — with its main
characters starting up a new agency of their own — may bring
us a few of those crazy scenes. As for the larger cultural
revolution predicted by Della Femina, it's four decades later
and we're still waiting.

The Four Lessons of Lou Dorfsman

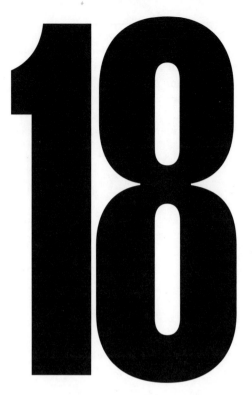

First appeared in Design Observer, October 23, 2008.

Working as an in-house designer for a big corporation doesn't sound glamorous, and staying in the same place for more than forty years doesn't sound like a path to career success. But Lou Dorfsman, who joined the Columbia Broadcasting System in 1946 and rose to become its vice president and creative director for advertising and design until his retirement in 1991, may have had the best job in the American design industry.

Over the course of his career, Dorfsman was responsible for everything at CBS, from its advertising to the paper cups in its cafeteria. Every bit of it was executed with intelligence, verve, glamour, and taste. Trying to get good work done from inside a giant institution is supposed to be hard. How did Lou Dorfsman make it look so easy?

When I learned the sad news last week that Dorfsman had died at the age of ninety, I pulled a book down from my shelf that I've referred to now and then through the years: *Dorfsman & CBS: A 40-Year Commitment to Excellence in Advertising and Design.* Flipping through its 216 pages, I was struck once more by the range and timelessness of the work illustrated inside. And I found an interesting passage, where authors Marion Muller and Dick Hess describe

Marion Muller and Dick Hess, *Dorfsman & CBS: A 40-Year Commitment to Excellence in Advertising and Design* (New York: Amshow & Archive, 1987).

"the do-it-yourself education of Lou Dorfsman," which began shortly after he joined the company as advertising assistant to the legendary Bill Golden, creator of the CBS Eye logo.

It turned out after all that, while working as Golden's assistant, Lou had learned an extremely important lesson about the origin of ads. He had observed that while he and Golden were sitting in their shirtsleeves scaling photos and cutting type apart, certain Ivy Leaguers in three-piece suits were sitting upstairs in conferences making decisions about the very projects he and Golden were producing. It was obvious to Lou that he could do a more intelligent and meaningful job if he were "up there" where the problems were being discussed.

So this is how he did it. Here are the four lessons of Lou Dorfsman.

Lesson 1: Mind the client's business.

Dorfsman began his career at CBS at the age of twenty-eight, working side by side with Bill Golden, his hero and mentor. After a few years, with the rise of the new medium of television, the corporation divided itself into separate units, the CBS Television Network and the CBS Radio Network. Golden took charge of advertising and design for television, the up-and-coming, exciting part. Dorfsman was made art director of the radio unit, the company's "orphan child."

Dorfsman ignored the gloom and doom surrounding the seemingly fading medium of radio and threw himself into meetings with the radio division's sales reps, understanding its wide range of audiences: not just the listening public, but advertisers, affiliates, and government agencies. Dorfsman produced hundreds and hundreds of unglamorous small-space print ads. Almost every one is an ingenious gem. Many feature beautiful illustrations, including a 1952 ad that marked Andy Warhol's first commercial appearance in print. All of them unflinchingly and entertainingly make the case for CBS Radio. When Golden died unexpectedly at the age of forty-eight in 1952, Dorfsman was promoted to creative director of CBS television. Five years later, he was named head design director of the entire Columbia Broadcasting System.

Lesson 2: Learn to identify opportunities.

Through his career at CBS, Dorfsman never sat around passively waiting for requests from his internal clients. Instead, he pushed them, inventing projects that he thought needed to be done. Taking pictures at National

Football League games in New York to promote CBS's local sports coverage, it occurred to him that there was a bigger story: documenting the technological feat of broadcasting multiple games each Sunday all over the country. The result was *Field of Vision*, a twelve-by-twelve-inch, 132-page book that reproduced, in gorgeous black-and-white rotogravure, photographs of each of the seven football games televised across the United States on the afternoon of November 4, 1962. The book emphasized the prowess of CBS's sports division, made a much sought-after gift for football fans, and was credited with helping to secure the network's exclusive contract to cover NFL games the following year.

A few years later, Dorfsman topped that feat with a hardcover book commemorating CBS's coverage of the 1969 moon landing. At 168 pages long, *10:56:20 PM EDT, 7/20/69* featured a spectacular blind-embossed-with-moon-craters dust jacket and a subtitle ("The historic conquest of the moon as reported to the American people by CBS News over the CBS Television Network") that made clear Dorfsman's goal: to associate CBS inextricably with the grand events that defined the nation. Today, both books are collectors' items; neither would exist at all except for Lou Dorfsman's initiative.

Lesson 3: Assume responsibility.
You can tell that Dorfsman identified passionately with his employer's success. He valorized every one of CBS's shows as if they were separate clients, each with individual importance. It's fascinating: to my eyes, each ad appears to have been done from scratch, with its own unique look and feel; the only consistent element is excellence.

Dorfsman didn't hesitate to be an advocate for programs he cared about. He is credited with saving *The Waltons*, a well-reviewed but low-rated show in the early '70s, by conceiving a single ad with the headline "This program is so beautiful it has to die," which exhorted viewers to support it. It ran once in three newspapers. Quoting *Dorfsman & CBS*: "According to Lou, the ad changed his life. He was never really certain how to measure the effectiveness of advertising. Now he had concrete results. CBS was inundated with letters and petitions bearing thousands of signatures. *The Waltons* remained on the air and by the end of the season was the number-one CBS show."

Dorfsman, who began his career as an exhibit designer for the 1939 New York World's Fair, never limited his ambitions to print and broadcast. He designed the CBS news booths at presidential nominating conventions starting in 1964 and created some of the first modern news sets for daily broadcasts the following year. Dorfsman didn't worry about his job description. He just did what needed to be done.

Lesson 4: Define the company's character.

In 1965 CBS moved into a new headquarters building on Sixth Avenue, a black granite skyscraper designed by Eero Saarinen. Quickly nicknamed "Black Rock," the tower was conceived as a defining symbol for the company by its leaders — and Dorfsman's main patrons — CBS chairman William Paley and president Frank Stanton. Dorfsman understood that this new home was an opportunity to emphasize the company's commitment to excellence. So he contributed to the design of every detail, from the barricades that surrounded the site while the structure was under construction, to the art on the walls in the hallways, to the signage in the lobbies, to the freshly printed letterhead and business cards that greeted the CBS staff the day they moved in.

In contrast to the eclectic approach Dorfsman took to the design of the network's outward-facing advertising and promotional material, the graphic standards at headquarters were almost obsessively rigorous. Dorfsman commissioned two new fonts from Freeman Craw, CBS Didot and CBS Sans, and these were deployed everywhere throughout the building, including door numbers, elevator buttons, and wall clocks, eighty of which had to be dismantled and reassembled with new faces installed. Dorfsman's typographic eclecticism reemerged in his career tour de force, his solution for a forty-foot-long blank wall in the corporate cafeteria. There he collaborated with his longtime friend Herb Lubalin to create an all-type, three-dimensional collage combining words related to food and culinary paraphernalia into a relief sculpture that was dubbed the "Gastrotypographicalassemblage." A combination of enthusiastic excess and clinical precision, the wall was hailed as Dorfsman's ultimate achievement. But I must confess, I am just as impressed — if not more — by the fact that he convinced the NYC safety authorities to allow him to use the elegant (and definitely non-code-compliant) CBS Didot font for the building's fire exit signs.

Lou Dorfsman with the Gastrotypographical-assemblage, 1966.

There is no one today — anywhere — that can match the breadth and depth of design authority Lou Dorfsman exercised in his years at CBS. Certainly there is no one like him there today. He retired from the company in 1991. The building was renovated shortly thereafter, and new tenants moved in to join CBS. The Gastrotypographicalassemblage was dismantled and put into storage, where it has been slowly decaying. The good news: there is a movement afoot to restore it led by the ambitious team at the Center for Design Study, which is actively seeking financial support.

A few years ago, we had an appointment at a midtown address that was new to me, 51 West Fifty-Second Street. When the taxi pulled up, I said to my colleagues, "Hey, this is the CBS Building!" And it was. I had never been inside. We were there to see one of the new tenants, not CBS. But the bronze signs in the elevator lobby were still set in CBS Didot. They looked worn, but they were as beautiful as ever, forty years later. Rest in peace, Lou Dorfsman. You will be missed.

As of 2014, the Gastrotypographical-assemblage has been permanently installed at the Marriott Pavilion and Conference Center at the Culinary Institute of America in Hyde Park, New York.

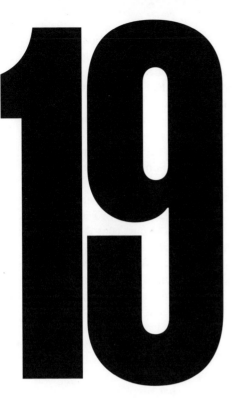

19

That Elusive Silver Bullet

Several years ago, *Business Week* launched a magazine dedicated to communicating the value of design and innovation to the business community called *INside Innovation*. The fact that it was designed in part through an unpaid design competition seemed more than, um, ironic to many readers, and they responded with a vengeance.

With that battlefield's embers finally cooling and the bruises barely healed, an email arrived in my inbox, inviting me "to learn some basic design skills" in order to "create attractive, eye-catching letterheads, logos, flyers, brochures, business cards, and more." Well, okay! Let's check out the website:

Everyone at one time or another has had to create a document of some sort. Whether it was a poster for your son's 7th grade presidential election campaign or your boss's directive to create a flyer for distribution by fax. The question is, do you have to be a trained graphic designer to create these documents? No, you don't. You only need to have a set of guidelines to follow, one of which is to open your mind and let your creativity out to play. It's probably been a while since the two of you got together. There is a world out there to explore with your two hands and one brain, so roll up your sleeves and put on your thinking cap.

First appeared in Design Observer, August 8, 2006.

Course description for "Graphic Design for Non-Designers," offered by bwcourses.com. No longer available.

Do you have to be a trained graphic designer to feel incredibly depressed? No, you don't. But it helps! The offer, by the way, is from *Business Week*.

Here we go again, right? But wait, there may be more here than meets the eye. Maybe the fault isn't with *Business Week*, or any of those mean, uncaring other people out there. Maybe, instead, it's us.

What stings here, I think, isn't just the specter of do-it-yourself. We're used to that. Some of us even applaud it. Once graphic designers possessed unique technical expertise: the names of fonts, the phone numbers of typesetters, the formula for calculating the precise length of a 200-word manuscript set on a 14-pica-wide column of 12-on-14-point Bodoni Book. Today, anyone can do it. If some untrained-in-graphic-design parent wants to support Junior's political ambitions, out comes the Photoshop and some awful typeface, and before you know it the printer is cranking away. (Of course, Junior, if he's got a brain in his head, has already launched his viral video and won't get around to hanging your pathetic old-skool posters. But it's the thought that counts!) For graphic designers, our craft is now a commodity.

It's a little depressing that there are some designers who can count on a little respect. Do you have to be a trained product designer to create a new sports car? Do you have to be a trained architect to design a new house? Despite *Divine Design with Candace Olson* and *Pimp My Ride*, the answer is still yes and yes. You don't see *Business Week* offering any fun courses in industrial design or architecture, at least not yet.

So what's an embattled graphic designer to do? During my three-year term as president of AIGA, the national professional organization for graphic designers, our members consistently ranked one priority above all others: proving the value of design to the general public and, specifically, the business community. To put it bluntly, we were all searching for some magic formula that would make clients predisposed to respect us and to demonstrate that respect by paying us large fees. We wanted design to have "a place at the table." We yearned for a silver bullet that would slay our insecurities once and for all. The silver bullet took a variety of forms. Perhaps the process of design was too mysterious to be credible: Would agreeing on a standard twelve-step sequence reassure clients that there was valuable science behind the art? So many amateurs out there: Shouldn't we be licensing graphic designers so clients could distinguish the professionals from the dabblers? And, oddly, so many credible firms participate in unpaid competitions: Can we make it, if not against the law, then at least professionally embarrassing?

But none of this has ever worked. Graphic designers use too many different processes — those that use a process at all, that is — for any single methodology to make sense to more than a fraction of practitioners. Licensing has been discussed for years and has yet to make any real headway; there's just no way to come up with a basic body of knowledge that could serve as a basis for determining meaningful qualifications. And simply demanding to be paid for your work is different than establishing your work's value.

Business Week's Bruce Nussbaum, finding himself at the center of the anti-free work maelstrom earlier this summer, responded with an observation that has stuck with me. In a competitive world, he wrote, "value is not created by rules or prohibitions but by what one brings to the game. Architects, writers, industrial designers, painters, journalists, baseball players, screenwriters and many other creative professionals understand that. Heck, the entire business community around the globe understands that."

Admit it: Nussbaum has a point. As a class, we designers long to wrap ourselves in the bulletproof cloak of our profession, thinking that if a place at the table is reserved for something called "design," maybe we can slide into that empty seat. But the game doesn't bring the player; the player brings the game. Every great designer I've ever met has gotten respect the old-fashioned way: by earning it. The means to that end are glorious in their variety. There is no one true path to victory, no silver bullet. I know some designers who are incredible strategists, others who are charismatic witch doctors, still others who are patient teachers, and a few who are just plain magicians. Each successful designer has to prove him- or herself with every new project and every new client. And, perhaps, with each new success the job gets a little easier for the rest of us.

It's time to stop being defensive. You may never find that silver bullet. But you can always improve your aim.

Would It Kill You to Smile?

20

First appeared in
Design Observer,
March 11, 2008.

My lovely wife,
Dorothy, 1977.

My lovely wife, Dorothy, finally finished a project that
she's been planning for years: to organize all those old
photographs, boxes and boxes of them, that we've been
accumulating in our basement for over a quarter of a century.
Most of these pictures are filled with smiling babies,
smiling toddlers, smiling little kids, and smiling adults. The
rest of these pictures are filled with nonsmiling adolescents.
Nonsmiling, sullen, disaffected, alienated-looking ten- to
twenty-year-olds. Some of these were our own children.
Some of them were relatives. Some of them were even us.

There must be something wrong with us,
I remember thinking. Where is the joy of youth, the carefree
spirit of eternal promise? Is there something inherently
depressing about our family?

Then I discovered we were not alone.
I discovered bershon.

Bershon was first introduced to a wide audience
by writer and blogger Sarah Brown, who remembered it as
a word from her own teenage years. Her definition is still
the best:

The spirit of bershon is pretty much how you feel when you're 13 and your parents make you wear a Christmas sweatshirt and then pose for a family picture, and you could not possibly summon one more ounce of disgust, but you're also way too cool to really even DEAL with it, so you just make this face like you smelled something bad and sort of roll your eyes and seethe in a put-out manner.

Sarah Brown, "Stream of consciousness post that makes no apologies yet comes full circle because I am magic," Que Sera Sera, May 21, 2004.

What a relief! So it's not an obscure affliction limited to subjects of the pictures in our basement. Bershon is everywhere. There's a Flickr group called I'm So Bershon, and there it is, over and over again. "Every photo of me from high school can be summed up in that one word," said blogger Heather Armstrong at Dooce. When Finslippy's Alice Bradley heard about bershon, her mind flashed back to her own adolescence, "when I was so consumed with distaste for everything and everyone I was forced to live with or near that I could not wipe that look off my face, no matter how I tried. I think I even slept with it on."

The Bershon Flickr group still exists and is as entertaining as ever.

Heather Armstrong, "Begging for commentary," Dooce, August 22, 2006.

Alice Bradley, "This one's for you, Sarah Brown," AliceBradley.net, March 21, 2007.

On reading that the Department of Homeland Security would be searching for passengers with suspicious expressions like disgust, anger, and sadness, Defective Yeti's Matthew Baldwin suggested, "In addition to having to forgo your iPod and hair gel you will now be required to check in your teen prior to boarding." Threat Level Bershon! Exactly. If any doubt whatsoever remains, simply rent a copy of *Ferris Bueller's Day Off* and study Jennifer Grey's performance. She conducts a virtual master class on the Fine Art of Bershon over the entire course of the movie.

Matthew Baldwin, "Threat Level Bershon," Defective Yeti, August 17, 2006.

Once I became aware of bershon, it was tempting to start classifying everything as bershon. But there are rules, delineated here by blogger Suebob Davis:

Suebob Davis, "Can we talk about Bershon?" Suebob's Red Stapler, August 26, 2006.

1. Babies with cranky faces are not bershon. Bershon implies a certain self-conscious world-hating attitude that only develops with time and hormones. Little kids may appear to be bershon, but we are projecting.

2. Photos of someone who is kind of uncomfortable but who is about to crack up are not bershon.

3. People who are just bored are not bershon.

4. People who are stoic are not bershon.

5. Old people, in general, are not bershon, though there may be exceptions.

6. Animals are not bershon. Animals are animals.

Although bershon can be experienced and expressed anywhere, it seems to be especially associated with the act of being photographed. ("God, will you please just take the stupid picture?") You don't have to be an adolescent to qualify. There are hundreds, if not thousands, if not millions of images of languid, bored, even stupefied-looking supermodels out there, all of them amply fulfilling the spirit, if not the letter, of the laws of bershon. And don't even get me started about author photographs. "John Updike, Bernie Siegel, David Halberstam, Dominick Dunne, Barbara Grizzuti Harrison and Caryl Phillips all lean forward uncomfortably, their chins or cheeks supported by a fist or hand. (Presumably their own hands, but who knows?)" Dick Teresi once observed in a *New York Times* story titled "Haul Out the Old Cliches, It's Time to Shoot an Author Photo." He concluded, "They all look like failed lounge acts appearing at your local piano bar. Mr. Updike appears ready to launch into an angst-laden version of 'Sometimes When We Touch.'"

Dick Teresi, "Haul Out the Old Cliches, It's Time to Shoot an Author Photo," *New York Times*, December 12, 1993.

In the days when I used to design corporate promotional literature, I used to dread the moment when we'd have to take the deadly CEO portrait. Titanic kings of commerce, totally in control in the boardroom and the executive suite, predictably would collapse into caricatures of rumpled unease before the camera, all the while grumbling, "How long will this take?" Herculean feats would be required to make these symphonies of corporate bershon ready for publication. I remember one group portrait for a well-known but volatile investment bank that required so much retouching and alterations — all in the days before Photoshop, mind you — that it may as well have been a picture of the Soviet Politburo leadership circa 1932.

But men — and boys — really don't have what it takes. Their way of dealing with a photograph is to scowl or make a horrible face. Bershon, ultimately, is a girls' game. For its quintessence, examine one of the most famous examples of all, Robert Frank's photograph "Elevator — Miami Beach," which appears on page 99 of his landmark 1959 book *The Americans*. The vaguely exasperated look on the operator's face, her eyes just short of rolling, the unspoken message clear as a bell: Lord, get me out of here. Sexy, too. This is what every girl is going for when she goes for bershon.

Robert Frank, *The Americans* (Göttingen, Germany: Stedl, 2008).

And who can blame her? I leave you with the last sentence from the legendary introduction that Jack Kerouac wrote for Frank's book. "And I say: That little ole lonely elevator girl looking up sighing in an elevator full of blurred demons, what's her name & address?" So keep trying, girls. Right now you're surrounded by jerks. But somewhere there's a Jack Kerouac who's desperately trying to find you.

You're So Intelligent

Baxter, the protagonist in John Cheever's short story "The Chaste Clarissa," is vacationing on a Cape Cod island. He discovers to his pleasure that a nearby house is to be looked after all summer by his neighbor's extraordinarily beautiful but stupid new wife — the Clarissa of the story's title — while his neighbor is in Europe. Baxter, a practiced seducer, sets his sights on Clarissa, but to no avail. He tries everything: flattery, chivalry, presents, but Clarissa responds coldly. Until, by accident, responding absently to still another of her inane offhand remarks, he murmurs, "You're so intelligent."

First appeared in Design Observer, September 5, 2007.

"You don't mean that," she answers. He assures her that he does. "I can't be intelligent," she says. "No one ever takes me seriously until they get their arms around me." Baxter assures her that, no, he finds her ideas fascinating and would love to hear more of her opinions. And as she spills them out, he knows he has her, and that's how the story ends. "'You're very intelligent,' he said, now and then. 'You're so intelligent.' It was as simple as that."

John Cheever, "The Chaste Clarissa," New Yorker, June 14, 1952. Later collected in The Stories of John Cheever (New York: Alfred A. Knopf, 1978).

Which brings me to today's theme. Designers of the world, it's as simple as that. You're so intelligent!

Upton was asked about the fact that 20 percent of Americans could not find their own country on a map. Overwhelmed and nervous, she responded: "I personally believe that US Americans are unable to do so because, uh, some, uh, people out there in our nation don't have maps and, uh, I believe that our education like such as in South Africa and, uh, the Iraq, everywhere like such as, and, I believe that they should, our education over here in the US should help the US, uh, or, uh, should help South Africa and should help the Iraq and the Asian countries, so we will be able to build up our future. For our children."

The criticism of Upton was somewhat cruel and unfair. She later enjoyed a measure of fame as an actress in music videos and television commercials.

I thought of the Chaste Clarissa last week while we were all distracting ourselves with one of those perfect end-of-summer bits of nonsense, the public meltdown of Miss South Carolina, Lauren Caitlin Upton, during the essay question section of the Miss Teen USA competition. Like many others who had spent their high-school years being essentially invisible to the cheerleading squad, I found it reassuring to note once again how seldom beauty and intelligence seem to coexist. Yet, in a way I cannot explain, I sensed what was coming when Ms. Upton revealed several days later to the sympathetic hosts of the *Today* show that she was not, in fact, dumb, but would be attending football powerhouse Appalachian State University, where she would be studying, yes, graphic design.

Perhaps design is the field of mindless prettiness. But hasn't it always been so? After all, most of us entered the profession not because we've determined after long thought that it represented a more effective way of influencing the course of world events than, say, law or medicine. Instead, somewhere along the way, we discovered we liked making things look good, and that we were better at it than other people.

Yet in all the years I was involved with AIGA, I heard the members demand one thing over and over again, and from this I got a pretty clear idea of what designers want. And it wasn't to be better designers; interestingly, almost every designer I've ever met has been serenely confident in his or her ability to make things look good, thank you very much. No, what designers wanted then and want now, more than anything else, is respect. Respect from clients. Respect from the general public. Respect from — let's go right to the cliché — our moms. We want to be seen as *more than mere stylists*, we want to *set the agenda*, to be *involved earlier in the strategic process*, to be granted a *place at the table*. In short, just like the Chaste Clarissa, we want to be taken seriously.

Like many designers, for years I used a tried-and-true tactic to hoist my way up the respect ladder, a technique I will here call Problem Definition Escalation. If you've listened carefully to the lyrics to "Gee, Officer Krupke" in *West Side Story* you already know how this works. The client asks you to design a business card. You respond that the problem is really the client's logo. The client asks you to design a logo. You say the problem is the entire identity system. The client asks you to design the identity. You say that the problem is the client's business plan. And so forth. One or two steps later, you can claim whole industries and vast historical forces as your purview. The problem isn't making something look pretty, you fool, it's world hunger!

I'm not sure when I got tired of this. The first few times I was asked to offer my opinion about my client's business strategy, I was flattered. I was even more pleased when my advice seemed to be — a dream come true — taken seriously. But I noticed I was spending more and more of my time in meetings, volunteering ideas about things that I wasn't any more qualified to put forward than what a lot of the people in those same meetings were offering about my design work. Finally, I found myself at a design conference listening to still another demand that clients give us designers that coveted place at that legendary table where all the big decisions are made. Sitting next to me was one of my favorite clients, someone I treasure for her levelheadedness and good humor. "I've spent hours at that table," she whispered to me. "It's not that great, you know."

I forget the theme of that particular conference, but, like so many others, it may as well have been "Designers: You're So Intelligent." Like Clarissa, designers yearn to be respected for our minds. Like Clarissa, we take our real gifts — our miraculous fluency with beauty, our ability to manipulate form in a way that can touch people's hearts — for granted. Those are the gifts that matter and the paths through which we create things that truly endure.

You can take anything I say with a grain of salt. After all, it's coming from someone who put out a design book with seventy thousand words and not a single picture. But here's my advice: designers, you don't have to be dumb. Just don't be so afraid of being beautiful.

Michael Bierut, 79 *Short Essays on Design* (New York: Princeton Architectural Press, 2007).

There Is
No Why

First appeared in
Design Observer,
July 31, 2008.

A review of *Man on
Wire*, directed by James
Marsh, 2008, based on
Philippe Petit, *To Reach
the Clouds: My High
Wire Walk Between the
Twin Towers* (New York:
North Point, 2002).

The best design movie of 2008 is not about a typeface. It's about a tightrope walker.

Man on Wire, a thrilling new documentary directed by James Marsh, tells the story of Philippe Petit's 1974 high-wire walk between the two towers of the World Trade Center. As a fifty-year-old designer who spends more time in meetings than at my (imaginary) drawing board, I find it conveniently reassuring to value concept over execution. *Man on Wire* shows how easy it is to have an idea, and how hard — and sometimes even miraculous— it is to see it realized.

Petit was a teenager in Paris browsing magazines in a dentist's office when he saw a rendering of the then-unbuilt World Trade Center. He was electrified. He was already an obsessed magician, juggler, and high-wire artist. To an aspiring tightrope walker, the idea of two 110-story towers, side by side, suggested only one thing. Petit drew a line between the image of the two towers. All that remained now was the execution.

Making the walk happen took years of planning. Petit sums up his own attitude with characteristic aplomb: "It's impossible, that's for sure. So let's start working."

He moved to New York and began visiting the construction site, at one point obtaining access to the top of the towers by posing as a French journalist. He made drawings and took photographs. Returning home, he built a full-sized model of the WTC roofs in the French countryside to practice the walk. Getting all the necessary equipment up to the tops of the towers was not a one-man job. He recruited a group of confederates, a colorful multinational troupe who offer conflicting present-day memories throughout the film, and who each played a different role in what they privately called the coup. The plan was not just bold but actually rather insane: their solution for the hardest part of the whole scheme, for instance, getting the wire from one tower to the other, a span of nearly two hundred feet, was to use a bow and arrow. It worked. Amazingly, it all worked.

Philippe Petit, August 7, 1974.

Man on Wire's biggest, most satisfying surprise is seeing what Petit actually did when the moment of truth finally arrived and he stepped out into the void. I have to admit, I'd always assumed that he simply edged his way inch by inch across the expanse between the towers, teeth gritted and knuckles white, finally making it with relief to the other side. Was this what I expected from past exposure to "death defying" circus acts, where the danger is always exaggerated while the crowd holds its collective breath? Or, more likely, was I simply projecting how I—and, admit it, you — would have attacked the challenge?

What happened was quite different. Philippe Petit was out on the wire for more than forty-five minutes, crossing back and forth between the towers eight times. One of my favorite characters in the film, Port Authority Police Department Sergeant Charles Daniels, a mustachioed New York '70s cop straight out of *Dog Day Afternoon*, later described to news cameras what he saw when he was sent up to persuade Petit to surrender:

Dog Day Afternoon, directed by Sidney Lumet, was released the year after Petit's walk and featured a huge cast of uniformed extras.

I observed the tightrope "dancer" — because you couldn't call him a "walker" — approximately halfway between the two towers. And upon seeing us he started to smile and laugh, and he started going into a dancing routine on the high wire. And when he got to the building we asked him to get off the high wire, but instead he turned around and ran back out into the middle. He was bouncing up and down. His feet were actually leaving the wire, and then he would resettle back on the wire again. Unbelievable, really.

It had taken six years of work and planning to get to that moment, and Philippe Petit never wanted it to end.

His greatest dream, unbelievably, had come true. He was twenty-four years old.

He finally surrendered to the police. In the film he remembers that the only moment he actually feared for his safety was when he was being hustled down the WTC stairs. Back on earth, he was mobbed by reporters, all with the same question: Why?

"There is no why," he said. "When I see three oranges, I juggle; when I see two towers, I walk."

Like many in the theater, I was crying at this point. It was all so senselessly brave and beautiful. And, of course, there was another reason: although it's never mentioned in the film, you are constantly reminded — especially as you watch Petit and his accomplices plan their audacious but benevolent "crime" — that the World Trade Center towers no longer exist.

When my wife and I first moved to New York in 1980, Dorothy's first job was in World Trade Center Tower Two. Alas, only the twelfth floor. I visited her after she started, and we went up to check out the view from the Observation Deck. We never saw Petit there, although in the face of public acclaim after his coup, he had been given a lifetime pass. But we saw something else, a little hard to see but clearly visible once you knew what to look for: Petit's autograph, the date of his triumph, and a little drawing of two towers connected by a single line, a replica of the idea that started it all.

Along with so much else, that autograph is gone now. But Philippe Petit is still with us, living in Woodstock, New York, and serving as artist in residence at the Cathedral of St. John the Divine. And, thanks to *Man on Wire*, so is the timeless lesson of the power of a simple idea, beautifully realized.

The
Graphic
Glass
Ceiling

In 2006, I was the moderator of a presentation and panel discussion at the 92nd Street Y, "The Art of the Book: Behind the Covers." The panelists were Milton Glaser, Chip Kidd, and Dave Eggers. The organizers seemed pleasantly surprised by the turnout: over nine hundred people showed up on a Monday night to hear three people talk about book design.

After a visual presentation from each participant, all three joined me on the stage for questions submitted from the audience. There were seven questions in all. The fourth question to the all-male panel was as follows: "Why do you — all three of you — suppose there are so few female graphic designers — or at least so few female 'superstar' graphic designers? Is there a glass ceiling in graphic design?"

I read the question to the panel. There was a moment of uncomfortable silence. What would your answer be?

Many still remember what happened next. Chip Kidd made a quick joke about Larry Summers, who lost his job at Harvard partly by ruminating a little too freely on a related topic. After another pause, Milton Glaser offered an answer. He spoke carefully and even hesitantly.

First appeared in Design Observer, December 11, 2006.

The account here is
from Jill Priluck, "Elder
Heckler and the Ghost
of Larry Summers Live
from the 92nd Street Y,"
Gothamist, December
6, 2006, and Priluck,
"The Glaser Conundrum,
Continued," Gothamist,
December 9, 2006.

A possible reason, Glaser said, was that many
working women chose to "get pregnant, have children, go
home, and take care of their children. And those essential
years that men are building their careers and becoming
visible are basically denied to women who choose to be at
home." There was "no substitute" for a mother raising her
child, he added. "Unless something very dramatic happens
to the nature of the human experience then it's never going
to change." About day care and nannies, he said, "None of
them are good solutions."

Jill Priluck at Gothamist reported what
happened next:

*The crowd was silent except for a hiss or two and
then Eggers piped up that he and his wife both work from home
and share child care responsibilities — but added that maybe
New York was different (although we don't think Eggers really
believes this). Then it was clear to everyone in the room that
it was time to move on.*

On stage, I remember feeling...well, I remember
feeling there sure are a lot of guys up here. As I recall,
I eventually volunteered that, in fact, cover design was a
part of our field that had provided a route to success for
several notable female designers, including Louise Fili,
Carin Goldberg, and Knopf's Carol Carson and Barbara de
Wilde, not to mention (as noted by our questioner) my
own partner Paula Scher. There didn't seem to be much else
to say. Luckily, there were other, and easier, questions to
answer. Next?

I began getting emails about the event, and
particularly its "Larry Summers moment," the next day, as
well as links to other reviews that raised the same question.
On Youngna Park's blog, Glaser's comments were rendered
like this:

Youngna Park,
blog entry,
December 6, 2006.
No longer available.

*There are no women at the top of the [book designing]
field because women give up that time to have babies and
families. [ed. note: Milton! whatttttt are you talking about?!!]*

It occurs to me now that I might have also said that
evening that three of the world's best book designers — no,
make that the three best book designers in the world — are
all women: Julia Hasting, Lorraine Wild, and Irma Boom.
But this misses the point. Because the issue isn't about
talent, or ability, or accomplishment. It's about celebrity.

"Superstar" designers — and that's what we're
talking about; read the question again — aren't just good
designers. They're celebrity designers. And celebrity is a

very specific commodity. It certainly helps to be good at what you do to be a celebrity designer (although celebrities in other fields don't always seem to have this requirement). But that's only a start. You also need to develop a vivid personality, an appetite for attention, and a knack for self-promotion. Accept every speaking engagement. Cough up a memorable *mot juste* for every interviewer. Make sure they spell your name right every time. This is time-consuming work, particularly on top of your regular job, which presumably consists of doing good graphic design. Naturally, if you choose this route, it helps to be free of the distractions of ten to twenty years of caring for children, to say the least. In many ways, Milton Glaser's observations were shocking only in their obviousness.

We all know that women face challenges in the workplace that go far beyond being denied spots on panel discussions. According to a 2004 study, women make only 75.5 cents for every dollar earned by men. In 2005, the US Equal Employment Opportunity Commission handled over 23,000 charges of sex-based discrimination. Just a few months ago, the London School of Economics estimated it will take 150 years to eliminate economic inequality based on gender worldwide. These are real problems.

Institute for Women's Policy Research, "Pay Equity and Discrimination," 2015. Over the past eleven years, this figure has improved slightly. The American woman now makes eighty cents for every dollar earned by a man.

Yet, you have to start somewhere. Glaser answered the question on the card, but the real question was the unspoken one: "Why is it that you guys up there are always... guys?" There is no good answer for this, and it doesn't seem we should have to wait 150 years to come up with one. It's depressing for a profession that's more than half female to keep putting up 100 percent male rosters, at the 92nd Street Y or anywhere else. And I say this with no small degree of self-consciousness, as a member of a firm where only 10 percent of the partners are women. This is what made me squirm last Monday night, and it's what makes me squirm today.

The 150-year estimate is from Alan Manning, "The Gender Pay Gap," *CentrePiece* 1, no. 11, Summer 2006.

This figure has improved slightly too. As of this writing, 21 percent of Pentagram's partners are women.

Celebrity is good for certain things. It puts the butts in the seats at a panel discussion on book design, for instance. But it's not the only thing, and based on the reactions of those people in the audience at the 92nd Street Y, it might be time for something more.

What
Lella
Knew

First appeared in
Design Observer,
November 13, 2010.

Thirty years ago this summer, I graduated from design school in Ohio and moved to New York to take a job at Vignelli Associates. Even then, Massimo Vignelli was a legend. Other designers who heard where I would be working always seemed to have a story about him. Only a few of these were true, but most were outrageous. I knew next to nothing about Lella Vignelli, Massimo's wife and partner, alongside whom he had been working for his whole career. I remember running into a former Vignelli Associates intern. "Oh, wait till you meet Lella," he said, mysteriously.

It was at the end of my first day when I was presented to Mrs. Vignelli so she could examine firsthand the office's newest, youngest, most poorly dressed, and least experienced underling. "Oh, you are the kid from Cincinnati," she said with an enigmatic smile, giving that last word a slight emphasis as if in her mind it explained everything. God only knows how I looked to her. To me, she looked like a movie star. (Sophia Loren was the obvious comparison.) Over the next ten years, I would get used to Massimo. But around Lella, I would never quite escape the feeling that I was just a rube from Hicksville.

I quickly came to understand the relationship between these two brilliant designers. Massimo would tend to play the role of idea generator. Lella served as the critic, editing the ideas and shaping the best ones to fit the solution. Massimo was the dreamer, focusing on the impossible. Lella was ruthlessly practical, never losing sight of the budgets, the deadlines, the politics, the real world. It was Massimo's worldview that had defined my studies in design school. Lella's concerns were entirely foreign to me. So I may as well say it right now: I learned an enormous amount from Massimo about how to be a good designer. But I learned how to be a successful designer from Lella.

Although Massimo hired me, it was Lella who gave me my first break. After months and months of making photostats, doing mechanical artwork, assembling comps, and executing Massimo's amazingly accurate sketches, I was called in to meet a new fashion client from the West Coast. Coming out of the meeting, I knew that Massimo would have some ideas of his own, but I decided for once to develop my own approach as well. After working after hours for a week or so on my own solution, I was called into a meeting with the Vignellis to plan our first design presentation. "Well," I said sort of sheepishly, "I've been doing some thinking about this." I spread out my designs —

Lella Vignelli, 2003.

all pretty detailed by this point — and Massimo and Lella scrutinized them. "These are great," exclaimed Massimo, picking up his pencil. "Of course, you might change the main typeface, and probably make this line here a little heavier — " "Massimo, stop!" said Lella. "Don't you see the kid has got it all worked out already?" Massimo laughed. "You're right," he said. "Let's do it your way." And we did — thanks to Lella. Looking back now, I realize it wasn't the greatest design in the world, but it was the first real thing I could call my own.

Lella taught me about the value of design, literally. "Don't either of you start talking about money," she would often joke as Massimo and I would go into a first-time client meeting. She knew that we would tend to give the work away for free just for a chance to see it realized. Once, all three of us were in a meeting with a client who wanted Vignelli Associates to design a shoe box. At the end of the meeting, the client asked how much we would charge. Lella looked quickly at the two of us: *leave this to me.* I did the math in my head. Five sides, not counting the bottom, say $1,500 apiece, that makes $7,500 in fees. Then Lella spoke:

"Thirty thousand dollars." "That sounds about right," said the client. After the meeting, Lella asked me what I would have charged, and I told her. "See?" she said triumphantly. "You just made $22,500 just by keeping your mouth shut!"

For some of the time I worked at Vignelli Associates, Lella was bothered by back problems and occasionally would spend days in bed. Or rather, on her back in her office. Like the rest of the fourteenth floor of 475 Tenth Avenue, Lella's suite was furnished almost entirely with chairs, tables, couches, and lamps that she had designed with Massimo. I remember more than once being summoned for conferences with Lella in that office, which she conducted with supreme elegance from a reclining position on her Poltronova sofa. Often these would happen at year end, when raises were announced and bonuses were distributed. Naturally this was Lella's job. "Listen, kid, we have decided to give you an increase," she would announce in her languid accent. One wouldn't know whether to say thanks, bow, or genuflect. At least once I remember approaching the sofa to kiss her ring. I was only partly joking. But what else could you do?

I was young and naive when I started out. I thought that good design was its own best argument. You simply would show it to clients, and how could they resist? I assumed that the mechanics of a successful design practice — payrolls, leases, taxes, balance sheets — all took care of themselves. I learned from Lella that talent and passion were crucial, but that alone they were not enough. If you really wanted to make a difference in the world as a designer, you needed to also have brains, cunning, confidence, and relentless drive. These traits turned abstractions into reality, converted doubtful clients into passionate advocates, and transformed trivial notions into ideas of consequence.

Lella Vignelli died on December 22, 2016.

Massimo has often defined their working relationship like this: "I'm the engine, and Lella is the brakes." The first time I heard this as a young designer, it was clear to me which was more important. If you were a designer, wouldn't you want to be the engine, powerful, propulsive, driving forward? It was only years later that I remembered something my high-school driving instructor once said: "You don't get killed in a car accident because the car won't start. You get killed because the brakes fail."

So thank you, Lella, for keeping Vignelli Associates, and the Vignelli design vision, alive and thriving for all these years.

Speech, Speech

First appeared in
Design Observer,
January 23, 2007.

Does this sound familiar?

Your client has a message to communicate: an argument, a sales pitch, a call to action. Your job is to give it form. You're an expert at this. You know how to take a complicated bunch of ideas and reduce them to their arresting, memorable, engaging essence. You come up with some big ideas that you're convinced will work, and, detail by careful detail, you bring those ideas to life. But there's a problem: your work is second-guessed by a bunch of middle managers, some of whom are insecure, some of whom have their own agendas to inject, some of whom just like to say no. Despite all that, you refine and revise, hoping to keep the strength of your original idea intact. Finally, your work is approved, and it goes out into the world. If you're lucky, it really makes a difference: minds are changed, passions are fueled, your client looks great. And, somehow, hardly anyone out there knows you were involved at all.

It sounds a lot like graphic design, doesn't it? But I'm talking about something else: speechwriting. To a surprising degree, the two professions are remarkably similar.

My introduction to the world of speechwriting came through an unlikely (for knee-jerk liberal me) source:

Peggy Noonan, *What I Saw at the Revolution: A Political Life in the Reagan Era* (New York: Random House, 1990).

Peggy Noonan's 1990 book *What I Saw at the Revolution*, her account of working as a White House speechwriter for Ronald Reagan and George H. W. Bush. By the end of her tour of duty, she was associated with some of Bush Senior's most parodied lines: "a thousand points of light" and "read my lips: no new taxes"; today she's a ubiquitous Republican pundit.

But in 1984 Noonan was still not far from her scrappy Irish-Catholic working-class roots, working her way up the White House ranks, taking on small assignments and looking for her big break. That came five months into her job, when she was asked to write a speech that Reagan was scheduled to deliver on the fortieth anniversary of D-Day, before the cliffs of Pointe du Hoc at Normandy. It was a plum assignment. In one of the best parts of her book, she describes how she constructed the speech, building one vivid bit of description on another: if you're a designer, you'll recognize the pure pride of craftsmanship when you hear it. Amidst a lot of useless advice ("We want something like the Gettysburg Address," more than one nervous staffer told her), a fellow writer kept telling her to remember something: they'll be there. Noonan realized that he meant the aging Rangers who scaled the cliffs on D-Day — and not scattered throughout the crowd, but sitting together in the front row, just five feet from the president. It was a crucial insight, and from it Noonan derived the key moment of the speech:

Many recordings of this speech are available online. The full text can be found at historyplace.com, "Ronald Reagan on the 40th Anniversary of D-Day," The History Place Great Speeches Collection.

When one Ranger fell, another would take his place. When one rope was cut, a Ranger would grab another and begin his climb again. They climbed, shot back, and held their footing. Soon, one by one, the Rangers pulled themselves over the top, and in seizing the firm land at the top of these cliffs, they began to seize back the continent of Europe.

Two hundred twenty-five came here. After two days of fighting only ninety could still bear arms.

Behind me is a memorial that symbolizes the Ranger daggers that were thrust into the top of these cliffs. And before me are the men who put them there.

These are the boys of Pointe du Hoc. These are the men who took the cliffs. These are the champions who helped free a continent. These are the heroes who helped to end a war.

I don't care what you think about Reagan, Noonan, Republicans, or the military-industrial complex: that's a speech.

It made Noonan famous around the White House. She became "the girl who does the poetry." She got more

important speeches to write, and with them came
more important people to oversee her work. The fun of the
early small jobs was replaced by the tension of higher stakes.
She began to "hate the comments, the additions and deletions
and questions...sending a speech out...to be commented
on by presidential aides, and their secretaries and their
secretaries' cousins." Her frustrations will be familiar to you,
as will her fantasy that one day the Top Guy will demand
to know who's been watering down his speeches and demand
"Get me Noonan." Her dream client had gone bad.

She got an opportunity with one more speech,
the one that consolidated her legend. On January 28, 1986,
the space shuttle *Challenger* exploded shortly after takeoff,
killing all seven astronauts aboard, one of whom was
Christa McAuliffe, the first member of the Teacher in Space
Project; because of her, many schoolchildren witnessed
the disaster as it happened. Reagan was scheduled to give
his State of the Union address that night. It was canceled,
and instead the president delivered a speech that Peggy
Noonan wrote that afternoon; time was short, there was
little time to review it and, hence, as Noonan says, "no time
to make it bad." It was short, extraordinarily moving, and
ended with a quote from the poem "High Flight" by John
Gillespie Magee:

> *The crew of the space shuttle* Challenger *honored
> us by the manner in which they lived their lives. We will never
> forget them, nor the last time we saw them — this morning,
> as they prepared for their journey, and waved good-bye, and
> "slipped the surly bonds of earth" to "touch the face of God."*

The full text of this
speech can be found
at history.nasa.gov,
"Explosion of the Space
Shuttle Challenger:
Address to the Nation,
January 28, 1986, by
President Ronald
W. Reagan."

A deluge of mail and calls followed. But does it
surprise you to learn that during the attenuated review
process, someone from the National Security Council
suggested that the end be changed — quoting, of all things,
a then-popular AT&T commercial — to "reach out and
touch someone"? Noonan described this as "the worst edit
I received in all my time at the White House."

In 2006, the Library of America released the
landmark *American Speeches*, which collects, in two volumes,
over one hundred speeches from Patrick Henry to Bill
Clinton. But, as William F. Buckley Jr. pointed out, nothing
is said about their genesis. We have to turn elsewhere
to unravel the mystery of how much of JFK's inaugural
address ("Ask not what your country can do for you...") was
written by the president and how much by speechwriter
Ted Sorensen; or to learn that the climax of Martin Luther

Ted Widmer, editor,
*American Speeches:
Political Oratory
from the Revolution
to the Civil War*
and *American Speeches:
Political Oratory
from Abraham Lincoln
to Bill Clinton* (New
York: Library of America,
2006).

King Jr.'s "I Have a Dream" was an improvised departure from the prepared script.

I've worked with many writers over the years. Some of my favorites have been former speechwriters. In my experience, they really know how to work with a designer. They know they have to fight for an audience's attention; they know that what matters is not word count but persuasion; they know that words do not just provide information but reveal the essence of a person or an organization. And they know to be appalled — but never surprised — when someone on the client end tries to ruin everything with a barrage of inept suggestions.

As I write this, George W. Bush — a man whom even his supporters would not hail as a great orator — will deliver his seventh State of the Union Address. A small army of writers is busy trying to put together an address that will wipe out memories of Bush's last outing, the less than persuasive unveiling of his latest plan for Iraq. "A mediocre speech that was flat," speechwriter emeritus David Gergen told the *New York Times*. "It was solid, but they miss Gerson." Gergen was referring to Michael J. Gerson, who left the White House in the summer of 2006. Gerson, according to the *Times*, is credited with Bush's best speech, the one he delivered to the joint session of Congress nine days after the September 11 attacks.

It's been a long time since George Bush has delivered a speech like that. But don't blame his speechwriters. Maybe they're working for a bad client.

Sheryl Gay Stolberg, "Clock Ticking, Speechwriters for Bush Seek Perfect Pitch," *New York Times*, January 22, 2007. The speech was, alas, not well received. ("He offered up a tepid menu of ideas that would change little," wrote the *Times*.)

Vinyl Fetish

The Cooper-Hewitt National Design Museum holds parties in its beautiful garden on Friday nights during the summer, each one of which features a guest DJ. I was talking to someone there and suggested — half jokingly — that I thought I would make a good guest DJ since I had what was, to my knowledge, the best collection of rap and dance twelve-inch records of any middle-aged white guy in Sleepy Hollow, New York.

Now, this claim may or may not actually be true, but the Cooper-Hewitt Museum decided to put me to the test. As you may have heard, they asked me to be the DJ for the after-party at the 2006 National Design Awards.

So, a few weeks before, I went down in the basement and brought up three heavy boxes of records that hadn't seen the light of day in more than twenty years. And I wondered: Would they still work?

When I first moved to New York City in the summer of 1980, I picked up a new habit. I started going to nightclubs, and I started buying records. Like any self-respecting '70s-era college student, I already owned a serious collection of LPs that I had dragged with me from one dorm room to another. But this was something new.

First appeared in Design Observer, October 9, 2006.

I still bought, say, the latest Elvis Costello or the new Talking Heads, but my real passion was searching for some song I had heard on Friday night at Danceteria, like "Chant No. 1 (I Don't Need This Pressure On)" by Spandau Ballet (well before they entered their treacly "True" phase). Or "Holy Ghost" by the Bar-Kays (featuring the stupendous drum break that was sampled to anchor "Pump Up the Volume" by M/A/R/R/S). Or "Alice, I Want You Just for Me!" with its insistent exclamatory punctuation, by Full Force, who also recorded under the name Cult Jam when they backed up Lisa Lisa on the irresistibly singsongy "Head to Toe." Or "Don't Make Me Wait" by the Peech Boys, or "(We Don't Need this) Fascist Groove Thing" by Heaven 17, or "Da Butt" by Experience Unlimited (lyrics by Spike Lee!).

Twelve-inch single of "The Adventures of Grandmaster Flash on the Wheels of Steel," Sugar Hill Records, 1981. Inscribed "To my buddy Micheal [*sic*], Grandmaster Flash" by Joseph Saddler.

But what came to obsess me was what today we'd call old school hip-hop, but what I then just called rap. "What are all those light-blue records?" a visitor to our teeny apartment once asked, indicating the line of identically clad Sugar Hill discs that I had lined up on my shelf back in 1984. Yes, like most of white America, I'd started with "Rapper's Delight" by the group that launched Sylvia Robinson's label, the Sugarhill Gang, but soon it was on to the Sequence ("Funk You Up"), the Funky 4 + 1 ("That's the Joint"), Mean Machine ("Disco Dream," which I won by being the first "Name It and Claim It" caller to Frankie Crocker's show on WBLS), and, of course, the performers that defined the movement, Grandmaster Flash and the Furious Five. And in early '80s New York, it was more than records. We saw Flash perform live three different times; his 1981 studio release "The Adventures of Grandmaster Flash on the Wheels of Steel" didn't come anywhere near replicating the experience of watching the virtuoso cut to the beat in real time. But records were what I had, and, like Shrevie in *Diner* (1982), boy, did I love my records.

In Barry Levinson's 1982 movie *Diner*, the character Shrevie (played by Daniel Stern) has a fight with his beleaguered wife Beth (played by Ellen Barkin) that culminates with the lines "Just don't touch my records! Ever!"

It wasn't the looks. Part of what made my collection remarkable was how...well, ugly it was. This was not a fertile field for record cover designers. I found a few exceptions in those boxes in my basement: Pedro Bell's ghetto psychedelia for "Atomic Dog" by George Clinton, Peter Saville's now-legendary sleeve for Joy Division's "Love Will Tear Us Apart," and Maira Kalman's debut as an illustrator on M&Co's cover for David Byrne's EP *3 Big Songs* (remixed from his score for Twyla Tharp's *The Catherine Wheel*). But most of the covers — Sugarhill's rainbow-hued tornado, Enjoy's illegible silver-on-red graffiti, West End's pink/maroon/orange/beige(!) skyline — are as seemingly disposable as the music they contained. For the most part, this was silly, danceable music dominated by exhortations to throw your hands in the air, et cetera. Flash's later collaborations with Furious Five member Melle Mel, "The Message" and "White Lines," were true Reagan-era protest songs that suggested the harder, darker strains that would overtake the genre in the mid-'80s with the rise of Run-D.M.C., Afrika Bambaataa, and, of course, Public Enemy. I didn't like this as much, and my mania subsided at about the time I got a CD player.

I never really worked as a professional DJ back then. I just had a fairly big record collection and would be asked to lug my boxes to friends' parties and play songs so people could dance. A few times, strangers asked me to play records at their parties, and I'd get paid for that, although not much. See, actually having the records counted for something in those days, as did knowing the difference between, say, the "Party Version" of Taana Gardner's "Heartbeat" and the "Club Version" (184 seconds). I remember someone at a party offering me $150 for my copy of "Hey Fellas" by those pioneers of DC go-go music, Trouble Funk. He said he'd been looking for it everywhere. I didn't sell it, of course: I was zealously guarding my private corner on the Trouble Funk market. So that record's been down in my basement with the rest of them for twenty years. Like all the others, it still works.

Of course, today you can download a dozen different versions of "Hey Fellas." My corner on the Trouble Funk market is, I guess, worthless. The boxes, however, are as heavy as ever. See you on the dance floor.

The playlist for the set I DJed at the Cooper-Hewitt Museum on October 18, 2006, was as follows:

Get Up I Feel Like Being a Sex Machine (Live in Augusta, Georgia)/ James Brown; Genius of Love/ Tom Tom Club; Double Dutch Bus/ Frankie Smith; Me No Pop I/Coati Mundi; Da Butt/Experience Unlimited; Hey Fellas/Trouble Funk; We Need Some Money/ Chuck Brown and the Soul Searchers; That's the Joint/Funky 4 + 1; 8th Wonder/Sugarhill Gang; Push It/Salt-N-Pepa The Breaks/Kurtis Blow; White Lines (Don't Do It)/Grandmaster Flash and Melle Mel; The Message/ Grandmaster Flash and the Furious Five; Kiss/Prince and the Revolution; Let It Whip/Dazz Band The Groove Line/ Heatwave; Shake Your Body (Down to the Ground)/ The Jacksons; Straight Up/Paula Abdul; Atomic Dog/ George Clinton; Alice, I Want You Just for Me!/Full Force; Chant No. 1 (I Don't Need This Pressure On)/Spandau Ballet; In the Name of Love/ Thompson Twins; Tainted Love/Where Did Our Love Go/Soft Cell; She Blinded Me with Science/Thomas Dolby; Soul Makossa/ Manu Dibango; Jam Hot/Johnny Dynell and New York 88; Car Wash/Rose Royce; We Are Family/Sister Sledge; Don't Leave Me This Way/Thelma Houston; Never Can Say Goodbye/Gloria Gaynor

Now You
See It

First appeared in
Design Observer,
December 20, 2006.

One Sunday in late November, I opened up the *New York Times* and was pleasantly surprised to find an illustration by my partner Abbott Miller on the front page of the paper's Book Review section. I hadn't seen it in process in the studio; so much work happens here that I see a lot of it only when the rest of the world does. I liked it. It was cool-looking, enigmatic. Ten vaguely Victorian-style illustrations of acrobats, precise vertical red hairlines, and a Baldessariesque black dot. What did it mean? Who knew? I gave it a long look and then turned to the rest of the paper.

Liesl Schillinger,
"Dream Maps," *New
York Times*, November
26, 2006, a review
of Thomas Pynchon,
Against the Day (New
York: Penguin, 2006).

I admired the illustration again when I read the section more carefully, including "Dream Maps," Liesl Schillinger's review of Thomas Pynchon's sprawling new novel *Against the Day*. Schillinger was largely positive ("his funniest and arguably his most accessible novel"), which was interesting to me since many of the other reviews I had read were mixed, to say the least. I looked at the other reviews, and the rest of the paper, and put the whole thing aside.

A few days later, I was taking a stack of newspapers out to the curb for recycling. The Book Review was on top. I put the bin down, glanced one last time at Abbott's illustration, and then I saw it at last: PYNCHON.

Maybe other people saw it all along. Good for them. Me, I felt both dumb and pleased: dumb that I had missed it for so long and pleased that I had finally unlocked the puzzle, and in the nick of time, too, with the recycling truck just a few hundred feet up the block. A few days later, I had a chance to talk to Nicholas Blechman, the accomplished designer who had recently replaced the legendary Steven Heller as art director of the Book Review. I complimented him on the illustration and asked if I was...well, stupid: Did everyone else see the "trick" right away?

Nicholas seemed to be ready for the question. "When I got the illustration," he said, "I called up Abbott and asked if he intended to make it any easier to read. He told me no, that he liked it as is." Nicholas then showed it to his editor, who had no trouble reading it: PYNCHON. Just to make sure, the editor showed it to some others; again, no problem. And so it ran, to confuse and delight me and, I suspect, a few others out there.

Editors, as many designers know, tend to be rather literal when it comes to illustration. So I was surprised — as, perhaps, was Nicholas — that such an oblique image was approved without protest. Do editors deserve more credit for visual adventurousness than they usually get?

Not necessarily. What was happening here was something else, something that Elizabeth Newton would understand. As a graduate student at Stanford University, Newton conducted a series of experiments that she described in her 1990 dissertation, "Overconfidence in the Communication of Intent: Heard and Unheard Melodies." Her experiment was described like this in the *Stanford Social Innovation Review*:

[College students were asked] to participate in an experiment in one of two roles: "tappers" and "listeners." Tappers received a list of 25 well-known songs and were asked to tap out the rhythm of one song. Listeners tried to guess the song from the taps. The tappers reported that they could clearly "hear" the lyrics and complete musical accompaniment as they banged away. When they were asked to predict how many songs listeners would guess, they predicted 50 percent. However, listeners heard only a series of seemingly disconnected taps. Indeed, of all the songs tapped out, listeners correctly guessed only 3 percent.

The conclusion? If you already know the answer, you tend to underestimate the difficulty of the question. When you tap out the rhythm of "Happy Birthday" while the

Illustration for "Dream Maps," Abbott Miller, 2006.

Chip Heath, "Loud and Clear," *Stanford Social Innovation Review*, Winter 2003.

melody plays in your head, it sounds clear as a bell. To a listener, however, you're just banging away with neither rhyme nor reason. Once you know something, it's hard to remember what it was like not to know it. Blechman's editors already knew what Miller's acrobats were doing: they were illustrating Liesl Schillinger's review of *Against the Day*. They saw Pynchon because they were looking for him.

Business consultants have come to call this phenomenon "the curse of knowledge," and it's central to the challenges that designers face with their clients. This is as common at the highest levels of corporate identity strategy as with a single commissioned illustration. As Chip Heath and Dan Heath explain in the December 2006 issue of *Harvard Business Review*, "Top executives have had years of immersion in the logic and conventions of business, so when they speak abstractly, they are simply summarizing the wealth of concrete data in their heads. But frontline employees, who aren't privy to the underlying meaning, hear only opaque phrases." (Of course, sometimes those abstractions summarize not a "wealth of concrete data" but recycled bromides and muddy thinking, and frontline employees know bullshit when they hear it.)

The curse of knowledge is especially true when the subject is logo design. In this case, context is everything, and some designers are clever enough to create what might be called a preemptive context. Take Lucent Technologies, for instance. Their 1995 logo, a scrawled red circle created by Landor, was unveiled to employees as the Innovation Ring. Now, there's no such thing, of course, as an innovation ring, and if there were, there's no reason to think it would look like the Lucent logo. This is simply a construct that was invented, with appropriate supporting rhetoric ("a continuous cycle of discovery, creativity and knowledge"), to preempt not just blank stares but other possible interpretations, which might include, say, a Red Doughnut Drawn by a Small Child. Then, after ten years of quite respectable performance, the Innovation Ring was retired when its owner merged with Alcatel. The new logo? Not just some scribbles in a purple circle! Think of it instead as the Infinity Circle, representing "endless possibilities for the future of the combined company, and its commitment to being a strong, stable and enduring ally for our customers around the world." Now that the melody's implanted in your head, you presumably will be better equipped to follow the tune.

Chip Heath and Dan Heath, "The Curse of Knowledge," *Harvard Business Review*, December 2006.

Lucent Technologies logo (also known as the "Innovation Ring"), designed by Landor Associates, 1996.

It's easy to dismiss this as facile salesmanship; I've come to appreciate it as a useful way to manage the curse of knowledge. Yet sometimes clarity is not just elusive but downright impossible. And every once in a while, it may not even be desirable. "'The fascination of what's difficult,' to steal from Yeats, is what first drew readers to Pynchon's novels," notes Schillinger in the review of *Against the Day* that was illustrated by those mysterious acrobats. The gap between seeing something and not seeing it can be narrowed but never entirely closed. There are pleasures to be had in making the leap across.

I Love
the '80s

First appeared in
Design Observer,
June 4, 2012.

I graduated from college in June 1980 and moved to
New York City the following week. I had just spent five
years at the University of Cincinnati's College of Design,
Architecture, and Art learning that appearances mattered,
that nothing was more important than the way things
looked, that every detail counted. And knew something else
as well: that this hard-won level of connoisseurship would
subject me and my fellow designers to a lonely struggle
that would probably last a lifetime. We understood that we
were destined to care about these things and hardly anyone
else would. Such was the lonely life of a designer. Then, on
Sunday, September 16, 1984, everything changed. I realized
that the battle was won. Suddenly the whole world seemed
to care about design. That evening marked the debut of
Miami Vice.

Yes, *Miami Vice.* The quintessential '80s TV show,
the epic entertainment that had been built, legend had it,
on a two-word premise, scrawled on a notepad by NBC
Entertainment head Brandon Tartikoff and passed to
veteran writer Anthony Yerkovich: "MTV Cops." There had
been cop shows before, there had been stylish shows before,
but none exhibited the obsession with surface gloss that

came to characterize *Miami Vice*. It was common knowledge that the show's executive producer Michael Mann had dictated a blanket edict — "No earth tones" — to the show's production designers, and that every aesthetic decision on *Miami Vice* had to conform — or else. A cover story in *TIME* in 1985 described the philosophy in depth. "There is a very definite attempt to give the show a particular look," episode director Bobby Roth told the magazine. "There are certain colors you are not allowed to shoot, such as red and brown.... I found this house that was really perfect but the color was sort of beige. The art department instantly painted the house gray for me." The two stars, James "Sonny" Crockett (Don Johnson) and Ricardo "Rico" Tubbs (Philip Michael Thomas), moved through a world of near-perfect heightened abstraction.

Richard Zoglin, "Cool Cops, Hot Show," *TIME*, September 16, 1985.

This mania for appearance, which no doubt struck some of *TIME*'s readers as idiosyncratic at best and insane at worst, was completely understandable to me. Upon arriving at Vignelli Associates for my first job as a junior designer, I learned that Massimo Vignelli had arranged for all of the window air-conditioning units to be sprayed with Krylon matte black paint, transforming the ugly (beige!) Fedders boxes into something resembling MoMA-ready Braun devices — sort of. Naturally I took a can back to my apartment so my own cheap unit could get the same treatment. Why stop there? The office was soon populated with matte black tape dispensers, adjustable lamps, and pencil holders. "The same attention," reported *TIME*, "is lavished on the show's fashions. On a typical episode, Crockett and Tubbs wear from five to eight different outfits — always in shades of pink, blue, green, peach, fuchsia and the show's other 'approved' colors."

Exactly, approved colors! Finally the world was coming around to my way of thinking. Was this really any different from the realm of architecture, where postmodernists like Michael Graves were on the rise and the cream and mauve paint was still drying on his 1982 Portland Building? Architecture even featured in the opening titles of *Miami Vice* itself, where millions every week saw the iconic palm tree in the upper-story atrium of Arquitectonica's brightly colored Atlantis condominium building. Meanwhile, the hot news in graphic design was coming from California. In San Francisco, the "Michaels" (Manwaring, Vanderbyl, Cronan, and Mabry) were marrying European modernism with the West Coast version of Miami chromatism. In Los Angeles,

April Greiman was turning up the intensity with DayGlo colors that would soon find their full expression in the digital realm, courtesy of the newly introduced Macintosh. And the world had seen graphic postmodernism writ large in the program that Deborah Sussman and Paul Prejza had developed for the 1984 LA Olympics, brimming with festive visual confetti designed to last for only a few weeks before a worldwide television audience.

More revolutionary than the visual appearance of *Miami Vice* was the underlying premise that somehow we had reached a moment in time where substance had ceased to matter. "The show is written for an MTV audience," another director told *TIME*, "which is more interested in images, emotions and energy than plot and character and words." Indeed, the most powerful moment in that 1984 pilot wasn't a gun battle or a courtroom confrontation, but a nearly wordless three-minute sequence where Crockett and Tubbs drive through the damp Florida night to the sound of "In the Air Tonight" by Phil Collins, neon reflecting off the hood of their black Ferrari Daytona Spyder 365 GTS/4. The legendary "Ba dum ba dom ba doom BOOM BAM BAM" of Collins's drum break at 3:17 was no less powerful for all its studio artificiality, and went on to define the sound of the '80s for much of pop music.

The signature Phil Collins drum sound, developed with producer Steve Lillywhite and engineer Hugh Padgham, is called "gated reverb." Unlike most other studio reverberation effects, it is not meant to simulate any kind of echo that occurs in nature.

Was I crazy to think it was all coming together exactly as I had dreamed in college, a world in thrall to the frisson of pinks and blues, of shiny black surfaces shimmering with squares and triangles? At Vignelli Associates, I became the unofficial "new wave" specialist. One of our established lighting company clients was an investor in a new experimental furniture line coming out of Milan. Without fully understanding what I was getting into, I was assigned to create the invitations for the New York launch of the Memphis movement. Each invitation involved applying a preprinted sticker with the Memphis logo onto a preprinted glossy black postcard that had itself been sprayed (by me) with Krylon fluorescent paint and scribbled on (by me) with red, yellow, and orange China markers. There were one thousand invitations. The handwork this production required took a full weekend. At its conclusion I was fairly delirious. Whether this was from contemplating the promise of a new aesthetic era or three days straight of inhaling aerosol fumes it was hard to say.

For me, this era of design wasn't about communicating messages, or serving society, or even problem solving. It was simply about manipulating colors and shapes, about engaging in the pleasures of the surface, as if these things had meaning in and of themselves. And although I loved the design work I saw all around me, it has not worn well. An exhibition on postmodern design was on view earlier this year at the Victoria and Albert Museum, and it was widely panned. Typical was the view of Stephen Bayley, who scathingly borrowed an epitaph for PoMo from Alexander Pope, saying it had "a brain of feathers and a heart of lead."

Half true. Design in the eighties was shallow. But it wasn't without soul. All those little discoveries I made, superimposing just the right orange on just the right teal, getting a curve exactly right, making something look perfect: those moments were thrilling for a young designer. The last piece in the V&A's installation was the video for New Order's "Bizarre Love Triangle," directed by New York artist Robert Longo in the style of his *Men in the Cities* lithographs. The song took me back, as songs do, to my own innocent youth, particularly the line "Why can't we be ourselves like we were yesterday?" I left the museum a little misty-eyed and a little embarrassed, remembering those days when the way something looked seemed to mean so much. I wonder if it will ever be that way again.

Postmodernism: Style and Subversion 1970–1990 was on view at the Victoria and Albert Museum from September 24, 2011, to January 15, 2012.

Stephen Bayley, "Irony Bites," *Architect's Newspaper*, October 14, 2011.

"Bizarre Love Triangle" was written by Gillian Gilbert, Peter Hook, Stephen Morris, and Bernard Sumner and was released on November 5, 1986.

Battle Hymn of the Tiger Mentor, or Why Modernist Designers Are Superior

First appeared in Design Observer, January 31, 2011.

The title, intended as an ironic reference to that of Amy Chua's book, was taken a bit too seriously by some.

Here are some things I was not allowed to do as I began my first job:

Use any typeface other than Helvetica, Century, Times, Futura, Garamond #3, or Bodoni.

Use more than two typefaces on any project.

Use more than three sizes of typefaces on any project.

Begin any layout without a modular grid in place, including a letterhead or a business card.

Make visual references to any examples of historic graphic design predating Josef Müller-Brockmann or Armin Hofmann.

Incorporate any graphic devices that could not be defended on the basis of pure function.

When I arrived as the most junior of junior designers at Vignelli Associates in 1980, my portfolio couldn't have been more eclectic. Filled with excitable homages to everyone from Wolfgang Weingart to Push Pin Studios, my design-school work begged for a diagnosis of Multiple Designer Personality Disorder. You might have expected me to rebel against the strictures to which I was subjected by my first employer. Instead, I willingly submitted to them. For ten years. And, as a result, I am a better designer today.

You may react to this with horror. That was certainly the reaction when the now-ubiquitous Amy Chua burst on the world several weeks ago with her *Wall Street Journal* essay "Why Chinese Mothers Are Superior," an excerpt from her memoir *Battle Hymn of the Tiger Mother*. The essay, which has been called the "Andromeda Strain of viral memes," made a no-holds-barred case for subjecting the young to draconian rules. No TV, no sleepovers, no video games. Instead, ten-hour violin lessons. Chua also advocates zero tolerance for A-minuses on tests and even (heads up, graphic designers!) the rejection of less-than-adequate handmade birthday cards. In an age of permissive parenting, the Tiger Mother struck a nerve: as of this writing, the original essay has received 7,600 comments and counting.

Amy Chua, "Why Chinese Mothers Are Superior," *Wall Street Journal*, January 8, 2011.

Amy Chua, *Battle Hymn of the Tiger Mother* (New York: Penguin, 2011).

The "Andromeda Strain" quote is from Elizabeth Kolbert, "America's Top Parent," *New Yorker*, January 31, 2011.

All of this got me thinking about my own strict upbringing as a designer. I was completely nonideological when I graduated from college. I didn't regard Helvetica-on-a-grid as the apotheosis of refined reductivism, as did the Swiss modernists or the founders of Unimark. But nor did I see it as the embodiment of Nixon-era corporate oppression, as did designers like Paula Scher. To me, it was just another style.

But it was a style I liked, and I submerged myself happily in its rigors when I took my seat at my first job. The rules weren't written down anywhere or even explicitly communicated. They were more like unspoken taboos. Using Cooper Black, like human cannibalism or having sex with your sister, simply wasn't done. For many young designers in the studio, the rules were too much. They resisted (futilely), grew restless (eventually), and left. By staying, I learned to go beyond the easy-to-imitate style of Helvetica-on-a-grid. I learned the virtues of modernism.

I learned attention to detail. Working with a limited palette of elements leaves a designer nowhere to hide. With so little on the page, what was there had to be perfect. I learned the importance of content. Seeing Massimo design a picture book was a revelation. No tricky layouts, no extraneous elements. Instead, a crisply edited collection of images, perfectly sized, carefully sequenced, and dramatically paced. Nothing there in the final product but the pictures and the story they told.

I learned humility. I was a clever designer who loved to call attention to himself. The monastic life to which I had committed left no room for this. It became my goal, instead, to get out of the way and let the words on the page

Invitation to
*The Masters Series:
Massimo Vignelli* at the
Visual Arts Museum,
New York, 1991.

Rob Roy Kelly,
*American Wood Type
1828–1900: Notes
on the Evolution of
Decorated and Large
Types* (New York:
Van Nostrand Reinhold,
1969).

Michael Bierut and
Peter Hall, editors,
*Tibor Kalman: Perverse
Optimist* (New York:
Princeton Architectural
Press, 1998).

do the work. Ultimately, I learned about what endures in design. Not impulsiveness and self-indulgence but clarity and simplicity.

There was another side to modernism, though: its legacy as the great leveler. Massimo once told me that one of the great aspects of modernist graphic design was that it was replicable. You could teach its principles to anyone, even a nondesigner, and if they followed the rules they'd be able to come up with a solid, if not brilliant, solution. To me, this was both idealistic — design for all — and vaguely depressing, a prescription for a visual world without valleys but without peaks as well. Sometimes impulsiveness and self-indulgence were no more than that, but every once in a while they were something you might call genius. I worried about genius.

So I permitted myself the occasional indulgence after I had been at Vignelli for a while. Once I did a freebie poster using Franklin Gothic for AIGA. "Why did you use that typeface?" asked Massimo, sincerely baffled. I think he would have been satisfied if I said that I had lost a bet, or that I was drunk. Instead, I just, um, felt like it. I mean, Ivan Chermayeff used Franklin Gothic all the time! Was it really that bad? Another time, designing a catalog for an exhibition of vintage photographs of the American West, I created a cover that imitated a nineteenth-century playbill. What pleasure it was to work with a half-dozen typefaces out of Rob Roy Kelly's fantastic book, *American Wood Type*. In so doing, I managed to actually break at least three rules at once (unauthorized typefaces; too many typefaces at once; and, perhaps worst of all, historical imitation). Massimo pronounced the result "awful," a word he could (and still can) provide with a memorable inflection while seeming to gag. I still like that cover.

By the time I left Vignelli Associates in 1990, I felt I was ready to move far beyond the limiting strictures of modernism. The period of graphic self-indulgence that followed is now a bit painful for me to contemplate. After a time I came to appreciate the tough love that my favorite mentor had so painstakingly administered for a full decade. The turning point came in about 1996, when I received a call to design a book for Tibor Kalman. This was the monograph that would become *Tibor Kalman: Perverse Optimist*. I was surprised and pleased. As a designer at Vignelli Associates, I had followed the work of M&Co with interest and admiration, noting how often they broke every design rule

in the world with cheekiness and impunity. I arrived at
my meeting with Tibor, brimming with notions about how
my book design would embody the irreverence of the
M&Co worldview.

Tibor listened patiently to my ideas — there were
lots of them — and then paused for a long time. "Well, yes,
you could do some stuff like that," he responded carefully.
"Or, we could do something like this. You could work out a
good clear grid. We could edit all the images really carefully.
Then you could do a really nice, clean layout, perfect pace,
perfect sequence. You know," he added with a smile, "sort of
like a Vignelli book. And then we could fuck it up a little."

I then realized that, whether you credit (or blame)
your mother or your mentor, you can never fully escape
your influences. The rules you grow up with are what make
you, as a person and as a designer. The trick is to remember,
every once in a while, to fuck them up a little.

Will the Real Ernst Bettler Please Stand Up?

First appeared in Design Observer, January 8, 2008.

Poster for Pfäfferli+Huber Pharmaceuticals, attributed to Ernst Bettler, 1959.

Can graphic design provoke real social change? Consider the example of Ernst Bettler.

In the late 1950s Bettler was asked to design a series of posters to celebrate the fiftieth anniversary of Swiss pharmaceutical manufacturer Pfäfferli+Huber. Aware of reports that P+H had been involved in testing prisoners in German concentration camps less than fifteen years before, he hesitated, and then decided to accept the commission. "I had the feeling I could do some real damage," he said later.

And indeed he did. He created four posters featuring dramatic, angular black-and-white portraits juxtaposed with sans serif typography. Alone, each poster was an elegant example of international style design. Together, however, a different message emerged, for it turned out the abstract compositions in the posters contained hidden letters. (The one here, for example, displays the letter A.) Hung side by side in the streets, they spelled out N-A-Z-I. A public outcry followed, and within six weeks the company was ruined.

So if you're looking for evidence that graphic design has the potential to change the world, you need look no further than the story of Ernst Bettler. But if you look a little

Now You See It

further, you'll discover something disturbing: Ernst Bettler never existed. The designer, the posters, the company are all entirely made up.

Ernst Bettler was introduced in 2000 in the second issue of *Dot Dot Dot*. Nothing about the article, "'I'm Only a Designer': The Double Life of Ernst Bettler" by the London-based writer and designer Christopher Wilson, identified it as anything less than fact. On the contrary, it was filled with convincing touches, including descriptions of each of the posters (only the "A" was pictured), portraits of a young "Bettler" in 1954 and today, and vivid details throughout. Here, for example, is Wilson's account of the reaction to the scandalous posters:

Christopher Wilson, "'I'm Only a Designer': The Double Life of Ernst Bettler," *Dot Dot Dot 2*, 2000.

The reaction of the usually passive local populace was immediate. The posters were torn down in the streets, the offices of the Sumisdorfer Nachrichten were buried beneath an avalanche of complaint letters, and demands were even made for the company's managers to stand trial. In under six weeks Pfäfferli+Huber were ruined forever. Even today, the sooty mark left on the front of the factory building by the long-gone metal logo is less visible than the ancient 'Nazi raus' spray-paint around the rusted gates. If World War II had in part been fought on the battlefield of design, then Bettler's involvement in the downfall of P+H stands as a testament to design's power to change things since then.

The design community knew an irresistible story when they saw it. *Adbusters* featured Bettler's feat in its September/October 2001 "Graphic Anarchy" issue: "It's one of the greatest design interventions on record," the magazine noted approvingly. Creativepro.com noted Bettler's "brilliantly subversive work." In Michael Johnson's admirable textbook *Problem Solved*, Bettler is saluted as one of the "founding fathers of the 'culture-jamming' form of protest," and to demonstrate his ingenuity his A poster is helpfully placed between typeset letters representing the never-seen others in the series.

The editors, "Graphic Anarchy," *Adbusters*, September/October 2001.

John D. Berry, "dot-font: Dot-Dot-Dot Dis," *Creative Pro*, May 18, 2001.

Michael Johnson, *Problem Solved* (London: Phaidon, 2004).

I bought the whole thing too, although I think I remember feeling something was off. I was a student of postwar Swiss design; why had I never heard of Ernst Bettler? What happened to the N and the Z and I posters? And, while like many others I found the idea of the downfall of P+H at the hands of a designer awfully satisfying, why would a subtle poster series be more effective than, say, a journalist's exposé? But it was Andy Crewdson, writing in his now defunct blog Lines and Splines, who finally did

As noted, Andy Crewdson's research on the origins of the Bettler story is no longer available online.

Rick Poynor, "The Ernst Bettler Problem," Eye.com, February 10, 2003.

Wolff is quoted by Carl W. Smith, commenting on Steven Heller's account of the event, "It's Easy to Criticize... Not," Design Observer, December 19, 2007.

Armin Vit, "Booksourcing: Posters," Speak Up, December 14, 2007.

After this essay was published, Christopher Wilson gave his own account of the saga, "And So to Bed," Dot Dot Dot 18 (New York: Princeton Architectural Press, 2009).

the research and discovered that there was no evidence that Bettler, or Pfäfferli+Huber, or even Contrazipan — the medication advertised in the poster — had ever existed.

Rick Poynor summarized the whole saga on the Eye website in February 2003. "What, then, is the point of the hoax?" he asked. "If the aim was to fool credulous browsers into perpetuating the story, then this latest development is a triumph. It's now a permanent feature in thousands of copies of an internationally distributed book produced by a major publisher, Phaidon, and it's likely to be taken at face value for years to come. It reveals how skimpy standards of research, validation and basic knowledge can be in design book publishing." But it also reveals something else: how desperately we designers crave evidence that our work has the capacity to truly make a difference.

At 2008's Designism 2.0 event, critic Michael Wolff infuriated many in the crowd by calling the work of some of today's most committed designers banal, trite, and ineffective. "The problem with using design as a disruptive force," he said, "is that everyone uses design as a disruptive force. So how do you break through the clutter? Someone figures it out, everyone copies, and you have to reinvent again." Design's value, he says, has been "inflated, and therefore devalued." What more resounding rebuttal could be imagined than the example of Ernst Bettler, the lone designer cunningly using his quiet skill to turn the machinery of evil against itself to devastating effect?

Bettler lives on today — perhaps more than ever, as Poynor feared. Do a search and you'll find him invoked on Myspace pages, fansites, and scholarly bibliographies. The same week of Designism 2.0, Bettler's P+H posters were nominated in a SpeakUp discussion on the world's most iconic posters. Not bad for a designer who never existed.

We need heroes, and we'll make them up if we can't find them any other way. It's been noted that one of the most compelling fictional heroes of all time, Superman, was invented by two midwestern Jewish kids in the 1930s. In a world where Nazi evil was spreading unchecked, how satisfying it must have been to invent a powerful figure who could burst from nowhere to take action on behalf of the most threatened and helpless.

The design world is full of Clark Kents. Are any of us ready to be the next Ernst Bettler?

Our Little Secret

The moment the New York graphic design community has long awaited is almost upon us. Tonight, Gary Hustwit premieres his sold-out-for-weeks documentary film *Helvetica*.

I was in the audience for a sneak preview at MoMA several weeks ago, and I'll give you my early review. The film is great. (And not just because I'm in it, nasal Cleveland accent and all.) Hustwit has structured the film's interviews to create a perfect short course in postwar graphic design. Luke Geissbuhler's cinematography is beautiful, and the music makes everything seem positively hip. I left the preview feeling thrilled to be a graphic designer.

Like many, I have high hopes that this will be the moment that our field finally breaks through to the general public. As I excitedly said to a friend, "Hey, this might do for typography what *Wordplay* did for crossword puzzles."

My friend, a nondesigner who has always found my enthusiasm for things like fonts a bit alarming, was a little less sure. "Maybe it'll do for typography," he said, "what *Capturing the Friedmans* did for pedophilia."

Hmm. I always have been a little sheepish about my obsession with type. And my friend isn't alone in sensing that this obsession has a vaguely prurient quality. More than

First appeared in Design Observer, April 6, 2007.

A review of *Helvetica*, a documentary film by Gary Hustwit, 2007.

Wordplay was a 2006 documentary directed by Patrick Creadon about the world of expert crossword puzzle solvers and constructors. *Capturing the Friedmans*, a 2003 documentary directed by Andrew Jarecki, told the story of a suburban family torn apart by accusations of child abuse.

Poster for *Helvetica*,
Experimental Jetset,
2007.

one interviewee in the film gets a little hot and bothered about things like counter space and x-heights. As Erik Spiekermann puts it: "Other people look at bottles of wine or whatever, or, you know, girls' bottoms. I get kicks out of looking at type. It's a little worrying, I must admit."

There was a time when we designers had this obsession all to ourselves. Before the introduction of the Macintosh computer and desktop publishing in the mid-'80s, the names of fonts were something that normal people encountered rarely. (Typically, this might happen if they stayed with their Alfred A. Knopf volumes all the way to the last page, where they'd encounter the often comically arcane "Note on the Type.") For the overwhelming majority of the population, the names of typefaces were as obscure as the Latin names of plants, and just as useful.

Anyone could design a poster or a T-shirt back then. What they couldn't do is typeset it. This was the technical feat that separated the professionals from the amateurs. Believe me: changing handwritten text into set type was magic, and we designers were the only ones who knew how to pull it off. For my first two and a half years of design-school projects, I used dry transfer lettering for headlines, and dummy copy in a few predictable sizes that we'd xerox out of books. Who could afford typesetting? A simple job would cost thirty-five or forty dollars back then, tough to come by on a student budget. Typeset words had true authority because they had real money behind them. And in the working world, the money got even more real: I remember seeing typesetting bills for annual reports that were in the high five figures.

As a young designer in my first real job in 1980, I learned that this made typography a high-stakes game. It went like this. You'd get a manuscript from a client, say twenty pages of Courier (although no one called it Courier, or even thought of it that way). You'd have to calculate how many characters were in the manuscript the old-fashioned way — no Microsoft Word, no word-count tools — by counting characters per line, then total number of lines, then doing the math. Next you'd have to decide what text typeface you wanted to use, what size, and what measure. Finally, you'd refer to a copyfitting table to see how long the columns would run: more math. If it seemed like this figure would fit the layout, you'd mark up the manuscript and send it to a typesetter. It would be back, set in beautiful type, the following morning, galley after crisp, clean galley of it.

If it fit, good for you. If it ran long, guess what? You just lost $250, stupid.

As was true for children of the Great Depression, these tiresome hardships led to deeply ingrained habits. It was a system that rewarded deliberate planning, not creative experimentation. You found yourself repeatedly specifying certain fonts just because you knew how they would set: after a few years I could make a pretty accurate guess about how long a typewritten manuscript would run in Garamond #3 (12 on 13, flush left, ragged right on a 30-pica column measure) just by looking at it. So I set a lot of Garamond #3. And your relationship with your typesetter was one of the most important in your life. For years, Earl from Concept Type was the first person I'd call in the morning and the last one I'd call before going home at night. He'd save my ass, too, calling me at home at 2:00 a.m. to confirm that I actually wanted that last subhead to be bold italic instead of just bold like the others. I knew his voice like I knew my wife's. I saw him only one time, at a Christmas party, and had that same horrible moment of disbelief and disorientation that I had when I saw a picture of my favorite radio disk jockey: but Earl doesn't look like that! It was him, though.

Earl is gone now, just like every typesetter I ever knew. Instead, we live in a world where any person in any cubicle in the world can pick between Arial and Trebuchet and Chalkboard at any time — risk free, copyfitting tables be damned — and where a film about a typeface actually stands a chance of enjoying some small measure of popular success. As my college-age daughter says, "All my friends are really into fonts." There isn't much other currency available, after all, in the realm of Myspace and Facebook. Is it still magic when everyone knows how the trick works?

I hope *Helvetica* is a smash. It deserves to be. But part of me still misses the days when it was just our little secret.

Alan Fletcher: Living by Design

First appeared in Design Observer, September 27, 2006.

Alan Fletcher, *Beware Wet Paint* (London: Phaidon, 1996).

The partners of Pentagram, *Living by Design* (New York: Whitney Library of Design, 1978).

Alan Fletcher, one of the five founders of Pentagram and one of the world's greatest designers, died on September 21, 2006, after a private eighteen-month struggle with cancer. He was less than a week short of his seventy-fifth birthday. His friend Colin Forbes deserves the credit for inventing Pentagram's unique organizational structure, which has endured now for nearly forty-five years and within which I've worked as a partner for twenty-five. But it was Alan Fletcher who showed by example, across three decades, how one could work, and live, within that structure. For him, design was not a profession or a craft, but a life. In an interview for his 1996 book *Beware Wet Paint*, he told Rick Poynor, "I'd sooner do the same on Monday or Wednesday as I do on a Saturday or Sunday. I don't divide my life between labour and pleasure." The title of another book from Pentagram could serve as a concise statement of his philosophy: *Living by Design*.

Alan Fletcher was born in 1931 in Nairobi and moved to London as a child. He studied art and design at four different schools — Hammersmith, the Central School, the Royal College of Art, and Yale — and worked in New York, Chicago, Barcelona, and Milan before returning to

London in 1959. Within three years, he had reunited with an old classmate from Central, Colin Forbes, and an American, Bob Gill, to establish a design firm that for many still embodies the excitement of London in those heady days, Fletcher Forbes Gill. In *Graphic Design: Visual Comparisons*, a book the studio published in 1963, Alan wrote, "Our thesis is that any one visual problem has an infinite number of solutions; that many are valid; that solutions ought to derive from subject matter; that the designer should have no preconceived graphic style." This idea-driven design approach ("Every job has to have an idea," he often said) brought success and growth. The addition of three more partners (and the departure of Bob Gill) led to the establishment of Pentagram in 1972. It was Alan that gave the firm its name. "Nobody liked it much but we settled on it anyway," he once said.

Alan Fletcher, Colin Forbes, and Bob Gill, *Graphic Design: Visual Comparisons* (New York: Reinhold, 1964).

At Pentagram, his work — and client base — was remarkably diverse: identities and signage programs for Reuters, the Commercial Bank of Kuwait, Lloyds, and IBM on one hand and small personal projects on the other. "I'm a split personality," he once told Poynor in an interview for *Eye*. "I do quite large, complex corporate identity jobs. I enjoy that, but I also enjoy sitting round doing my own little things, which are invariably the ones that don't pay." Eventually, he gravitated to the latter, and in the autumn of 1992 he went off on his own to focus on his creative obsessions. These were eventually compiled in his 2001 masterpiece, *The Art of Looking Sideways*, a staggering tour de force of visual acrobatics that clocks in at over one thousand pages.

Rick Poynor, "Reputations: Alan Fletcher," *Eye*, Winter 1990.

Alan Fletcher, *The Art of Looking Sideways* (London: Phaidon, 2001).

Alan was intimidating — many of us thought he looked like Sean Connery in a darker mood — but in person he was curious, enthusiastic, and endlessly passionate. Gathering up the courage to introduce themselves at parties, young designers often would be surprised to learn that Alan already knew their names and had been following their work. In fact, I was surprised at how many of my partners remembered their first meeting with Alan. He told Paula Scher, "So many people ask me if I've met you, I just lie and say yes." He told Jim Biber, "Colin said I'd like you. Why is that?" And he told me, "I hear you're supposed to be some kind of genius." He delivered that last one with more suspicion than admiration, to tell the truth.

His vast body of work, memorialized in a major retrospective at the London Design Museum that opened a few months after his death, managed to combine the rigorous simplicity of modernism with a dedication to wit, joy, and surprise that was intensely personal. "I like to reduce everything to its absolute essence," he once said, "because that is a way to avoid getting trapped in a style." Yet a Fletcher solution was always nothing if not stylish, refined, and precise, with always a bit more than the problem required: "I treat clients as raw material to do what I want to do, though I would never tell them that." What Alan wanted to do was what we all wanted to do.

I find myself thinking back to my first dinner with Alan, shortly after I joined Pentagram. I was seated at a table with some of my new partners, and the meal was winding down. Alan made a bet that none of us could duplicate a trick he was about to do. It involved two wine corks — Alan enjoyed activities that required the consumption of good wine — that had to be exchanged from one hand to another. "Ready?" he said. "Okay, watch." He held the corks between his thumbs and forefingers, and then traded them in one quick gesture. It didn't look like magic. It looked easy, something anyone could do.

"Got it?" Alan asked. "Now you try." So we did try. And try. And try. And he leaned back in his chair, sipping his wine with a faint smile on his lips, watching all of us attempt, without success, to imitate the effortless simplicity of Alan Fletcher.

This is called the "Pass-Through Cork" trick. Many tutorials for it are available on YouTube.

Fitting

A few weeks ago, I wanted to replace my old New Balance 992s, so I ordered a new pair on the internet. But as I was clicking the final "confirm sale" button, I had that feeling you get the moment before you hit your thumb with a hammer. I turns out I bought the right shoes but in the wrong width: I accidentally ordered them in 11E instead of 11D. Undoing the order was complicated to the point of impossible, and returning the package for a refund seemed even more so. I decided instead to send out an email to see if any of my friends could use a pair of 11Es.

What I got back surprised me. "What's all this D and E business?" "Wait, shoes have a width?" "How do you know your foot width, anyway?" and even "Does this have something to do with cup size?"

It turns out that no one seems to know one's precise foot measurement any more. So I've got a question: Haven't any of you people ever used a Brannock Device?

My first real job after high school was as a salesperson for Noble Family Shoe Store at Pleasant Valley Shopping Center in Parma, Ohio, in the summer of 1975. This was not a fancy boutique. Most of the shoes cost less than $10. I think the most expensive pair was $18.99.

First appeared in Design Observer, May 13, 2008.

Brannock Foot-Measuring Device, Charles F. Brannock, 1927.

Quoted in Reuven Fenton, "Shoe fitting device made since 1927 still a perfect fit," *Columbia Journalism School News Service*, March 13, 2007.

That whole summer, no one even tried on the $18.99 shoes.

I loved that job. I loved the rows of shoe boxes back in the stockroom. As in most such places, they were organized so that if a shoe wasn't available in the size the customer wanted, you could emerge with the boxes immediately to the left and right, with instructions to describe them as "something you might like even more." I loved saying things like "espadrilles" and "partial leather uppers." I loved pushing the high-margin extras at the cash register like polish and laces. (My girlfriend Dorothy had the same talent for selling add-ons in her job at Ponderosa Steakhouse down Broadview Road, where they gave the meat away for free but made millions on the sour cream for the baked potatoes.) But most of all, I loved handling the Brannock Device.

Charles F. Brannock only invented one thing in his life, and this was it. The son of a Syracuse, New York, shoe magnate, Brannock became interested in improving the primitive wooden measuring sticks that he saw around his father's store. He patented his first prototype in 1926, based on models he had made from Erector Set parts. As the Park-Brannock Shoe Store became legendary for fitting feet with absolute accuracy, the demand for the device grew, and in 1927 Brannock opened a factory to mass-produce it. The Brannock Device Co., Inc., is still in business today. Refreshingly, it still makes only this one thing. They have sold over a million, a remarkable number when one considers that each of them lasts up to fifteen years, when the numbers wear off.

I find Charles Brannock's single-mindedness about his namesake both touching and slightly frightening. He once wrote of a visit to a shoe salon in Chicago in 1959: "As I entered the store there was a salesman, evidently the one who was 'up' and greeted me, so I stopped, removed my hat and said, 'I will introduce myself, if I may,' and gave him my name, extended my hand and remarked that I was the inventor and manufacturer of the Brannock Foot-Measuring Device. He seemed genuinely pleased to meet me." One imagines him crisscrossing the country, lurking in shoe stores, waiting for the right moment to reveal his identity to his legions of delighted acolytes.

I would have been among that genuinely pleased legion. I am clumsy, incapable of operating even simple tools, unable to perform rudimentary household repairs.

Now You See It

The Brannock Device manages at once to look incredibly complicated while being totally simple to use: despite its seemingly daunting instructions, I mastered it in about a minute on my first day. Having such an exotic bit of machinery at my disposal took a job that's actually sort of demeaning — after all, I literally had to kneel in front of each of my customers — and transformed it into something akin to brain surgery. What people today feel about their iPhones, I felt about my Brannock Device.

I am not alone, of course. Twenty or so years ago, I was visiting Tibor Kalman at M&Co, and there it was on his desk: his very own Brannock Device. It was exactly the sort of thing he loved, and if you require proof, his testimony is available to this day on the Brannock website: "It showed incredible ingenuity and no one has ever been able to beat it. I doubt if anyone ever will, even if we ever get to the stars, or find out everything there is to find out about black holes." It's hard to tell now whether this hyperbole was intended ironically, but I don't think so. Some things just work perfectly. I wish more things did.

Alas, the Brannock site has been redesigned and this delightfully hyperbolic testimony by Kalman is nowhere to be found.

The Faux Ball Game

First appeared in Design Observer, March 31, 2008.

The 2008 baseball season begins this week. By coincidence, this will be the last season that New York's two teams, the Yankees and Mets, play in their current stadiums. Next year, both teams will move into brand-new venues that will include state-of-the-art amenities, high-tech electronic displays, expensive VIP suite areas, and every modern convenience — on the inside, at least.

On the outside, both stadiums, like almost every baseball park built since 1992, will make every attempt to convince us that they were built sometime in the first part of the last century.

In the last twenty-five years, Americans have designed, built, and enjoyed modern office buildings, modern libraries, modern museums, and modern houses. Why is it so hard to build a baseball stadium that looks like it belongs in the twenty-first century?

More than any other American sport, baseball is fueled by nostalgia. I have fond memories of rooting for the hapless Cleveland Indians in a remarkably hideous setting, the chilly and cavernous Cleveland Municipal Stadium. Built in 1931 with a seating capacity of nearly eighty thousand, the "Mistake by the Lake" routinely attracted fewer than twenty thousand fans to see the likes of Sam McDowell, Steve Hargan, and Rocky Colavito. But it had a lot more character than Cincinnati's cookie-cutter Riverfront Stadium, an airport-like facility built in 1970 where I would sit in alienated gloom during my college years watching the Big Red Machine roll over all comers amidst a smug crowd who expected no less.

For a long time, most new ballparks looked like Riverfront: Atlanta-Fulton County Stadium, St. Louis's Busch Stadium, Pittsburgh's Three Rivers, all charmless industrial facilities lacking any sense of place, specificity, or human scale. Then came Oriole Park at Camden Yards in Baltimore, and everything changed.

When it opened in 1992, Camden Yards was a revelation. Janet Marie Smith, the Orioles' vice president for planning and development during the park's construction, had encouraged project architect HOK Sport to design an "old-fashioned ballpark with modern amenities." As a result, in contrast to Memorial Park, the 1950 "concrete doughnut" stadium it replaced — but like beloved urban ballparks such as Wrigley Field or Fenway Park — Camden Yards was asymmetrical, to conform to the idiosyncrasies of the neighborhood street pattern, and scaled to bring the fans close to the action. And the ballpark was old-fashioned not only in spirit, but in the literal details; using a steel structural system that hadn't been used in stadiums since the '30s and clad in brick to match the restored B&O Railroad warehouse across the street, it was designed to look as if it had been built in 1912, not eighty years later. Sponsors and advertisers were encouraged to use vintage logos, all the better to scrupulously maintain the illusion.

William Gildea, "Friendly and Familiar Confines,"*Washington Post*, April 12, 1992.

The illusion proved irresistible. Camden Yards was a hit with critics and fans alike, and it launched a trend in ballpark design that has continued unabated to this day. In the wake of Camden, retro facilities rose in Arlington, Denver, Atlanta, San Francisco, Detroit, Houston, Pittsburgh, San Diego, Philadelphia, St. Louis, and Oakland. Cleveland Municipal Stadium was replaced by Jacobs Field in 1994. Cincinnati's Riverfront Stadium was replaced by Great American Ball Park in 2003. Both Jacobs (now Progressive Field, named for Progressive Insurance) and Great American (named for the Great American Insurance Group) were designed by the architects who started it all in Baltimore, HOK Sport. The firm has made the most of their success at Camden Yards; by 2012 they will have designed nineteen of the thirty major league baseball fields.

Which brings us to my hometown. HOK's portfolio includes our two newest ballparks, the new Yankee Stadium and the new home for the Mets, Citi Field. I can't say much about the design of Yankee Stadium. The House that Ruth Built is regarded by sports fans as a secular cathedral, and it goes without saying that the new facility, which is currently being built on a park adjacent to the current stadium, will replicate as many details as possible of the 1923 original. The weight of tradition is just too much.

The Mets, however, are different. I moved to New York in 1980, the perfect moment to become a Mets fan: the following years would see the arrival of Keith Hernandez, Ron Darling, Gary Carter, Darryl Strawberry, and Dwight Gooden, culminating in the thrilling championship year of 1986. The setting of these heroics, however, was the dismal and unbeloved Shea Stadium, opened in 1964 as a home for the then two-year-old Mets. "There's no redeeming architectural value in Shea," the American Institute of Architects' Fredric Bell told the New York Times. "If Yankee Stadium is like visiting the Metropolitan Museum, then Shea is like a visit to the dentist's chair." Mets fans have been waiting a long time for a new ballpark.

Ben Shpigel, "Shea in '64: The Planes Above, the Mets Below," *New York Times*, March 30, 2008.

And what are we getting? Well, this passage from the Mets website should sound familiar: "Inspired by tradition, Citi Field will be clad in brick, limestone, granite and cast stone, with the brick closely resembling the masonry used at Ebbets Field, both in color and texture. Exposed steel will be painted dark blue and the seats will be dark green." I find this all rather odd. Ebbets Field served as the home of an entirely different team, the Brooklyn Dodgers, until 1957. Camden Yards sits in the middle of Baltimore and picked up its design cues from its surrounding neighborhood. Citi Field sits in the middle of nowhere — Flushing Meadows, Queens — and it picks up its design cues from a ballpark that, before it was demolished nearly fifty years ago, was located nearly nine miles away.

But in reality Flushing Meadows is hardly the middle of nowhere, and has a potent design tradition of its own. Originally a city dumping ground memorialized as *The Great Gatsby's* "valley of ashes," it was cleared by parks commissioner Robert Moses for the 1939 New York World's Fair, and, twenty-five years later, the 1964

Now You See It

New York World's Fair. Its grounds were the site of some of the most iconic and entertaining visionary architecture ever built in North America: Wallace Harrison's Trylon and Perisphere, Norman Bel Geddes's Futurama at the General Motors Pavilion, not to mention the Unisphere, which still stands today within sight of the new Citi Field. Wouldn't any of these have made great precedents for a new pleasure dome to be built in Flushing Meadows? Or, to go a little further afield — but at least within the same borough — how about Queens's greatest piece of architecture, from the same year as Shea, no less: Eero Saarinen's TWA Terminal?

But instead, we have the fourteenth old-timey iteration of something that was an innovation a decade and a half ago, and now seems like nothing more than a default. HOK Sport is capable of bold, exciting architecture: just consider their Lansdowne Road Stadium in Dublin, Nanjing Olympic Sports Centre in China, or their work with Norman Foster at Wembley Stadium. The Mets are an atomic-age team, unburdened by the century of tradition that haunts their crosstown rivals. Their site is as close to a blank slate as anyone could imagine.

We all know that baseball fans love their nostalgic ballparks, and I certainly like the human scale and sense of place that the best of these venues provide. But do those values always have to arrive smothered in old-fashioned wrappings? Sooner or later someone has to take a risk on something new. In Flushing Meadows, all the conditions were right to take a chance on a home run. What a pity we have to settle instead for a sacrifice bunt.

In 2009, HOK Sport separated from its parent company and renamed itself Populous.

The Smartest Logo in the Room

First appeared in Design Observer, February 11, 2008.

Stephen J. Eskilson, *Graphic Design: A New History* (New Haven: Yale University Press, 2007).

After the 2002 collapse of the company under the weight of its fraudulent business practices, [Paul] Rand's "E" took on a whole new meaning. Rechristened the "crooked E," it inadvertently became the most powerful anti-logo of its time. No parodist of corporate identity could have devised a more startling outcome.

> *The Enron debacle created much soul-searching among the graphic design community, as artists pondered the ethical dimensions of their power to shape people's perceptions.*

Of all the things I read in Stephen Eskilson's *Graphic Design: A New History*, this passage startled me the most. Let the soul-searching begin!

Paul Rand took logo design very seriously, and his work in the field serves as the centerpiece of many of his books. Detailed accounts of the genesis of symbols for such companies as Morningstar, NeXT, and Ideo appear in *A Designer's Art; Design, Form and Chaos* and *From Lascaux to Brooklyn;* even rejected proposals, like those for The Limited and Ford, merit many pages of coverage. But Enron was designed too late in Rand's career to make any of his books. In Steven Heller's monograph, it's simply identified as one of Rand's last works, and it appears toward the very end, with no further comment, rounded up with a group of other, less notorious, logos.

Perhaps the only thorough account of the launch of the Enron logo appears in *Conspiracy of Fools*, Kurt Eichenwald's 746-page history of the company's rise and fall. According to Eichenwald, Enron chairman Kenneth Lay unveiled the logo to company employees in a special meeting in January 1997, promising "a new logo that would reflect the dynamic company Enron has become."

Kurt Eichenwald, *Conspiracy of Fools* (New York: Broadway, 2005).

Sadly, he mentioned the designer nowhere in his dramatic introduction. But maybe not! Because, well, wait for it:

Within hours, the world would laugh it off the stage. Houston faxed the logo to Enron's offices in Europe. But in transmission the middle, yellow prong disappeared, leaving the new design meant to celebrate Enron's triumphant ascension looking more like an electric plug. Worse, to the Italians it resembled an obscene hand gesture, one that meant about the same thing as shooting a middle finger at an American. The European executives roared with laughter: now they had a new way to win Italian customers.

Enron logo, designed by Paul Rand, 1996.

Back in Houston, dismay grew: the yellow prong also vanished when run through the copying machine. Somehow, Enron had spent millions of dollars on a new business logo without bothering to check if it worked in business. Soon the hallway signs went down, the new cards and letterheads were shredded. With no fanfare, another logo was introduced, replacing the yellow prong with a green one.

The symbol meant to carry Enron into the next millennium hadn't lasted a week.

Embarrassing, but not to its designer. Not only would he know nothing of Enron's ultimate collapse, Rand didn't even live to see the unveiling, having died weeks before in November 1996. It has yet to be revealed who performed the last-minute yellow-to-green substitution that briefly snatched the design from the jaws of defeat.

Nonetheless, faxability aside, the new symbol was rated a success. Identity consultant Tony Spaeth, for one, was enthusiastic about what he saw. "Enron would be Rand's last logo (it is likely that he knew this), and he said it was his best ever. That is a tall order," reported Spaeth in his annual assessment of new logo programs for the February 1998 issue of the Conference Board's magazine, *Across the Board*. "But it is a fine mark: bold, one big idea, but richer in layered ideas and associations than might appear at first glance.

Tony Spaeth, "Fresh Faces for 1998," *Across the Board*, February 1998.

Like great names, great marks often have more than one layer of possible meaning; this one is of course a big E, but one can also see in Rand's Enron ideas of household power as in a plug, industrial power as in stacks or towers, and connectivity (whether pipe or wire) between the E and N."

There has since been some debate as to whether Enron was actually Rand's last logo; certainly it was his last of real consequence. I personally never cared for the way the "pipeline" met the top of the first letter of Enron; it works fine for the N, but really needs a letter like U to work well at the top end. Unron, anyone? Also, I bet I would have preferred the doomed red-yellow-blue version.

But all of this is entirely missing Professor Eskilson's point. The issue he raises is not the Enron logo's aesthetics, or metaphoric incisiveness, or suitability to xerographic technology. Instead, it's the "soul-searching" that consumed the design community after the scale of the Enron debacle became known. Was one of our greatest practitioners complicit in legitimizing the activities of a massive criminal enterprise? Is Paul Rand our very own Leni Riefenstahl?

I actually don't remember any soul-searching. I do remember a bit of *hey-you'd-never-guess-who-designed-the-Enron-logo* gossip, but the reaction to the news was either schadenfreude or a bit of perverse pride, depending on one's opinion of the late Mr. Rand. If anything, the fact that the same person had designed the Enron logo and the IBM logo seemed to say nothing more than that good logos and good companies didn't necessarily go hand in hand. Rand himself implied as much in his 1991 essay "Logos, Flags, and Escutcheons," saying "A logo doesn't sell (directly), it *identifies*....A logo derives its *meaning* from the quality of the thing it symbolizes, not the other way around. A logo is *less* important than the product it signifies; what it means is more important than what it looks like." And for those seeking Riefenstahl parallels, Rand adds, "Design is a two-faced monster. One of the most benign symbols, the swastika, lost its place in the pantheon of the civilized when it was linked to evil, but its intrinsic quality remains indisputable. This explains the tenacity of good design."

So is this another instance where Stephen Eskilson's book gets it wrong? I'm afraid so. In fact, I would make a completely different argument: even if Paul Rand's logo helped legitimize Enron in its heyday, it played an even more important role in the aftermath of its collapse.

Paul Rand, "Logos, Flags, and Escutcheons," collected in Michael Bierut, William Drenttel, Steven Heller, and DK Holland, *Looking Closer: Critical Writings on Graphic Design* (New York: Allworth, 1994).

Enron's success was built on one fundamental trait: the fact that the way it made its money was essentially — perhaps intentionally — incomprehensible. Any resemblances to electrical plugs and pipelines in the Rand logo were, if not unintentional, then less than useful to Enron's management. They seemed much more comfortable with the completely abstract aesthetic of another iconic designer, Frank Gehry. "Enron shares Mr. Gehry's ongoing search for the moment of truth, the moment when the functional approach to a problem becomes infused with the artistry that produces a truly innovative solution," wrote Jeff Skilling in his introduction to the catalog of Frank Gehry's landmark 2001 exhibition at New York's Guggenheim Museum, for which Enron was a lead sponsor. "This is the search Enron embarks on every day, by questioning the conventional to change business paradigms and create new markets that will shape the new economy."

Questioning conventions! Changing paradigms! New markets! Whatever it all meant, somewhere in there Enron was making lots of money. Sorting out how it all went down the drain was such a baffling exercise that when Malcolm Gladwell convened an online discussion to try to figure out what it was, exactly, that Enron did that was legally wrong, he got nearly fifteen thousand words' worth of answers. You couldn't take a picture of Enron's crime: it all happened in the world of numbers and spreadsheets, of financial reports and affidavits. But there was something you *could* take a picture of, and that was Rand's logo. A company with a made-up name, incomprehensible business practices, and largely intangible assets suddenly had a vivid manifestation, a logo that once might have stood for nimbleness, balance, and connectivity, now given new life as "the crooked E."

"The flip side of the power and importance of a brand is its growing vulnerability," wrote the editors of the *Economist* in a riposte to Naomi Klein's *No Logo* titled "The Case for Brands" and subtitled "Far from being instruments of oppression, they make firms accountable to consumers." The editorial goes on: "The more companies promote the value of their brands, the more they will need to seem ethically robust and environmentally pure. Whether protesters will actually succeed in advancing the interests of those they claim to champion is another question. The fact remains that brands give them far more power over companies than they would otherwise have."

Jean-Louis Cohen, Beatriz Colomina, Mildred Friedman, William J. Mitchell, and J. Fiona Ragheb, *Frank Gehry, Architect* (New York: Guggenheim Museum Publications, 2001).

Malcolm Gladwell, "Enron," Gladwell.com, January 3, 2007.

The editors, "The Case for Brands," *Economist*, September 6, 2001.

And indeed, the general public had no more convenient target than Rand's logo to express their feelings about Enron. A 2002 contest to redesign the Enron logo received entries that reimagined the crooked E as, among many other things, a sinking ship, tombstones, the shadows cast by tombstones, skidmarks, a flaccid penis, a dead Republican elephant, a toilet-paper holder, and — perhaps as no surprise to Enron's Italian colleagues — a raised middle finger. Professor Eskilson got that part right: Paul Rand's creation was "the most powerful anti-logo of its time." Whether you believe this outcome was inadvertent or inevitable depends on what you think a logo is supposed to do. No one knew better than Rand, and I'm not so sure he would have been disappointed, or even surprised, by the outcome.

The value of a corporate identity is supposed to be hard to calculate, but in the denouement of its meltdown, the Enron logo proved far from worthless. In fact, at least one version of it — the three-dimensional, LED-illuminated, rotating sign from Enron's corporate lobby, known as the "Disco E" — was worth exactly $33,000. That's how much it went for at a liquidation auction in December 2002, sold for an unknown purpose to a mysterious stranger in a gray Ferrari who, ironically, has never been identified.

"Enron 'Disco E' goes for $33,000," *Houston Chronicle*, December 4, 2002.

Now You See It

36

Everything
I Know
about
Design
I Learned
from *The
Sopranos*

Last night, after eight years, eighty-six episodes, and
untold quantities of gobbagool, *The Sopranos* finished its
run on HBO.

First appeared in
Design Observer,
June 11, 2007.

And this is what we've learned.

On client relationships:
"When you're bleeding a guy, you don't squeeze him dry
right away. Contrarily, you let him do his bidding, suavely.
So you can bleed him next week and the week after,
at minimum."

One of my partners once described two designers
he knew. One was determined to maximize the profit of
every project he undertook, a quest that was accompanied
by massive arguments with clients and occasionally
lawsuits. Another would concede every reasonable point
to his clients, making less on each job, even losing money
every once in a while. Which one never had repeat business?
Which one worked with the same clients for decades?
Take a guess. Of course, clients don't want to be bled, but
they do appreciate a little suaveness.

On creative blocks:

"My advice? Put that thing down awhile, we go get our joints copped, and tomorrow the words'll come blowing out your ass."

Paulie's advice to frustrated amateur screenwriter Christopher is pretty much exactly the same as every book on creativity I've ever read: if you're struggling with a problem, put it aside and inspiration will come when you're not expecting it. While it may not be possible to follow Paulie's prescription to the letter — my lovely wife, Dorothy, is generally unsympathetic when I ask for this kind of assistance — going to a museum will usually do the trick.

On the creative professions:

"Event planning? It's gay, isn't it?"

On The Sopranos, interest in certain things, including but not limited to event planning, fashion design, literature, and certain psychological theories, is considered an indication of effeminacy. A not unsimilar macho attitude often obtains in corporate boardrooms when it comes to design. A lot of executive decision makers are comfortable with spreadsheets. Show them colors and shapes, on the other hand, and you can see the panic in their eyes as they frantically grope through their memories for that time they helped pick out the fabric covers in their beach houses. Part of your job is making these fellows comfortable with their softer sides.

On professional behavior:

"You don't think. You disrespect this place. That's the reason why you were passed the fuck over."

For reasons too complicated to explain here — aside from the obvious point that they sound somewhat alike — the design equivalent to disrespecting the Bing is doing spec work.

On appropriation:

"Fuckin' espresso, cappuccino. We invented this shit. And all these other cocksuckers are gettin' rich off us."

"Oh, again with the rape of the culture."

By his own admission, Howard Schultz was inspired by the coffeehouses of Venice and Milan when he created his own little version in Seattle. The designers of the graphical user interface at Apple were influenced by work developed at Xerox's Palo Alto Research Center. And some people think that the Flintstones are just the Honeymooners except set in the Stone Age. Imitation, influence, and iteration are crucial to design development. The only requirement is that the goal is transformation, not replication.

On the unintended consequences of technology:
"It sounds to me like Anthony Junior may have stumbled onto existentialism."

"Fucking internet."

Okay, advanced technology may have introduced the idea of a godless universe to the Soprano household. Designers, however, believe that advanced technology is our best proof that God exists — and that He lives in Cupertino, California.

On commitment:
"I came home one day, shot her four times. Twice in the head. Killed her aunt, too. I didn't know she was there. And the mailman. At that point, I had to fully commit."

I heard this back in design school, and I still forget it every now and then: if you're going to make something big, make it really big. If you're going to make it simple, make it really simple. Or really small, or really fancy. If you're going after a project, if you're trying to win a competition, if you're serious about getting the job done, don't bother unless you're willing to fully commit.

On aesthetics:
"Not in the face, okay? You give me that? Huh? Keep my eyes?"

Designers like to think that it's not about how it looks. It's about how it works, or how it communicates, or how it changes the world. All true, except it's also about how it looks. The artifacts we make are the Trojan horses that deliver our ideas to an unsuspecting public. Making them look beautiful — or engaging, or funny, or provocative — is anything but a superficial exercise.

We all get whacked now and then. Just make sure you get to keep your eyes.

When in Helvetica

Originally appeared in the *Wall Street Journal*, on March 26, 2011, as a review of Paul Shaw, *Helvetica and the New York City Subway System* (Cambridge: MIT Press, 2011).

Tourists first know cities by their grand architectural icons. Something as unglamorous as public transportation system graphics often are taken for granted, if not outright ignored. But these signs, directing us as subtly as a touch on the elbow, are the real voices of their cities. The typeface that calligrapher Edward Johnston created for the London Underground in 1916 is as emblematic of his city as Big Ben; Hector Guimard's art nouveau signs for the Paris Metro from 1900 are as Parisian as the Eiffel Tower.

By contrast, the signs that New York straphangers see every day as they wait for the uptown A train or the downtown 5 express might seem so blunt and functional that it's hard to imagine them inspiring passion. But they do, and as proof we have *Helvetica and the New York City Subway System*, an entertaining book from MIT Press by Paul Shaw that starts out as a sort of typographic detective story and turns into a history of the New York subway, a survey of global transportation graphics, and an authoritative overview of twentieth-century design in action.

What started Shaw on his research — and this is surely one of the best-researched books on modern design to date — was his irritation with the idea that the modern

New York subway system has always been associated with the typeface Helvetica. This belief, widespread among a small but growing subculture of font aficionados, was fueled by the attention that the typeface received on the fiftieth anniversary of its introduction in 2007. Gary Hustwit's documentary film *Helvetica* from that year surveyed the astonishing ubiquity of a lettering style that appears over the entrances of stores from American Apparel to Staples, on Lufthansa airplanes and New York City garbage trucks, and on Comme des Garçons bags and, yes, New York subway signs. But, as Shaw points out, it was not always so.

Page from New York City Transit Authority Standards Manual, 1970

New York's subway as we know it today was not created as a system at all, but was born in 1940 with the merger of three separate train lines: the Interborough Rapid Transit (IRT), dating to 1904; the Brooklyn-Manhattan Transit (BMT) lines, which began in 1908 as the Brooklyn Rapid Transit; and the Independent (IND) lines from 1932. Each had developed its own signs through the years, none of which were internally consistent. The oldest were the lovely mosaic signs that are still visible today in many stations, but these were quickly overwhelmed by a riotous plethora of black-and-white placards, most of which were hand-painted and all of which accrued like barnacles without any governing standards. By the '60s, using the New York subway meant navigating what a John Lindsay–era task force called "the most squalid public environment of the United States: dank, dingily lit, fetid, raucous with screeching clatter, one of the world's meanest transit facilities." The ugly and baffling signs underlined the city's loss of control.

Desperately seeking to bring order out of chaos, in 1966 the New York City Transit Authority turned to a brand-new firm called Unimark International. The firm's lead designers, Massimo Vignelli and Bob Noorda, hailed from Milan, where Noorda had just designed the graphics for the Metropolitana Milanese. At the heart of Paul Shaw's book is the story of what happened when these champions of European high modernism collided with the union labor at the TA's Bergen Street Sign Shop. If you can imagine a mashup of Antonioni's *Blow-Up* and the original Walter Matthau version of *The Taking of Pelham One Two Three*, you'll get the general idea.

Vignelli and Noorda conducted an exhaustive analysis of the foot-traffic patterns at several of the system's most convoluted stations and devised a system of coordinated directional signs that they were convinced would work across the system. Their original plan was to make these signs in Helvetica, Unimark's typeface of choice, as splendidly neutral as its Swiss homeland. Noorda had used Helvetica for the Milan transit system, and Vignelli soon would be deploying it enthusiastically for everyone from Knoll Furniture to JCPenney. The TA's signmakers, however, didn't have the fancy and exotic Helvetica at hand. They countered with a lettering style they did have, the prosaicly named Standard Medium. The Italian designers may have viewed this as akin to substituting Heinz ketchup for *ragù alla bolognese*, but they acquiesced.

The loss of Helvetica was the least of the designers' problems. Hoping to implement their recommendations personally, they were instead simply thanked for their advice while Bergen Street went to work. As a result, the introduction of the new sign system at the first stations in late 1967 was, in Vignelli's words, "the biggest mess in the world." New signs were installed, but the old signs were left up. The TA added still more signs, hastily made by hand, in an attempt to address the confusion. Symbolic of the confusion was the fact that the signmakers misinterpreted the drawings, not understanding that a black horizontal bracket was meant to secure the signs from above. Instead, they simply painted a black stripe along the top of each sign. The clash between modernist idealism and New Yawk–style practicality reached its apotheosis with the introduction of a new subway map by Vignelli in 1972. Inspired by Harry Beck's revered London Tube map of 1931, Vignelli distilled the labyrinthine tangle of lines to a colorful simplified geometry — with Helvetica this time. Striking as it was, the Vignelli design proved too simple for many and was replaced within four years by a more conventional map that resembles the one in use today.

Yet the sign system took hold. Unlike the map, there was no debate about its functionality, and as it was rolled out over more stations, commuters became familiar with the sans serif lettering and color-coded disks that identified the different lines. And by 1989, no-longer-exotic Helvetica was so easy to obtain that it was finally designated as the standard typeface for the consolidated Metropolitan Transit Authority. Contemporary font spotters might glimpse an occasional bit of Standard Medium in the subways. But, as Paul Shaw's remarkable and unlikely book makes clear, today this most New York of places is, at last, a realm dominated by a Swiss typeface specified by a pair of Italian designers, a testimony to the city as melting pot and the strange turns that any major design project inevitably takes.

Designing through a Recession

First appeared in Design Observer, December 24, 2008.

This advice generally applies to all recessions.

It actually doesn't seem that long ago that my only problem was getting all the work done and finding people places to sit. Back in the middle of that seemingly endless string of sixty-hour workweeks, not one, not two, but (um) several clients called to ask if I wouldn't mind billing them in full, in advance, for work we hadn't yet begun, just so they could commit their budgets and get the money off their books. And then at least one of them just seemed to forget about the project altogether.

I mentioned this at the time to a friend who's been a hedge fund manager from before the time when anyone had ever heard of hedge funds. "Yeah, that's the kind of shit that happens just before everything goes horribly wrong," he said, looking pained. "That's why I'm getting out."

Even if you don't know much about the economy, you've probably noticed that something went horribly wrong in 2008. And 2009 doesn't look much better. I've been working as a designer for over twenty-eight years, and depending on how you count, this is either my fourth or fifth recession. Here's what happens, and a few things you can do about it.

What happens in a recession:

1. Everything slows down.

On October 19, 1987, I was talking on the phone to a client about a potential project. Suddenly she went silent and then said, "Wow. The stock market just went down seven hundred points. Let me get back to you." It was a long time before she got back to me. In a recession, it takes forever to get things off the ground. Clients take their time gathering (lots of brutally competitive) proposals, interviewing (lots of hungrier-than-usual) prospective design firms, calling back and forth with minute (and trivial) revisions to the proposals, and finally selecting the (perhaps not-so-lucky) design firm to get the assignment. Then they go back and renegotiate all the terms of the proposal. Then they delay the start of work several times, put the project on hold several more times once it's underway, and generally take lots of time to brood over every decision every step of the way. Once the project is delivered, they wait longer to launch, print, or build it. And then when you submit the invoice...well, you get the idea.

2. Everyone acts busy.

Yet, in the midst of all this molasses-like slow motion, everyone acts busier than ever. One reason is that because of layoffs, fewer people are around, and those left behind have to do the work of their fallen colleagues. But another reason is that everyone knows that it's idle people who get laid off, so looking busy is the best defense. Things that used to be settled with an email need a phone call, what used to be a phone call is now a meeting, a thirty-minute meeting now takes four hours, and so forth. If you're afraid of losing your job, asking your design firm to visit with three dozen iterations of a brochure cover to spread out on a conference room table certainly seems like a way to signal to the powers that be that you've got way too much on your plate to be axed.

3. Nothing is certain.

Even if you've just presented three dozen iterations, your client can still get fired, and your project can still be put on hold. This makes planning anything completely maddening. I remember back in the 1991 recession going to a meeting in suburban Washington, DC, with one of my partners for a new business presentation to a senior marketing person at a client company with a name you'd recognize today. We presented ourselves all bright and cheerful to the receptionist and said, "We're here for our ten o'clock meeting with Ms. McGillicutty [not her real name]." The receptionist looked blankly at us for a minute, then looked vaguely terrified, then asked us to sit down in the lobby, then moved us to a small conference room. After a long time, a young fellow came in and said, "Hello, I'm Joe Blow [not his real name]. Ms. McGillicutty can't be here, and she asked me to help you." We showed this polite but baffled guy our wares and left. What everyone knew, and no one wanted to say, was that Ms. McGillicutty had been fired sometime between making the appointment and our arrival. Needless to say, we didn't get the assignment, which had probably been eliminated along with Ms. McGillicutty. Joe, however, was quite skillful in the situation, and, if he's still there, is probably busier than ever.

What you can do about it:

1. Be frugal.
Whether you're a freelancer at a kitchen table or a principal in a big consultancy, you've got overhead — not the work you do, but the other stuff you need (or think you need) to do the work: the printer paper, the rent, the $120,000-a-year business development consultant. This is a chance to get back to basics. Ask yourself: What do I really need to do my work? Then get rid of everything else.

2. Be careful.
In your desperation to compete for work, you'll be tempted to do things that you might not do when times are good: take on work for a shady client, start a project without a contract, ship a finished job to someone who's fallen behind on an agreed payment schedule. Do not do these things. Not only will they not help, they will almost certainly end in tears, probably your own.

3. Be creative.
The modern design studio can't help but subscribe to the cult of ASAP. But while working at full speed is great for profit margins, it's not so good for quality control. A design solution almost always benefits from a second, third, or fourth look. Take advantage of the slower pace of a recession by remembering what it was like in design school to spend

a full semester on a single project. What seemed then like torture may now feel like a luxury, and your work will benefit. And don't forget that recessions are a great time for the kind of research and development that manifests itself in self-initiated projects, work that takes a longer view than the next deadline. As Michael Cannell wrote in the *New York Times*, "However dark the economic picture, it will most likely cause designers to shift their attention from consumer products to the more pressing needs of infrastructure, housing, city planning, transit and energy. Designers are good at coming up with new ways of looking at complex problems." In the same article, Cranbrook's Reed Kroloff agreed, saying we could be "standing on the brink of one of the most productive periods of design ever."

Michael Cannell, "Design Loves a Depression," *New York Times*, January 3, 2009.

4. Be sociable.

In boom times, no one has time to talk. "Let's have lunch" can be an empty pleasantry, and even if you make a date with a friend, it will be rescheduled three times before you both silently agree to forget about it altogether. Congratulations! You now have time for lunch. (Somewhere cheap, of course.) Use the gift of time to reconnect with others. But don't, if you can help it, think of this as merely something as deliberate and goal-oriented as networking. This takes the fun out of it for both you and your date. If you make time for people you like with no agenda except the simple joys of human companionship, trust me, something good will come of it.

5. Be patient.

My friend the ex–hedge fund guy (he did get out in time) told me recently, "In the middle of every boom, people say, 'This one is different, it's never going to come down.' But it always does." This was true with dot-coms, and it was true with real estate. "In recessions, they fear the same thing: this one is different. But it will eventually turn around after all the crap gets worked out." And it will, eventually. Just hold on tight.

You may have noticed something interesting: all of these tips for what to do in a recession will work just as well in good times. Or even better. So the final lesson is to use this downturn as a learning experience. If you've got this discipline to survive, or even thrive, in the next year or so, you'll be mastering skills that will serve you well forever. Good luck.

When Design Gets in the Way

First appeared in Design Observer, June 19, 2009.

For more background, see Joshua David and Robert Hammond, *High Line: The Inside Story of New York City's Park in the Sky* (New York: FSG Originals, 2011) and Janette Sadik-Khan and Seth Solomonow, *Streetfight: Handbook for an Urban Revolution* (New York: Penguin, 2017).

I have a confession: I am sort of sick of the High Line.

The product of a design competition with over seven hundred entries, designed to within an inch of its minutely cultivated life, and surrounded by some of the chicest real estate in town, the half-mile southern stretch of this elevated New York City park has been so deliriously popular that crowd control has become a serious problem.

Nearly as popular, but much less celebrated by design cognoscenti, is an urban intervention about two miles north. At the beginning of the summer, New York transportation commissioner Janette Sadik-Khan closed two sections of Broadway to traffic, including five blocks at Times Square, creating new pedestrian malls overnight. Then, Tim Tompkins of the Times Square Alliance, realizing that people might want to sit somewhere, bought 376 rubber folding chairs for $10.74 apiece from Pintchik Hardware in Park Slope. Done and done, and instantly — without the High Line's international design competition, logo, $170 million budget, and five years of painstaking deliberation — millions of people had a new way of enjoying the city.

This raises a question: When it comes to fulfilling simple human desires, can design get in the way?

Consider the behavior of one of my big corporate clients, a client with, God bless them, a seemingly healthy respect for design and the design process. This client would convene an internal task force to consider ways to, say, improve customer service. The task force would come up with a decent idea, for instance: let's make a rule that from now on we'll pick up the phone on our customer help line after no more than three rings. So far so good.

Then I would get a call. This proposal, now designated an "initiative," needed a name. The team has been brainstorming, I'd be told, but none of the names so far had generated enough enthusiasm. Quik Pik Help Line. Rapid Ring Response. Customer First. And so forth. Could I help?

Usually, at this point, I would ask if they might consider, you know, just answering the phone in less than three rings and not making such a fuss out of it. No, I'd be told. "We need to build buy-in around this initiative with the internal stakeholders," my client would tell me carefully. "The thinking is that we need a brand identity for this concept before we introduce it to a broader audience." Well, okay. Eventually, after a great deal of internal debate and the presentation and rejection of several alternatives to the higher-ups, a name would be chosen: ServiceQuest 2010. And then would inevitably come another phone call: Could I design a logo for ServiceQuest 2010? Sigh.

Meanwhile, presumably, the phone would just keep ringing and ringing.

Now, far be it from me to argue against any kind of full-employment program for designers. But I do find it useful to start conversations with potential clients with a simple question: Are you sure you want to do this design project? Why is it necessary? Is this the easiest way to do it? Is it the best? Why does a designer have to be involved?

I like to think about how Ms. Sadik-Khan and Mr. Tompkins would have dealt with the less-than-three-rings initiative. How about a one-paragraph (or even one-sentence) mass email? Just answer the goddamned phones, people! Likewise, if they had run the High Line project, I'm guessing their first priority would have been access — not high design, not ingenious little moments, not formal affectations that may end up looking very 2009 about ten years from now — but simply getting people up there. I applaud the ambition of Friends of the High Line and their design consultants, and the result is quite rightly acclaimed.

When Design Gets in the Way

High Line founder Robert Hammond reflects on his process, with some second thoughts, at Laura Bliss, "The High Line's Next Balancing Act," Citilab, February 7, 2017.

However, I would love to see more design incrementalism, more Jane Jacobs–style fast prototyping to complement those slow-moving Burnhamesque Big Plans.

One last thing: a lot of people liked sitting in those $10.74 chairs, but a lot of people really hated the way they looked. So earlier this month they were replaced with more tasteful park chairs, the ones that Sadik-Khan and Tompkins evidently wanted all along but couldn't get in time. And what about the old chairs? With the customary improvisatory panache I've come to associate with this effort, they commissioned artist Jason Peters to create a sculpture out of them. It lasted for a weekend.

Management consultants like to enthuse about the importance of Big Hairy Audacious Goals. BHAGs are good for whiteboards and PowerPoint presentations. But sometimes — and maybe more than ever, these days — the best kind of audacity comes in small packages.

How to Be Ugly

I'm no purist when it comes to graphic design, and I thought I had seen it all. But that was before I saw Mike Meiré's redesign of German culture magazine *032c*.

First appeared in Design Observer, November 11, 2007.

Am I easily shocked? No. But with *032c*, Meiré builds a whole publication around what I now realize is the last taboo in graphic design: the vertical and horizontal scaling of type.

Dear God in heaven: at long last, is nothing sacred?

If you're unfamiliar with the work of Meiré und Meiré, you might just assume that *032c* was simply the output of a naive amateur. But Mike Meiré is a great designer, and he's been responsible for some extraordinarily beautiful magazines, including the innovative business journal *brand eins* and its predecessor *Econy*, both models of taste, precision, and understatement. Meiré knows exactly what he's doing, and what he's doing with *032c* is telling the world that we can take taste, precision, and understatement...and shove them.

Behold the style pendulum in the midst of another swing. The fits, literal and otherwise, that attended the unveiling of the London 2012 Olympics logo were a clear signal that ugly was getting ready for a comeback. It only took a day or two for the backlash to the backlash to set in; as the folks at the website Coudal told us, what we were witnessing were the birth pangs of the new brutalism. And lest anyone write this moment off as a mere anomaly, Wolff Olins, the design firm that created the 2012 campaign, quickly followed it up with the jammed-together-on-a-stalled-downtown-No.-4-train-at-rush-hour New York City tourism logo, as well as the hey-mom-when-did-you-learn-Photoshop Wacom identity, both of which extend new brutalism, or (in the case of Wacom) just plain ugliness, to new levels. When similar symptoms are detected at both hypertrendy German culture magazines and massive corporate-identity consultancies, a trend might be said to approach pre-epidemic stages.

This and subsequent quotes are from Patrick Burgoyne, "The New Ugly," *Creative Review*, September 2007.

Steven Heller, "The Cult of the Ugly," *Eye*, Summer 1993.

"Ugly is back!" With these words, Patrick Burgoyne confirmed the diagnosis in *Creative Review*, recalling the "mother of all rows" back in the early '90s that attended the publication in *Eye* of Steven Heller's now-legendary article "Cult of the Ugly." As for this time around, Burgoyne asks, "are we witnessing a knee-jerk reaction to the slick sameness of so much design or a genuine cultural shift?"

Whether reactionary spasm or irrevocable paradigm shift, if history is a guide, once the game is afoot, scores of designers will be eager to get with the program. Obviously, doing ugly work isn't difficult. The trick is to surround it with enough attitude, so it will be properly perceived not as the product of everyday incompetence, but rather as evidence of one's attunement with the zeitgeist.

Paraphrased from *Helvetica*, a documentary film by Gary Hustwit, 2007.

This is harder than it looks. Breaking rules is reactive and, perhaps, needlessly provocative. One approach is to declare a complete ignorance of the rules and cloak oneself in an aura of Eden-like innocence. David Carson provides a classic example with his monologue in *Helvetica*, recalling his unawareness, at the outset of his career, that some guys had spent a lot of time setting up a bunch of standards or something. Rules? What rules? Burgoyne updates this approach with his "charitable" explanation for the design of the truly alarming magazine *Super Super*, the appearance of which has been likened to a clown being sick. Creative director Steve Slocombe's lack of formal design training, he offers, "has left him unencumbered by the profession's history and therefore more able to seek out new forms of expression."

That's one way to put it. Not everyone, however, is so blissfully unencumbered. The alternative approach, then, is to elevate differentiation to the end that justifies all means. If you can't ignore the rules, break them. "We have created something original in a world where it is increasingly difficult to make something different," announced Wolff Olins chairman Brian Boylan in the midst of the brouhaha surrounding the London 2012 launch. "I became a bit tired of all these look-alike magazines," said Mike Meiré in *Creative Review*. "They're all made very professionally but I was looking for something more charismatic. I wanted to search for an interesting look that was beyond the mainstream."

At all costs, however, onlookers should be reassured that the results, no matter how careless looking, were achieved through the same painstaking attention to detail that one would associate with more conventional solutions. Maybe even more! "It takes perfectionism to get this kind of design just exactly not quite right," said Hugh Aldersey-Williams about the work of the late master of antidesign Tibor Kalman, whose former employees all have stories about spending endless hours on deliciously bad letterspacing. Similarly, when Meiré was asked about the stretched headline type in *032c* — a typographic effect seemingly mastered by everyone in my neighborhood who has ever lost a cat — he answered, "This was actually the hardest job to get right."

When ugly is done properly, the conventional-minded are properly outraged. This should never be admitted as the goal, however. "This is the most appropriate way to communicate to our audience," offered *Super Super*'s Steve Slocombe. Or, as Mike Meiré says, "It is what it is." But finally there may come a stage when the public's outrage is too much to ignore: at that point, claim that this was precisely the plan in the first place. "Its design is intentionally raw, which means it doesn't immediately sit there and ask to be liked very much," said Wolff Olins's Patrick Cox of the 2012 logo. "It was meant to be something that did provoke a response, like the little thorn in the chair that gets you to breathe in, sit up, and take notice." And what say you, Mr. Cox, when the inevitable complaint is lodged that a four-year-old could do it? "When people are saying that a child could have done it, or are coming up with their own designs, that's what we want: we want everyone to be able to do something with it." Check and mate.

So the New Ugly may be here to stay for a while. If you're familiar with art and design, you know the perils of condemning the shock of the new. After all, no one wants to risk being one of the bourgeoisie sneering at the unveiling of *Les Demoiselles d'Avignon* or booing at the debut of *Le Sacre du Printemps*.

But only some of the time does that little thorn in the chair turn out to be a Picasso or a Stravinsky. Most of the time, it's just a pain in the ass. Until further notice, be careful where you decide to sit.

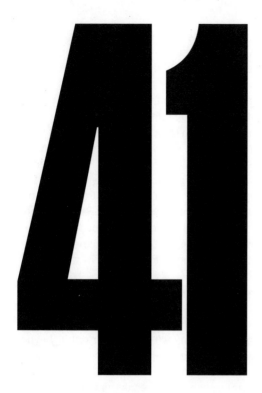

Five Ways to Design for a Cause

Graphic design, the field to which I've devoted my life, isn't mentioned often in popular fiction. A rare exception can be found in Richard Price's epic six-hundred-page 1992 novel *Clockers*. In it, Price tells the story of a young drug dealer, Strike, describing his desperate, day-to-day existence in harrowing detail. My profession makes its appearance while Strike is visiting his parole officer:

> *The walls of the waiting room were hung with black-and-white cautionary posters, encircling Strike with admonitions, the subjects ranging from AIDS to pregnancy to crack to alcohol, each one a little masterpiece of dread. Strike hated posters. If you were poor, posters followed you everywhere — health clinics, probation offices, housing offices, day care centers, welfare offices — and they were always blasting away at you with warnings to do this, don't do that, be like this, don't be like that, smarten up, control this, stop that.*

That three-word sentence stopped me cold: "Strike hated posters." Graphic designers, as everybody knows, love posters. The difference between these two points of view couldn't be more disturbing to me. I love posters. I love looking at them, and I love designing them. By the time I'd read those words, I'd spent countless hours designing many

Written as an introduction to Dmitri Siegel and Edward Morris, *Green Patriot Posters: Images for a New Activism* (New York: Metropolis, 2010).

Richard Price, *Clockers* (Boston: Houghton Mifflin, 1992).

of those "little masterpieces of dread." Bold. Black-and-white. Designed to, yes, blast away with their admonishing messages. I had to do some soul-searching. Who was I designing for, anyway?

The poster for the pro-bono cause is, frankly, a bit of a cliché in contemporary design practice. Like many others, I was always happy to take them on because of their meaty subject matter. Forget the struggle to find drama in inherently dull commercial subjects. Here, instead, were the great themes: life, death, good, evil, the very future of humanity. And my imaginary audience was, often, humanity itself. At least that's what I told myself. If I were completely honest, I'd admit that my real audience was one I know a little bit better: my fellow designers. Or perhaps an even more cynically limited subset: fellow designers who judge design competitions.

Right around the time I first read Richard Price's words, I was ready to make some changes. Design for designers is great, but the real challenge in doing cause-related work is communicating with the larger public beyond our small circles. It's harder in every way: harder to compete with all the other noise, harder to reach the people who can really make a difference. This means thinking differently, in five specific ways.

1. Be clear about your purpose.

If you're acting as a communicator, be clear about what you're communicating. "Building awareness" can be a cop-out, an excuse to separate cause and effect. What do you want your work to accomplish? How will you know if you're successful? Make your goal action, and determine the most direct way to provoke it. Be outrageously ruthless.

2. Know your audience.

Who are you trying to reach? Don't start until you have an answer to this question. A message that doesn't ring true — visually, verbally, and in every other way — will get dismissed or, even worse, ignored. Understand the context of the people who will be seeing your work. The more you can master that language, the more your message will get through.

3. Try not to use design as therapy.

When horrible things happen, feeling bad is an understandable reaction. Helping makes us feel better.

Figure out the best way to help. Is making a poster the best way? Sometimes, donating your talent is great. Often, simply donating money is better.

4. Don't be "creative."

The brilliant Chilean architect Alejandro Aravena says, "Creativity is what you do when there is not enough knowledge. If you have knowledge, you do not need creativity." Don't use work for social causes as a showcase for your cleverness or as an excuse to stretch your creative muscles without the constraints of demanding clients. Do your research, get the knowledge you need, and then find the fastest, most bullshit-free route from point A to point B. If you can be clever on the way, go ahead. But not at the expense of getting your point across. Be your own demanding client.

Alejandro Aravena is quoted in "Creativity, Controversy and Change at DI2010," Design Indaba, March 12, 2010.

5. No matter what, be optimistic and positive.

The best designs and the most effective campaigns are inspiring, not depressing. Don't admonish; don't talk down to people. At its best, our work can serve as a rallying cry and give voice to people who might otherwise feel isolated and silent. Use your work to visualize the future, and lead the way with enthusiasm and passion.

A committed designer will respond creatively to an urgent challenge on his or her own terms. Each solution is a chance to demonstrate that design can be a potent tool for communication and social transformation. And if you look hard enough, and think even harder, you too will find your own way.

Designing Obama

First appeared in
Design Observer,
October 25, 2009.

Originally written as an
introduction to Scott
Thomas, *Designing
Obama* (Albany, CA:
Post, 2009).

I was talking recently with a group of graphic designers. The subject was good work: not doing it, but how to get it accepted. Designers like to complain. We cast ourselves as embattled defenders of good taste and inventive ideas; arrayed against us are armies of insensitive clients, determined to thwart us, whose pigheadedness can only be defeated by dedication, cunning, and guile.

We traded war stories for a while, but one seasoned designer in our midst was silent. We finally asked him what tricks he used to get good work done. "Well, I guess I'm lazy," he said. "I just make sure all my clients are smart people with unique messages and good products. The rest is easy."

The rest is easy. Looking back at the design work that led to Barack Obama's historic victory in November 2008, I wonder if that was the trick. Although much has been made — rightly so — of the ingenious and adaptable "O" logo developed by Sol Sender's team, Obama himself was his own best logo. Young, African American, charismatic — change wasn't just a message, it was the candidate's very embodiment. When it was all said and done, Barack Obama was a smart guy with a unique message and a good product. And what designer wouldn't wish for that in a client?

Selling change isn't easy in a world that tends to prefer the comfort of the familiar. We all know what a revolution looks like: handmade signs, scrawled graffiti, the voice of the people. But Obama's campaign was the opposite. Reportedly, the candidate resisted at first. "He did not initially like the campaign's blue and white logo — intended to appear like a horizon, symbolizing hope and opportunity — saying he found it too polished and corporate," reported the *New York Times*. But David Axelrod and his team prevailed. They must have known that the revolution, when it finally came, would have to be wrapped up in the most comprehensive corporate identity program the twenty-first century has yet seen. And it worked, as *Designing Obama*, the book by Scott Thomas, design director of new media for Obama for America, reveals.

Jeff Zeleny and Jim Rutenberg, "A Delegator, Obama Picks When to Take Reins," *New York Times*, June 16, 2008.

Like every other graphic designer I know, I watched the live images of campaign rallies from Toledo to Topeka to Tallahassee with a growing feeling of awe. Obama's oratorical skills were one thing. But the awe-inspiring part was the way all of the signs were faithfully, and beautifully, set in Hoefler and Frere-Jones's typeface Gotham. "Trust me," I told *Newsweek* back in February 2008. "I've done graphics for events — and I know what it takes to have rally after rally without someone saying, 'Oh, we ran out of signs, let's do a batch in Arial.'" But it isn't just strict standards and constant police work that keeps an organization on brand. It's the mutual desire for everyone to have every part of the effort look like The Real Thing. At the height of the campaign, my daughter asked me if I could design a flyer for a friend's Obama benefit party at a little bar in Hoboken, New Jersey. We took the text and reset it in Gotham, downloaded the O logo, and put it together in minutes. "Wow," my daughter said. "It looks like Obama's actually going to be there!" Exactly.

Andrew Romano, "Why the Obama 'Brand' is Working," *Newsweek*, February 27, 2008.

The same thing was happening all over the country. In a world where access to digital media and social networks is becoming increasingly ubiquitous, Obama '08 became the first open-source political campaign. Shepard Fairey's "Hope" poster — an icon that's destined, if you ask me, to occupy the 2008 slot of any historical timeline drawn up a hundred years from now — sits at the top of an astonishingly vast collection of posters, websites, buttons, flyers, and YouTube videos, some generated by professionals, some by ordinary citizens, all of whom were motivated by the urge to create a sense that their candidate was actually going to be there.

Political operatives will study this campaign and its design program for years, trying to unlock its secrets. Many will copy it. But few will capture its magic. It seems so simple, doesn't it? A good logo, consistent typography, get everyone to join in. They'll have all the ingredients in place except the hardest one: the client. You need a smart person with a unique message and a good product. Then, like the fellow said, the rest is easy.

43

Graphic Design Criticism as a Spectator Sport

1. There's Something Wrong with Vinny

It's an imaginary summer Saturday afternoon in suburban Cleveland in, say, 1969 or so. I am twelve years old. My father is cutting the back lawn, and so is our next-door neighbor Vinny. Each of them decides at the same time to take a break under a small tree that stands at the border between our yards. They talk about the weather, the Cleveland Indians, typical stuff. Then Vinny says, "Hey, Lenny, did you notice that new packaging for Tropicana?"

My father is taken aback for a moment. "What, you mean Tropicana, the orange juice?"

"Yeah," says Vinny. "Did you notice they changed the packaging?"

My father is baffled. "The packaging? You mean the carton it comes in? The way it looks?" Vinny nods. My father looks doubtful. "I can't say I have."

"Well, they changed it, all right," says Vinny with a slight edge to his voice. "There used to be curvy lettering, and a picture of an orange with a straw through it. Now it's plain lettering and the orange and the straw are gone." Vinny looks at my father's blank expression. "I can't believe you didn't notice."

First appeared in Design Observer, January 14, 2013.

"I don't know, I'll have to, um, take a look. It sounds like..." My father isn't sure of his words here: "...quite a change."

"Well, I don't like it," declares Vinny. "In fact, I'm going to write a letter to the company and tell them how much I hate it. You should take a look and write something, too."

My father nods, and then looks over his shoulder. "Well, listen, Vinny, I think I'd better check in with Anne Marie. Take it easy." My dad walks back to the house and into the kitchen, where my mom is at the sink. They both look out the window at the backyard. "Anne Marie," says my dad, "I think there's something wrong with Vinny."

Of course, this never happened, at least not in 1969. But forty years later, Vinny would not be seen as someone to be watched carefully and perhaps medicated, but rather as a spokesperson for a highly desirable audience. In 2008 PepsiCo Americas Beverages commissioned Arnell Group to redesign the packaging for its flagship juice brand, Tropicana Pure Premium. Thanks to the internet and social media, what followed the introduction of the new packaging was not a few unnerving backyard conversations with eccentric neighbors, but an outpouring of complaints from consumers, as well as demands that the suddenly beloved previous packaging be reinstated. The *New York Times* told the story.

Stuart Elliott, "Tropicana Discovers Some Buyers Are Passionate About Packaging," *New York Times*, February 22, 2009.

It was not the volume of the outcries that led to the corporate change of heart, [PepsiCo North America president Neil] Campbell said, because "it was a fraction of a percent of the people who buy the product."

Rather, the criticism is being heeded because it came, Mr. Campbell said in a telephone interview on Friday, from some of "our most loyal consumers."

"We underestimated the deep emotional bond" they had with the original packaging, he added. "Those consumers are very important to us, so we responded."

The response was to throw out the new package design and return to the old. The people had spoken, and not for the last time.

2. Everybody Wants to Go to Harvard

Earlier last year, the University of California quietly unveiled a new logo. Much has changed since 2008, including the notion that you can quietly unveil a logo. The logo was, eventually, inevitably noticed. After Tropicana, after the "epic fail" Gap debacle, after the seizure-inducing London 2012 affair, no one should have been surprised by what happened next. In fact, you almost had a sense that we all knew our roles in the drama to come: New logo? Game on! Graphic design criticism is now a spectator sport, and anyone can play.

The review on Brand New, Armin Vit's amazingly popular logo review website, was mixed. The new UC logo was contemporary and abstract, and sat at the center of a smart and attractive new visual system, a very professional job by the university's in-house design team. Significantly, it was meant to represent the University of California system, the holding company, in effect, for UCLA, UC Berkeley, UC Davis, and the other schools in the network. All of them would keep their existing logos. Brand New commenters tend to be other graphic designers. Some liked it, some didn't.

"IC, UC, We all C for California," Brand New, November 20, 2012.

There was no such ambivalence on the part of the UC community of students, faculty, and alumni. They basically went crazy with rage. A petition on Change.org — "Stop the new UC logo" — got over fifty-four thousand signatures. The outcry spread to the general press coverage, where it was described as "one of the worst logo rebrands in history," "revolting," and "a fiasco." Some in the graphic design community attempted to rally around the embattled designers, including Armin Vit, who wrote a none-too-subtle response to the critics that included the suggestion: "Shut up. Seriously. Shut up."

Reactions are from "The University of California Debuts One of the Worst Logo Rebrands in History," The San Francisco Egotist, December 11, 2012; Priscilla Frank, "UC Logo Fail," The Huffington Post, December 13, 2012; and Christopher Knight, "New UC Logo on Suspension after Much Well-Deserved Criticism," Los Angeles Times, December 14, 2012.

The university held its ground for a week or so before capitulating. Said Daniel M. Dooley, UC's senior vice president for external relations: "While I believe the design element in question" — you can almost hear him choking on the word logo — "would win wide acceptance over time, it also is important that we listen to and respect what has been a significant negative response by students, alumni, and other members of our community." "Pleasant news," said the opponents. "Awesome victory."

Dooley decried the "false narrative" that had surrounded the controversy, specifically the idea that this newfangled modern thing would replace the century-old traditional university seal. (The official line was that the seal would continue to be used on old-looking stuff like diplomas.) As usual, no one had expressed much passion for the good old seal until it was threatened by the arrival of the new logo. Suddenly, people were lining up to testify to its virtues.

Dooley's quote is from Larry Gordon, "UC Drops Controversial New Logo," Los Angeles Times, December 15, 2012.

The University of California seal, of course, is nothing more than a banal pastiche of the kind of stuff of which university seals are always made: open books, celestial bodies, slogans, type arranged in circles. Which is exactly the point. As one surprisingly revealing Brand New commenter, a UC alumnus, said, "Please take the time to look up the websites and logos of Oxford, Cambridge, Harvard or Princeton, they all feature the seal or coat of arms of the university to the left of the institution's name. Lesser and/or newer learning institutions will tend to have newer, more corporate designs because a seal or traditional coat of arms would not be a good fit, almost usurpatory in fact." In short: don't you dare mistake my alma mater for one of those second-rate places that doesn't have a proper seal as its symbol. (Cruelly, the same commenter pointed out with undisguised distaste the logo of Armin Vit's own college, "a second-tier private school in northern Mexico called 'Anáhuac University.'" In this case, Vit is right: shut up.)

Original University of California seal and proposed update, 2012.

But all the UC logo dissenters remind us of how different designers are from regular people. Designers tend to overvalue differentiation and originality. We are taught this in design school. The best solutions are created ex nihilo, break new ground, resemble nothing else in the world. Everyone wants to stand out, or else what's the point? But this isn't true. Most people don't want to stand out. They want to fit in. More precisely, they want to fit in with the people they like, or want to be like. At one point in the debate, Armin Vit linked to a Google image search result of university seals. Did anyone wonder why they all look the same?

When people imagine going to college, what most of them are imagining is going to a place like Harvard. If you're not going to Harvard, it's best not to have some funny-looking logo reminding you of that fact. Once you've graduated, the university seal stands for the experience you've bought and paid for. Changing it after the fact is like coming into people's houses, taking away the things they own, and replacing them with things they didn't ask for and don't want. No wonder they get mad.

3. When the Chips are Down

In October 2011 the exhibition *Graphic Design: Now in Production* opened at the Walker Art Center. Co-organized by the Walker and the Cooper-Hewitt National Design Museum, the show surveyed a wide range of contemporary work with a strong bias toward small-batch work by sole practitioners, small studios, and people with no professional design training. The work on view, by designers and artists like Daniel Eatock, Keetra Dean Dixon, Metahaven, Mike Perry, and Christien Meindertsma, was strong and provocative, and the show was largely well reviewed.

Most of the exhibited pieces were experimental and designed for extremely limited audiences, if they were designed with audiences in mind at all. The biggest exception was an area devoted to contemporary identity design. Elsewhere viewers were invited to contemplate the mysteries of, say, the "poster" Daniel Eatock created by setting a blank piece of paper on dozens of upended Magic Markers. In the entrance corridor they confronted the familiar, frankly commercial logos of Starbucks, Comedy Central, AOL, and Popeyes Chicken & Biscuits. The contrast was stark and rather disorienting.

This area was curated by Brand New's Armin Vit and Bryony Gomez-Palacio, whose online commenters are invited to vote on each new identity presented. At the Walker, the installation's designers created a charming low-tech homage to Brand New's digital polling system: visitors could vote on the redesigns by placing poker chips in two transparent tubes in front of the "before" and "after" versions of each logo, creating a bar-charted popularity contest in real time each day the exhibition was on view.

After the Walker, the next stop for *Now in Production* was the Cooper-Hewitt National Design Museum in New York. This represented a challenge. The Cooper-Hewitt is in the midst of a multiyear renovation, and the museum building is closed. This means that alternate venues had to be found for all its exhibitions. The New York team found an interesting one: Governors Island, a 172-acre decommissioned military base and national park eight hundred yards off the southernmost tip of Manhattan, reachable only by ferryboat on weekends during the summer. The exhibition opened in Building 110 on Memorial Day weekend.

Building 110, located adjacent to the point where the ferries load and unload, is not particularly suited to museum-quality exhibitions; its low ceilings and rough surfaces are quite different from the clean, well-lit galleries at the Walker. But it had two notable characteristics. Not only was it the only air-conditioned building on the island during one of the hottest New York City summers on record, it housed the island's only indoor bathrooms. To get to the bathrooms, one passed down a long corridor like that in a typical public school. The Cooper-Hewitt's exhibition designers had the inspired idea to start the show in the corridor, and it was there that they located the logo-voting apparatus. This guaranteed that it would be seen not just by a self-selected audience of graphic design enthusiasts, but by a cross-section of the general public: moms with strollers, skateboard kids, joggers, tourists.

It was fascinating to watch their reactions and the shifting tabulations. I was surprised by how often the civilians got it "wrong," voting enthusiastically for the cartoony old version of the Comedy Central logo, the needlessly fussy and insecure pre-redesign Starbucks, the dated *Clarissa Explains It All*–era Nickelodeon splat. After a few hours of air-conditioned anthropological observation, a number of precepts emerged, almost all of which rang as true in my professional experience as in Building 110.

First, in logo design, people prefer complicated things to simple things. Simple things look too easy to do, and it baffles people that professionals must be enlisted to design something like the *USA Today* logo, which is basically a blue circle. "How much did they pay for this?" and "My four-year-old could do this" are responses so predictable you wonder if they're hardwired into people's brains. (Invoking the Target circle or the Nike swoosh as a counterargument is a red herring: imagine the four-year-old designers that would be invoked if Target unveiled its Unimark-designed dot-in-a-circle logo today.)

Second, people prefer literal things to metaphoric things. People like actual splats on their Nickelodeon logos, not metaphoric splats, actual drawings of Saturn on their Sci-Fi Channel logos, not metaphoric alternate alien spellings. And they react with suspicion, if not outright contempt, when designers refer to the mystical characteristics of colors and shapes, to meanings that are open to interpretation or that will emerge only upon examination. (A rare and legendary exception to this is the hidden arrow in the FedEx logo. Everyone loves that arrow!)

Third, and most crucially, people prefer the thing they're used to rather than whatever new thing you're foisting on them. Now, some will point to evidence that people like new things when the new thing is really good: in debates like the one over the new University of California logo, many will argue that the problem was that the new logo wasn't well designed. In a piece on what he calls the "crowdsmashing" phenomenon, *New York* writer Paul Ford argues that people, in fact, like change. He equates change with "novelty," naming as examples "tablet computers with smaller screens, iPhones with bigger screens, new Batman movies, 'Gangnam Style.'" Sorry, change isn't introducing an iPhone with a bigger screen that you can voluntarily purchase. Change is replacing a perfectly good map application on your iPhone with a new one. And you know how that turned out.

Paul Ford, "Crowdsmashed," *New York*, December 21, 2012.

4. Please Tell Me This Is a Joke

I know from personal experience how much consumers dislike change, and I have a clue why. Several years ago, Pentagram received an assignment to redesign the logo for the Big Ten college athletic conference. This wasn't change for change's sake. The existing logo incorporated a number eleven, FedEx arrow-style, to acknowledge the fact that the number of teams in the conference did not correspond to the conference's name. Now the conference was expanding to twelve teams, requiring a new logo, and ideally one that didn't incorporate its own obsolescence.

Big Ten logo, Pentagram, 2010.

If there's one group that gets even more agitated about logos than college alumni, it's sports fans. That made this particular job, which combined both, a perfect storm. Moments after our new logo (which incorporated the number 10 into the word "big") was unveiled, the reaction started pouring in, almost all negative: "epic fail," "looks like it took 25 seconds to make," "the gayest thing I've ever seen," and, of course, the inevitable conclusion that it looked like "a four-year-old from Chicago designed it in her sleep." What is it about four-year-olds, anyway?

Then there were the emails that were sent to us directly. "You should be completely embarrassed." "Lame and boring." "So bad." "Please tell me this is a joke." "My thirteen-year-old could have done better with a blank piece of paper and a pencil." (This last represents a kind of progress, at least.)

Reasoning that people who took the time to look up our email address and send a note — no matter how filled with swear words — deserved a response, we replied with regret for their disappointment in our work and our hope that the logo would grow on them. And we always ended with an acknowledgment of the passion of our correspondents; as I told *Fast Company*, "It's that exact same passion that fills the seats at every game." Almost every person we answered wrote back. Some softened their

Stephanie Orma, "Why Do College Sports Fans Hate the Big Ten's Smart New Logo?" *Fast Company Design*, December 27, 2010.

criticism, some did not, but all expressed surprise that anyone wrote back at all. Clearly, part of the anger this change aroused was based on the idea that it was being imposed on them by remote, detached "experts" with no concern for the feelings of loyal fans, fans who have their own unique histories with their brands, histories that had abruptly been rendered null and void.

And this sense of alienation, more than anything else, is the fuel for the rising tide of logo crowdsmashing. Here *New York*'s Paul Ford got it exactly right: "People don't like their stories messed with. You expect a certain continuity, and when the opposite happens...you react out of proportion to external measures of the offense but very much in proportion to the internal anxiety and anger you might feel." In this case, our (wonderful) client held firm, the anger subsided, and two years later people do seem to be getting used to the logo.

5. How Many Psychiatrists Does It Take to Change a Lightbulb?

Whether it's from the general public or the professional design community, this kind of criticism always has an underlying tone: I could have done better. And you know what? You may be right. But designing a better logo usually isn't the hard part.

"UPS Says Bye-Bye to Rand," Speak Up, March 25, 2003.

Six years before Tropicana outraged its brand loyalists with its new package, another company changed its logo to great outcry. The company was UPS, the logo was the "package, bow, and shield" mark designed by Paul Rand in 1961, and the outcry was mostly limited to the design community. But loud it was — so loud, in fact, that it became the hottest subject to date on Speak Up, a fledgling blog created about a year before by two young Mexican émigrés who have been so central to our story, Armin Vit and Bryony Gomez-Palacio. The discussion ran to 169 comments, overwhelmingly negative: the redesign by FutureBrand was "crap," "shit," "pointless," "stupid," "hideously unoriginal," and so forth, and those quotes are from only the first dozen or so comments. Many of the commenters proceeded from an assumption that a logo by Paul Rand, especially one with forty years of history behind it, should not on any account be changed. Many of them were also certain that if it had to be changed, they could do better.

I read these comments with mixed feelings because of something that was not widely known. From late 1996

Now You See It

to early 1999, I worked with a team at my firm on our own redesign of the UPS identity. We were hired for a simple reason: surveys kept showing the company was inaccurately perceived as being slower, more inflexible, and less technologically adept than their competition. If a logo from the Kennedy administration carried around by eighty-thousand-plus boxy brown trucks wasn't reinforcing this perception, it certainly wasn't changing it. The mission was to disrupt external perception by somehow changing the face of the company. But how?

We came into the project similarly intimidated by the Rand legacy. On top of that, I personally had sentimental feelings about the brown truck, which seemed to me as much an American design icon as the Coke bottle. So my first idea was my favorite idea: don't change the logo or the trucks at all. Instead, repaint ten thousand trucks each in red, orange, green, purple, yellow, and blue, and leave the remainder brown. If UPS already "owned brown," this would give them the next best thing: owning the entire spectrum. And imagine how fun it would be to spot a new color on the road. You could just hear the happy voices of America's children shouting, "There's an orange one!" I called this The M&M Strategy, and after I unveiled it at the first design presentation, I poured a big bag of M&M's into a glass bowl in the middle of the conference table, convinced I had hit a home run.

For more on my M&M Strategy, see Karrie Jacobs, "Learning to Love Brown," *New York Times*, August 20, 1998.

The client didn't buy it. Nor did it buy any of the design proposals we would make over the next two years of work. We received a lot of encouragement and intelligent guidance, and were paid well and treated with respect. Some of the recommendations almost got across the finish line. I remember a presentation to top management in a carefully guarded facility where one of the options had gotten far enough to be painted on a spare UPS truck. It looked great. If you ask me, everything we presented looked great. But none of it was accepted. (I learned along the way that we were not alone: at least two other well-known firms had been similarly engaged before us and were similarly unable to attain the ultimate consummation.) Our suspicion was that the client simply was not ready to make a step this dramatic. I was reminded of the joke about the number of psychiatrists required to change a lightbulb: one, but the lightbulb has to really want to change.

About four years later, UPS finally was, evidently, ready to change, and the Rand logo was superseded at last by the swooshy, shiny, gradated logo that we all know today and that at the time was so widely criticized by the design community. But not by me. Did I like it? Not really. (I agreed with my colleague Tracey Cameron, who had studied with Rand at Yale and called it "The Golden Combover.") Was it better than the logos we had presented? Not necessarily. But FutureBrand had done something that we and the others had failed to do: they had convinced the client to accept their solution.

The basic starting point of Graphic Design Criticism as a Spectator Sport is "I could have done better." And of course you could! But simply having the idea is not enough. Crafting a beautiful solution is not enough. Doing a dramatic presentation is not enough. Convincing all your peers is not enough. Even if you've done all that, you still have to go through the hard work of selling it to the client. And like any business situation of any complexity whatsoever, that process may be smothered in politics, handicapped with exigencies, and beset with factors that have nothing to do with design excellence. You know, real life. Creating a beautiful design turns out to be just the first step in a long and perilous process with no guarantee of success. Or, as Christopher Simmons put it more succinctly, "Design is a process, not a product."

Christopher Simmons, "It's Not About the Logo," Teaching Design, December 13, 2012.

I do not propose here that this complex process should be an excuse or a crutch. Few things in the design world sound as sad as "the client made me do it." Nor do I argue that the final result shouldn't be held up to scrutiny. We should be judged by what we make. But perhaps the question in these logo discussions could be more than: Could I do better? Perhaps we could also ask: What was the purpose? What was the process? Whose ends were being served? How should we judge success? But we seldom look any deeper than first impressions, wallowing instead in a churning maelstrom of snap judgments. Should we be surprised when the general public jumps right in after us?

6. I Had a Dream

Ah, the general public. Years ago, people like my dad and our neighbor Vinny would have been no more likely to have a backyard conversation about orange juice packaging or university seals than particle physics or the Treaty of Westphalia. Yet I dreamed of a day when regular people like my dad would be aware of graphic design, of typefaces, logos, packaging, when these things would be discussed as seriously as movies or books. And look how it all turned out.

Thoughtful criticism of graphic design once seemed to have a bright future. Ten years ago, a growing number of blogs on the subject provided more than any curious person could absorb, led by the pioneering Speak Up. In 2009 Vit and Gomez-Palacio, finding the traffic generated by frantic logo debates too irresistible to ignore, closed it down and launched Brand New, replacing the discursive, eclectic writing of their earlier site with the addictive, shallower thrills of up-down votes on logo after logo after logo.

That same year, *I.D.* magazine closed after fifty-five years in print. Last week, F+W Media fired the senior staff of the United States' oldest design publication, the seventy-three-year-old *Print*, and announced they were moving the magazine's operations to Cincinnati. (Although this was supposedly in the service of "synergy," it's more like a wayward Soviet diplomat being summoned back to Moscow, where a posting to Siberia was usually followed by an appearance before the firing squad.) From 1994 to 2006, I helped edit five anthologies of graphic design criticism, culled from magazines, journals, and blogs, nearly 1,400 pages of thoughtful, in-depth writing about our field. With the drying up of so many oases of intelligence, I wonder if it would be possible to scrape together enough content for a sixth volume.

"Pretty pictures can no longer lead the way in which our visual environment should be shaped. It is time to debate, to probe the values, to examine the theories that are part of our heritage and to verify their validity to express our times." That was Massimo Vignelli, writing in 1983, in a call for criticism that is yet unfulfilled. What do we settle for, thirty years later? A seemingly endless series of drive-by shootings punctuated by the occasional lynch mob, conducted by anonymous people with the depth of barroom philosophers and the attention span of fruit flies.

Massimo Vignelli, "Call for Criticism," in *Looking Closer 3: Classic Writings on Graphic Design*, Michael Bierut, Jessica Helfand, Steven Heller, and Rick Poynor, editors (New York: Allworth Press, 1999).

All this is happening at a time when more people than ever are engaged with design, and where designers, when given a chance, can be articulate, inspiring advocates for the power of design. We need these voices more than ever. Maybe it's time to stop shouting from the sidelines and actually get back on the field.

Spoiler Alert! or Happy Father's Day

First appeared in Design Observer, June 21, 2009.

The Taking of Pelham One Two Three, written by Peter Stone, directed by Joseph Sargent, 1974.

Warning: the following article contains spoilers for the plots of Citizen Kane *(1941)*, Double Indemnity *(1944)*, Stalag 17 *(1953)*, Some Like It Hot *(1959)*, The Longest Day *(1962)*, and The Taking of Pelham One Two Three *(1974)*.

I enjoyed the remake of *The Taking of Pelham One Two Three*, but like many others, I like the 1974 original better: the gritty vérité of 1970s New York, the terse understatement of Robert Shaw's Mr. Blue, and, best of all, the deadpan, sly performance of Walter Matthau.

This was one of my father's favorite movies. He especially liked the clever way that the scriptwriters dispensed with the complicated expository material that explained the workings of the NYC Metropolitan Transit Authority's command center. As the movie begins, Matthau's character is giving a tour to a delegation of Japanese businessmen, and this tour provides an excuse for the expository business that sets the stage for the action that follows. The delegation reacts to everything with smiling, cordial, seeming obliviousness, and Matthau abides this inconvenience with mounting comic exasperation, at one point calling them monkeys to their face. So it's a particularly funny moment a bit later, when the leader of the group bows politely and, in perfect English, thanks Matthau for such a fascinating tour.

I know my dad got a real kick out of this, because the first time we watched *Pelham One Two Three* together, at the first appearance of the Japanese tour he leaned in toward me and said, with barely disguised glee, "Walter Matthau doesn't realize they understand everything he's saying!"

Dad couldn't help it. He was a natural-born spoiler. Even if you were the only person in the room with him, my dad always took care to deliver his spoilers in a near-whisper. He loved movies, and nothing made him happier than when one of his favorites made an appearance as a rerun on late-night TV. "Come in here, you've got to see this," he'd beckon, and you'd settle down next to him on the couch to watch, say, *Stalag 17*. He'd watch Billy Wilder's prisoner-of-war drama in rapt silence until he couldn't stand it anymore. Then he'd turn to you, point at the screen, and murmur solemnly, "Watch that light cord."

Stalag 17, written by Billy Wilder and Edwin Blum, directed by Billy Wilder, 1953.

"But why, Dad? What light cord? Why is it important?"

My dad would just narrow his eyes mysteriously and say, "Just watch." Now, if you haven't seen *Stalag 17* yet, I won't try to explain why the light cord is important, because it would sort of, you know, ruin the movie for you. But when it was finally revealed, Dad would simply turn toward me and nod sagely: See?

He wasn't always that explicit. Watching another Billy Wilder movie, *Double Indemnity*, at the first appearance of Barbara Stanwyck, he would simply mutter with grim resignation, "This is not going to end well." Sometimes he would just wait for a favorite line. "Here it comes," he would say during Keenan Wynn's change-for-a-pay-phone confrontation with Peter Sellers in *Dr. Strangelove* ("If you don't get the President of the United States on that line, you know what's going to happen to you? You're going to have to answer to the Coca-Cola Company.") "Is that just great?" he'd say afterward. It was especially satisfying (or maybe excruciating) when the line came at the very end, like in *Some Like It Hot*. He would repeat "Nobody's perfect!" for the rest of the day. Occasionally, I would manage to see a movie without the benefit of his advance counsel. After I told him I had finally seen *Citizen Kane* in a college film class, he could only nod enthusiastically, clap me on the back, and exclaim, "Hey, Rosebud is the sled, right?"

Double Indemnity, written by Billy Wilder and Raymond Chandler, directed by Billy Wilder, 1944.

Dr. Strangelove or: How I Learned to Stop Worrying and Love the Bomb, written by Stanley Kubrick, Terry Southern, and Peter George, directed by Stanley Kubrick, 1964.

Some Like It Hot, written by Billy Wilder and I. A. L. Diamond, directed by Billy Wilder, 1959.

Leonard Bierut was a partner in a company that sold printing equipment. He was in charge of sales, and I realize now how well suited he was to that job. A good salesman gives his prospect the sense of being an insider, of knowing information that others aren't privy to, of getting a deal that no one else knows about. That came easily to him; introducing a potential customer to a Heidelberg was not that different than introducing me to *The Longest Day* ("Pay attention to that little clicker. It's going to be important later.") He was absolutely honest, genuinely liked people, and loved talking about the stuff he had to sell. From the time I was a child, I remember how he could take a complicated pile of cast iron and grease and turn it into a story. "The man who invented this thing died insane," he told me once on his shop floor, pointing to a Linotype machine. This sounded disturbing to me. "But why, Dad?" "Well," he would say, "just look at it!" To this day I secretly want to own a Linotype machine.

The Longest Day, written by Cornelius Ryan, directed by Ken Annakin, Andrew Marton, and Bernhard Wicki, 1962.

Despite the popularity of this legend, it doesn't seem to be true. By all accounts Ottmar Mergenthaler died of tuberculosis.

Dad was somewhat alarmed when I announced my intention to become a graphic designer; almost all of the commercial artists he had ever seen were pasting up bowling alley score sheets in the back of print shops. But he made some inquiries, and before long he was slipping me spare copies of *Print* and *Communication Arts* that he had managed to cadge from his ad agency accounts. He knew just enough about what I did to be an enthusiastic cheerleader but not so much that he could tell whether my work was any good. Take my word for it: if you ever get a chance to benefit from this combination of informed but unequivocal approval, I highly recommend it.

For a guy who loved to know how the story ends, my dad's story ended way too soon. Leonard Bierut died at the age of fifty-nine. It was my thirtieth birthday. I miss him every day. Happy Father's Day, Dad.

Now You See It

**My
Handicap**

All of us start with youthful dreams. But sooner or later you realize that you've turned into something different than what you imagined.

First appeared in
Design Observer,
July 20, 2008.

I always wanted to be a designer. I learned early on that being a designer involved, among other things, affecting a manner of dress, speech, and general attitude that would signal to other designers that you shared their access to the creative muses. At the same time, these same cues would enable nondesigners to dimly apprehend that there was something special about you that commanded a certain level of respect and even awe.

To be honest, I was never much good at this even when I was in my twenties, and now that I'm about to cross over into my second half-century on earth, I may as well admit defeat. I'm not special. I look, talk, and act exactly like a million other middle-aged, upper-middle-class, balding, white, suburban businessmen.

But there is one difference. I don't golf.

I've come to know a little bit about demographics, customer profiling, and market segmentation, and I can tell I'm supposed to care deeply about golf. As befitting my station in life, I spend a lot of time in airports, and there I'm besieged with pictures of golfers. Occasionally these images actually promote a particular golf course or golf-related product, but more commonly golf is used as a metaphor, usually for business success. The key card I was entrusted with by the Crowne Plaza Hotel on a recent layover at LAX is a good example. The photograph on it shows two men standing side by side on, I think, a putting green. One, wearing an odd apron-type thing that I'm guessing identifies him as a caddy, examines something in his hand. The other, gripping a club, stands alertly at his side. Beneath this, some type: PHILOSOPHY work together. After a great deal of study, I noted that the first four letters of "philosophy" are bolder than the others. Could this mean something? A visit to Google ("phil+crowne+plaza") and, aha: it turns out that the guy with the club must be someone named Phil Mickelson, pro golfer and Crowne Plaza spokesman. A profoundly rich tapestry of layered codes, all intended to predispose me to the comforts of the Crowne Plaza, all completely lost on me.

Lest you get concerned, although I've never heard of Mr. Mickelson, even I know the most famous golfer in the world, Tiger Woods. If you spend any time in airports or paging through business magazines, you quickly realize that Woods is assumed to be a surefire aspirational figure for guys like me. He's everywhere. His endorsement contracts are legion, including sports-related brands like Nike, Gatorade, and Titleist, and general consumer companies like General Motors, American Express, TAG Heuer, and Gillette.

Accenture and other sponsors ended their relationships with Tiger Woods after he was involved with sex scandals in 2009.

For me, the most inescapable expression of Woods's authority is the one deployed since 2003 by management consultant Accenture in their "Be a Tiger" campaign, which links photographs of the golfer in action with abstractions like Distractions, Focus, and Hindsight. "As perhaps the world's ultimate symbol of high performance, he serves as a metaphor for our commitment to helping companies become high-performance businesses," Accenture says on its website. "Informed by findings from our comprehensive study of over 500 high performers, as well as our unparalleled experience, the advertising draws upon our understanding of the world's elite companies, and our ability to channel that knowledge on behalf of our clients." The tantalizing element here is that reference to those "500 high performers," carefully selected by Accenture for their passionate commitment to both business success and Tiger Woods, an opinion-shaping elite that obviously excludes — by a long shot — me.

Now You See It

It's no secret that golf and business success are inextricably linked. The *Wall Street Journal*, itself a stronghold of golf columns, golf metaphors, and golf advertising, ran a widely reprinted story last year titled "Business Golf Changes Course." "Business golf is a collusion that has developed over the years between business people and their clients," according to the *WSJ*. The old model, "foursomes of cigar-chomping white males closing deals at exclusive country clubs," has given way to today's business golfers, who claim that "the sport's primary value is to get away from an office environment to network and build relationships, in the hopes of doing deals down the road."

John Paul Newport and Russell Adams, "Business Golf Changes Course," *Wall Street Journal*, May 26, 2007.

Apparently, there is a small industry of consultants who stand at the ready to provide remedial assistance to people like me. These include a former KPMG marketing exec, Hilary Bruggen Fordwich, who "gives seminars at companies and one-on-one lessons to lobbyists and other executives on organizing golf retreats, avoiding business golf blunders and deciding when best to broach the business topic." Broaching the business topic — yikes! Indeed, every time I lose a potential project to one of the big identity consultancies, I always end up muttering the same thing: their goddamned new business team must have taken them golfing. Yes, while I'm sitting on my butt worrying about letterspacing, other people are out on the links, broaching things.

The sad thing about all this is that golf is, or should be, in my blood. My late father was a passionate golfer, playing once or twice a week at public courses in northeastern Ohio like Seneca and Briarwood. And he was good. Shooting a hole in one gets your name in the back of *Golf Digest*, and he did it not once, but twice. My brother Don is a serious golfer today.

But I'm not. A good part of my job is helping clients imagine how they could reach specific audiences most effectively. This means, too often, reducing people to stereotypes. As my father's son, being a nongolfer may be a last vestige of adolescent rebellion. Or it may be a denial that I've turned into a stereotype that I never chose. Or it may even be a way of resisting aging and, ultimately, death. No matter what, it is my handicap.

Positively Michael Patrick Cronan

First appeared in Design Observer, January 7, 2013.

I met Michael Cronan on my first visit to San Francisco in 1983. It was a trip that changed my life.

I had been working at my first job in New York for three years at that point. In those days, the East Coast graphic design scene was dominated by legendary names: Milton Glaser, Ivan Chermayeff and Tom Geismar, Paul Rand, Rudy de Harak, George Tscherny, and the one I was lucky to have been hired by, Massimo Vignelli. These well-known designers were all in their fifties, or sixties, or seventies. They had made their names as young Turks twenty, thirty, or (in the case of Rand) forty years before, and were showing no signs of stopping. They dominated New York like skyscrapers. And like skyscrapers, they cast long, deep shadows.

It was in 1983 that we got a client in San Francisco and I made my first business trip there. Using Massimo's name as a door opener, I decided to look up some local designers. And the hottest designers in town were the ones who were nicknamed "The Michaels": Manwaring, Vanderbyl, Mabry, and Cronan. Amazingly, everyone took my calls, which wouldn't have happened in New York. Even more amazingly, I was invited to join Michael Vanderbyl, Michael Manwaring, and Michael Cronan for lunch.

It was nearly thirty years ago, but I can still remember that lunch. It was a beautiful, sunny day. These guys were clearly good friends. They were so energetic, so supportive of each other, so enthusiastic about design and its possibilities. And more than anything else, they were so young. I remember thinking how much fun it must be to work in a town where the legends were not towering skyscrapers but just great guys a few years older than you were.

In the middle of it all was Michael Patrick Cronan. He was one of those rare people who was not just funny and smart but who could make you feel funny and smart yourself just by being in his presence. Even at that first meeting, he was full of ideas, full of questions, full of advice — even for a kid like me, someone he had just met and, for all he knew, would never see again.

As it turned out, we would see each other again — many times — over the next three decades. At each encounter I was enveloped in an all-consuming hug from this great bear of a man. I got to know his wife, Karin, and encountered his sons, Nick and Shawn, just often enough to be stunned by how fast they grew. Michael, on the other hand, didn't seem to age at all. His seemingly limitless supply of energy led him from venture to venture, most notably the clothing line he created with Karin, Walking Man. Like the designer, the garments were big, warm, and comforting; looking back, I suspect they may have been created just so anyone could have a Michael Cronan hug ready to go at a moment's notice, no further away than the nearest clothes closet.

To many people, he became most famous as a naming consultant, coming up with monikers for, among many other products, TiVo and Kindle. This surprised some people, but not me. Having led people through several painful "nomenclature exercises," I've learned the hard way that — even more than design — this particular field requires taking people on a journey that in the end requires nothing less than a blind leap of faith. And it's hard to imagine anyone better at instilling faith — faith in oneself, faith in one's judgment, faith that everything was simply going to turn out okay — than Michael Cronan. A positive attitude was the only kind of attitude he had.

It was that sense of faith that I took away from that sunny lunch thirty years ago with Michael and his two friends. Living in New York in the shadows of giants, I had grown unsure about my own ability to design and about my own prospects for success. The example of the Michaels — three guys who were just a little older than me, who were having a great time and had no doubt that the best was yet to come — changed the way I thought about the future. I returned to New York filled with energy, and optimism, and the blind, thrilling faith that everything was going to turn out okay.

Michael Patrick Cronan embodied that spirit, and it will live on in everyone he touched in his too-short life. He died in 2013 at sixty-one, following a five-year struggle with cancer, on that holiday that for so many of us symbolizes the moment for new beginnings, New Year's Day.

The Poster that Launched a Movement (or Not)

Occupy Wall Street began with a poster. *Adbusters* cofounder Kalle Lasn described the moment in an oral history of the movement published in 2012 in *Vanity Fair*.

> *We put together a poster for the July issue of* Adbusters. *The poster was a ballerina — an absolutely still ballerina — poised in a Zen-ish kind of way on top of this dynamic bull. And below it had the [Twitter] hashtag #OccupyWallStreet. Above, it said, "What is our one demand?" I felt like this ballerina stood for this deep demand that would change the world. There was some magic about it.*

The *Vanity Fair* article was illustrated with a half-page-spread photo of protesters retaking lower Manhattan's Zuccotti Park after being temporarily evicted on November 15. There were also portraits of many of the protagonists in the OWS movement. What wasn't shown was the poster that started everything. Six months into the movement, I had never seen it. Chances are, neither have you. Because the poster — so elliptical, poetic, and provocative, in that characteristic *Adbusters* way — didn't matter at all. The ballerina didn't matter. The bull didn't matter. The headline didn't matter. Only one thing mattered: that hashtag at the bottom.

First appeared in Design Observer, April 30, 2012.

The oral history of Occupy Wall Street appeared in Jaime Lalinde, Rebecca Sacks, Mark Guiducci, Elizabeth Nicholas, and Max Chafkin, "Revolution Number 99," *Vanity Fair*, January 10, 2012.

So, here is the question. In the age of social media, does political graphic design matter?

It all seemed settled in 2008. Then, the answer was an emphatic yes. Shepard Fairey created a poster, later adopted by the Obama campaign, that will certainly rank as one of the most ubiquitous and effective pieces of political graphic design of the decade, if not the century. The Obama campaign itself seized the methods of contemporary consumer brand management and deployed logos, colors, and typography with a sophisticated precision that was revolutionary in the usually flat-footed world of campaign graphics. And the accessibility of communications tools made it possible for millions of people to download the campaign's graphic assets and contribute their own designs.

Poster for Occupy Wall Street, 2011. Kalle Lasn (concept and copywriter), Pedro Inoue (creative director), Will Brown (art director), and Abdul Rehman Khawar (illustrator).

Four years later, everything seems different. Make no mistake, OWS has not lacked for graphic support, both professional and grassroots, including a response from the reliable Shepard Fairey. And over on the mainstream side of the political spectrum, the 2012 presidential contests predictably have generated a deluge of red-white-and-blue campaign graphics that in turn have been predictably subjected to analysis. But am I wrong that this year conventional graphic design seems like an inefficient way to make a point, never mind to create or fuel a grassroots political movement?

Consider, on the other hand, the genius of that simple #OccupyWallStreet hashtag. Three little words, with a call to action built right in. And also right there was the potential for an articulated brand architecture that any corporate identity expert could envy. "Occupy" sits in the master brand position. Fill in the blanks for a potentially infinite number of user-generated subbrands, from Occupy Amarillo to Occupy Zurich. Elsewhere in the OWS communications arsenal, we find other slogans ("We Are the 99%") and some visual tropes (the Guy Fawkes mask popularized by Anonymous, soon an emerging public face for the protest). But no typeface guidelines, no color standards, no official logos.

Of course, the goals of OWS have been elusive from the start, and clarity of message has almost always taken a backseat to the chaos of participatory democracy in action. I suspect that many of its supporters would insist that the last thing OWS needs is something as simple and reductive as a logo. Instead, many of the most effective contributions made by designers have taken the form of old-fashioned information graphics like those from Jake Levitas and Occupy Design, which range from visualizations of income disparity to icons identifying recycling stations at protest sites.

Perhaps, however, the inability of OWS to develop a coherent graphic language is symptomatic of a larger challenge. Can a grassroots movement mature into a viable political force? An answer may come this week. Occupy Wall Street has called for a "general strike of the 99%" on May 1, the traditional workers' solidarity day. What will the turnout be? Will spring weather bring, as some have predicted, a rededication to the cause? Or is the movement too diffuse to gain the traction it needs to move to the next stage?

One thing is certain. The graphic designer who has played the most dramatic role in the rise of Occupy Wall Street isn't Shepard Fairey or Jake Levitas. On September 24, 2011, a group of peaceful protesters in Manhattan was pepper sprayed by police officers. The incident was captured on video and posted to YouTube, where it has been viewed over 1.5 million times. "When the pepper-spray video came out, that was the hook," said an activist in the *Vanity Fair* oral history. "That's what made people focus on Occupy Wall Street." The central figure in the video is a woman named Chelsea Elliott, who was subsequently identified as...a freelance graphic designer.

Sometimes, the key to political change isn't designing a logo or poster. It's simply having the courage to show up and make your voice heard, no matter what the cause — and no matter what the risk.

The
Typeface
of Truth

First appeared in
Design Observer,
August 9, 2012.

The ingredients used by graphic designers — colors, shapes, typefaces — are fundamentally mysterious. What do they mean? How do they work? Why does one work better than another? What criteria should we use to choose?

This ambiguity can be maddening, especially to clients, who in desperation will invoke anecdotes and folk wisdom to help control an otherwise rudderless process. I've been told in meetings that triangles — to take one example — are the "most energetic" (or the "most aggressive"?) shape. I've been asked if it's true that white means death in Japan. Or is it black? Or red? Or China?

William Goldman,
*Adventures in the
Screen Trade: A Personal
View of Hollywood
and Screenwriting*
(New York: Warner, 1983).

To tell you the truth, I've always appreciated this ambiguity. Like other experienced designers, I appear to navigate this miasma of hearsay with confidence. For the truth is that in our field, to quote screenwriter William Goldman, "Nobody knows anything." Black can be ominous or elegant. Triangles can be trendy or timeless. And typefaces? Hmm! Typefaces can be…anything you want them to be, right? There are many reasons to pick any one typeface, all of them more or less arbitrary.

Now You See It

So imagine a client demands that text be set in "the most credible typeface." I would probably hide a smile and say there's no such thing.

But there is such a thing, says Errol Morris.

Several weeks ago, Morris, the Academy Award–winning documentary filmmaker and author, posted a simple quiz in his *New York Times* Opinionator blog. Ostensibly, the object of the quiz was to determine if the reader was an optimist or a pessimist. You read a short introduction about the likelihood of an asteroid hitting the earth, and then an indented passage from a book by David Deutsch, *The Beginning of Infinity*, in which he claims "we live in an era of unprecedented safety" and will likely be able to defend ourselves against such an impact. Morris then asked the reader to agree or disagree with the truth of that claim and to indicate the degree of confidence the reader had in his or her conclusion. The result, supposedly, was to determine how many of us are optimists (finding Deutsch's statement to be true) versus how many are pessimists (finding the statement to be false).

But it was all a trick. Morris was actually testing something completely different: the effect of fonts on truth. "Or to be precise," as he pointed out in his follow-up posts, "the effect on credulity. Are there certain fonts that compel a belief that the sentences they are written in are true?"

To find out, he had a colleague, Benjamin Berman, create a program that changed the font of the indented David Deutsch passage each time the article was first opened. Each person taking the quiz would read the passage in one of six randomly assigned fonts: Baskerville, Computer Modern, Georgia, Helvetica, Comic Sans, or Trebuchet. So the test had nothing to do, really, with optimism or pessimism. Instead, it was meant to find out if setting the passage in one typeface or another would lead people to believe it more.

Now, if you're like me, you already know what the least trustworthy typeface is, right? It's got to be Comic Sans: goofy, unloved, mocked Comic Sans. And it turns out we're right. According to Morris, people seem to be consciously aware of Comic Sans: it was in the news as recently as a few weeks ago, when it caused a minor dustup in the midst of the announcement of the discovery of the Higgs boson particle. This awareness seems to engender, in Morris's words, "contempt and summary dismissal." And good riddance, say I and countless other graphic designers.

Errol Morris, "Are You an Optimist or a Pessimist?" *New York Times*, July 9, 2012.

David Deutsch, *The Beginning of Infinity: Explanations That Transform the World* (New York: Viking, 2011).

Errol Morris, "Hear All Ye People; Hearken O Earth (Parts 1 and 2)," *New York Times*, August 8 and 9, 2012.

The Book of Common
Prayer, John Baskerville,
1762.

But what about the other side of the equation? Is there a font that inclines us to believe that a sentence that's set in it is true? After analyzing the research, Morris says the answer is yes. And that typeface is Baskerville.

To Morris's surprise, the results of the test showed a clear difference between the performance of Baskerville and other fonts — not just Baskerville and Comic Sans (no contest); or Baskerville and Trebuchet or Helvetica (a clear serif versus sans distinction); but even Baskerville and Georgia (a lovely, and arguably even more legible, serif by Matthew Carter). Compared to versions in the other typefaces, the passage set in Baskerville had both the highest rate of agreement and the lowest rate of disagreement. This led Morris to the inevitable conclusion: Baskerville is the typeface of truth.

John Baskerville loved typography, and it's believed that he lost his fortune in pursuit of it, sinking all the money he had into designing and printing complete editions of the works of Virgil and Milton, not to mention the Bible. He was an avowed antireligionist but had a deep and abiding faith in typography. "Having been an early admirer of the beauty of Letters," he wrote in his introduction to *Paradise Lost*, "I became insensibly desirous of contributing to the perfection of them." The typeface we today call Baskerville is based on the fonts he developed in the mid-eighteenth century at his foundry for his private presses. Ironically, a skeptic has created the typeface most likely to induce credulity.

John Baskerville,
preface to John Milton,
Paradise Lost, 1758.

"We have entered a new, unexpected landscape," Errol Morris writes at the conclusion of his article. "Truth is not font dependent, but a font can subtly influence us to believe that a sentence is true. Could it swing an election? Induce us to buy a new dinette set? Change some of our most deeply held and cherished beliefs?"

Whether or not a typeface can do any or all of those things, I do agree the landscape has changed. Once upon a time, regular people didn't even know the names of typefaces. Then, with the invention of the personal computer, people started learning. They had their opinions and they had their favorites. But until now, type was still a matter of taste. Going forward, if someone wants to tell the truth, he or she will know exactly what typeface to use. Of course, the truth is the truth no matter what typeface it's in. How long before people realize that Baskerville is even more useful if you want to lie?

49

Seven
Things
Designers
Can Learn
from
Stand-Up
Comics

The premise of HBO's hour-long special *Talking Funny* is
simple: invite four top-ranked comedians — Ricky Gervais,
Jerry Seinfeld, Chris Rock, and Louis C. K. — turn on
the cameras, and let them talk shop for an hour. There
are laughs, of course, but the most interesting parts focus
on the technical craft of getting those laughs. This is
serious business. Stand-up comedy is a high-risk creative
enterprise, executed in real time in front of a critical
audience. I didn't tune in looking for lessons for designers,
but I found seven.

And please note, they have nothing to do with
being funny.

1. It's all about the basics.
"I love jokes so much," says Jerry Seinfeld toward the
beginning of the show. "I love them so much." He loves
them because they're the indestructible building blocks of
comedy. The others agree. "So many of these young guys
think it's all attitude," says Chris Rock. "But you have to
have jokes under your weird persona, under your crazy
glasses, under your crazy voice." Design has basic building
blocks too: scale, proportion, hierarchy, contrast. Get those

First appeared in
Design Observer,
July 17, 2011.

Talking Funny, directed
by John Moffitt, 2011.

right first. Or, as Seinfeld concludes: "You can put in all kinds of furniture, but you have to have steel in the walls."

2. Once you've mastered the basics, make your work your own.

"Do you think you have to have a thing?" asks Ricky Gervais. "Well, you've gotta figure something out," responds Seinfeld. Between all the "things" and "somethings," we know exactly what they're talking about. Every successful comedian is different. The best have an immediately identifiable attitude, whether it's Henny Youngman, Demetri Martin, or the four participants in *Talking Funny*. The best designers are no different. Think of how many ways there are to design something like, say, a Vladimir Nabokov book cover. A good designer is a problem solver. A great designer can figure out a way to solve a problem that's completely unique. At one point, Seinfeld tells a Louis C. K. joke his way and asks, "Is that how it goes?" Louis C. K. replies, "Well, that's a completely Seinfelded version. You made it...nice." It's one of my favorite parts of the show.

3. Respect your audience.

Chris Rock says: "A lot of comedians have great jokes, and they're like, 'Why is this not working?' It's not working because the audience doesn't understand the premise. If I set this premise up right, this joke will always work." The comics talk about ensuring the audience — so demanding, so easily distracted — is with them for every joke during the act. This doesn't mean talking down or pandering. Rather, it's good old-fashioned respect. I sometimes tell students that every design needs a welcome mat and a doorknob. The first helps a person realize, "Hey, this is for me." The second gives them a way into the design. Good design, like good comedy, is about surprise. But surprise can't happen in a vacuum. It needs a context that establishes familiarity. If you respect your audience, you provide that context.

4. Know your tools.

The tools of a stand-up comic are words. Some are good for every job. Some are more powerful and should be used sparingly. All of them are potentially crutches. Louis C. K. says that Jerry Seinfeld once told him, "The F-word is like a Corvette." "And I thought," says Louis C. K., "that means that it's fast and it's cool and it's got power and thrust to it. But then I thought: wait a minute, this guy grew up on Long

Island and collected Porsches. So to him, a Corvette is a piece of shit, with a Chevy engine, just a flashy bullshit car." Your own favorite tool may be a typeface or a Photoshop effect or a certain color combination. Seinfeld says he stopped using the F-word when he realized it had become a crutch. Of course, one man's crutch is another man's secret weapon. Or, as Louis C. K. observes, "Where I grew up, a Corvette is an awesome car."

5. Honor your craft.
One striking running theme of *Talking Funny* is that each of the comics works extremely hard, creating challenges where they might just as easily coast. Chris Rock reinvents his entire show every year. Louis C. K. regularly takes his closing bit — the strongest part of his show — moves it to the beginning, and forces himself to create a new show designed to top the old climax. Ricky Gervais says, "Oh, it's not just being funny. It's being proud of your stuff and doing things that other people couldn't do." Louis C. K. adds that, for him, "Easy laughs, cheap laughs, they don't exist." Chris Rock: "How many unfunny comedians have ever sustained a career not being funny?" Mastery of craft is tied to perpetual self-improvement. And, just as in design, mere technique is never enough. Louis C. K. is nervous when he feels he's relying on technical skill: "This bit is working because I know how to do stand-up, not because it's something that's important to me." Hone your skills, but make certain they serve ends that are important to you.

6. Don't be afraid of failure.
Good comedians experiment constantly. Every time they test a new joke, they risk bombing. That's why they'll try out new material in smaller venues, polishing pieces in front of live audiences: they need to hear what's working and what's not working. Seinfeld admits that when he was starting out, "I was hitting five hundred. I would have a good show and a bad show, a good show and a bad show." His very first show was bad. "But success wasn't my objective." He was desperate to simply be on stage and was willing to risk failure every other night to get there. Designers take risks for the same reasons. Trying something new means not being sure of the outcome. But it's the only way that anyone working in a creative field can hope to make progress. Ambition is a strong enough antidote to fear. Louis C. K.

remembers how he idolized good comics: "I wanted to be one of them, and I didn't care if I sucked at it."

7. Finally, never forget you have a special gift.

Ricky Gervais, in a revealing moment, asks, "Don't you ever think, when we make people have this feeling of laughter and they pay us money: What if they discover they can do it themselves?" The other comics are rather stunned at this. Seinfeld shouts, "But they *can* do it themselves!" Gervais almost glumly asks, "Then why are they paying us?" Louis C. K. answers, "We're a high octane version of it. We're pros. They can play touch football, too." And Seinfeld adds: "But that doesn't hurt the NFL." We live at a time when the tools of design are more available than ever before. What client doesn't have a nephew who knows InDesign, or, better still, a spouse with a newly discovered enthusiasm for PowerPoint? Graphic design: Anyone can do it, right? Well, yes. But the professionals still understand what it means to do something well. And that confidence makes its own statement.

Near the end of the show, Chris Rock talks about what a pleasure it is to watch anyone do anything really well, even a great truck driver. "I just saw this guy park an eighteen-wheeler into this narrow space," he says. "And I said, I guarantee you, there's heart surgery that's not as hard as what this guy just did." Louis agreed. "I watched a guy pull into a loading dock, and I stopped and said, 'That was amazing.' And he was like, 'Yeah, I know, I know.'" If you're a designer, it's easy to forget that what you do is, in so many ways, amazing. Appreciate that gift in yourself. Appreciate the gifts of others. And look for lessons wherever you can find them.

This is not a simple story, but it has a simple lesson. It was destined to be a partnership as consequential in its way as some of the most storied in the design profession: think of Charles and Ray Eames, say, or Massimo and Lella Vignelli. But this one took a while to happen.

William Drenttel was born in 1953 in Minnesota. His family moved a year later to Southern California and he grew up about ten miles from Disneyland. To this day, his demeanor seems to combine the rectitude of someone from the upper Midwest with the laid-back attitude of a Los Angeleno. He went to college at Princeton University, spending a year studying in Paris, and graduated in 1977.

Jessica Helfand was born in 1960 and moved from suburban Philadelphia with her family when she was ten to live in Paris for five years. It so happens that Bill Drenttel spent his year abroad at the same time not that far away, but they never met. Jessica returned home and attended Yale University, studying graphic design and architectural theory. Unable to find a job upon graduation, she took a job writing soap operas for Procter & Gamble, finally becoming a junior scriptwriter on CBS's *Guiding Light*. She still credits this experience for providing her with an interest in narrative in design.

Written on the occasion of the presentation of the AIGA Medal to William Drenttel and Jessica Helfand. Originally appeared on aiga.org on April 19, 2013.

Bill, meanwhile, got a job as an assistant account executive at Compton Advertising, through a connection he met while working the counter at a Madison Avenue diner over the summer. His main client was Procter & Gamble. In the early 1980s Bill and Jessica worked in the same building, three floors apart — but still they never met. Bill was sent to Italy to launch P&G's new product, Pampers. He lived there for three years. At one point, he helped negotiate an agreement with media magnate Silvio Berlusconi to broadcast old P&G soap operas dubbed in Italian. As a result of this deal — struck with the future prime minister by her future husband — Jessica would be receiving residual checks for scripts ten years later.

Saatchi & Saatchi merged with Compton, and Bill was brought back to New York as a senior vice president. He became a consummate pitchman, crisscrossing the world and winning accounts with an ease that, eventually, would begin to disgust him. ("I actually came to hate advertising," he wrote much later.) He sold telecommunications and kitchen cleanser. In the midst of this, Bill was becoming increasingly fascinated by design. Charged with improving the stores of a national fast-food chain, he brought in the hottest designers in town, a small but soon-to-be-legendary studio called M&Co, led by Tibor Kalman and the firm's senior designer, Stephen Doyle. Bill and Stephen became friends, and one day the idea of going into business together came up. "It was an off-the-wall idea we both jumped on," Bill later told the *New York Times*. They quit their respective jobs, and Drenttel Doyle Partners was incorporated two weeks later. It was 1985.

William Drenttel, "I was a Mad Man," Design Observer, July 11, 2008.

Somewhere along the way, Jessica Helfand realized that she wasn't destined to be a soap opera writer; she had studied design and architectural theory, after all. Through a family connection, she got a ten-dollar-an-hour job at a small studio in midtown Manhattan called Designers III. She was the only employee, and only one of the three designers who gave the firm its name was still active. Her boss was demanding, scrutinizing her projects and sending her away each time with the command, "Move it up a hair." Eventually, after receiving this input, she would simply leave the room and wait, as she later wrote, "for what I believed to be the requisite amount of time anyone would require to actually make the 'move it up a hair' adjustment." Then she would return and the work would inevitably be approved. After eighteen months of this, she was accepted into the MFA graphic design program at Yale and left for New Haven to study with Paul Rand, Bradbury Thompson, and Armin Hofmann.

Back in New York, if Drenttel Doyle Partners wasn't an overnight success, it was the closest thing possible. Within a year, the firm created the design for *Spy*, a satirical monthly magazine with a tiny budget and an approach to typography (a "collage-like use of tiny type, sidebars, background tints and snippets of information whispering like groundlings in the margins") that was widely copied and continues to be enormously influential over twenty-five years later. Freed from restraint, Bill and Stephen were eager to define a new kind of studio, practicing a hybrid of design, advertising, marketing, and publishing that eluded quick definition. They redesigned the *New Republic*, repositioned the Cooper-Hewitt Museum as the National Design Museum, and launched the biggest real estate development in town, the World Financial Center, with a series of print ads that featured text from prominent writers and poets like David Rieff, Mark O'Donnell, and Dana Gioia.

Patricia Leigh Brown, "Style Makers," *New York Times*, May 14, 1989.

Jessica completed graduate school in 1989 and became interested in magazine design: here was a place to reconcile her interest in storytelling with the graphic design skills she had learned with Rand, Thompson, and Hofmann. She returned to Philadelphia to become design director for the *Philadelphia Inquirer Sunday Magazine*. This was a moment when the digital revolution was arriving, and one of its first beachheads was the world of publishing. Many of her colleagues viewed this strange new world with alarm. Jessica was fascinated by it. If you could create narratives for the television screen, why not the computer screen? "What we see on screen is obviously an issue of considerable importance to communication designers," she would later write. "Are we makers or managers? Controllers or curators? Editors or aesthetes? To what degree do the classic principals of design apply in an environment characterized by randomness and reciprocity, distribution across networks and democracy among netizens?" Well before the end of the twentieth century, Jessica placed herself squarely in the middle of a debate that still continues. She became a technology columnist for *Eye* magazine, and her writing there would become the heart of her first book, *Screen: Essays on Graphic Design, New Media, and Visual Culture*.

Jessica Helfand, *Screen: Essays on Graphic Design, New Media, and Visual Culture* (New York: Princeton Architectural Press, 2001).

Her interest in the changing profession took her to the 1993 AIGA Biennial Conference in Miami. It was unusually bleak and rainy, but there was at least one ray of light. They had met before in New York, but it was in Miami that Jessica Helfand got to know Bill Drenttel, recently divorced and celebrating his fortieth birthday. Jessica was guest editing an issue of the *AIGA Journal* and, upon returning to Philadelphia after the conference, called to ask if he was free for lunch to talk about story ideas. "No," he replied ("pretty quickly," according to Jessica). "But I'm free for dinner." They became friends, and then more, and in 1997 they decided to become business partners.

It was clear from the start this would be different. Bill and Jessica had experienced the scale of the international ad agency, the hot New York design firm, the bustling urban newspaper. In their new venture, they deliberately took the opposite direction. Their partnership would just be the two of them and a few helpers. Within a year, they moved to the remote town of Falls Village, Connecticut, where they had discovered a place they could live and work, the modernist 1932 painting studio of Radio City Music Hall muralist Ezra Winter. It was the studio that gave their business its name: Winterhouse.

Winterhouse, deliberately, followed no recognizable model. Yet the firm's output was prodigious. Winterhouse Studio was a design firm, and in that capacity Bill and Jessica designed magazines like *Poetry* and the *New England Journal of Medicine*; identities for the filmmaker Errol Morris and the Yale School of Management; and websites for the *New Yorker*, Nextbook, the *Paris Review*, and the New York University School of Journalism. But studio work for clients — even at this high level — comprises only a fraction of the work that Winterhouse does.

Jessica Helfand, *Reinventing the Wheel* (New York: Princeton Architectural Press, 2006).

Jessica Helfand, *Scrapbooks: An American History* (New Haven: Yale University Press, 2008).

The Bush Administration, *The National Security Strategy of the United States of America* (Falls Village, CT: Winterhouse Editions, 2003).

Under the imprint Winterhouse Editions, the firm copublished limited and trade editions of works by Thomas Bernhard, Paul Auster, and Franz Kafka. In addition to *Screen*, Jessica has written and designed two additional landmark books: *Reinventing the Wheel* and *Scrapbooks: An American History*. Each volume is, as expected, elegantly designed and impeccably produced. Not so expected? Learning that the National Security Act of 1947 required the Bush administration to prepare a comprehensive strategy statement for Congress each year, and believing that it deserved greater attention, Drenttel published and distributed that year's entire document at the height of the Gulf War in 2003. It too was elegantly designed and impeccably produced.

Now You See It

This impulse — not to wait for client work, but to respond with design when confronted with real-world needs — led Bill and Jessica to found Winterhouse Institute in 2006. The institute's initiatives are wide in scope and lasting in impact. They include the AIGA Winterhouse Awards for Design Criticism, a yearly ten-thousand-dollar prize for design writing; the Polling Place Photo Project, a initiative to document citizen experiences at polling places during the 2006 and 2008 elections; the development of comprehensive case studies in social design with the Yale School of Management; and the creation of conferences on the power of design for social change on behalf of the Rockefeller Foundation, the International Design Conference in Aspen, and the Mayo Clinic.

In the midst of this activity, all while running what has essentially been a two-person office, Bill has been president of AIGA, co-edited the *Looking Closer* anthologies of design writing, and taught design thinking and creative strategy at the Yale School of Management. Jessica has served on the US Citizens' Stamp Advisory Committee, as a guest artist at Wesleyan University, and as senior critic at the Yale School of Art and lecturer at Yale College. Together, Bill and Jessica were the first recipients of the Henry Wolf Residency at the American Academy in Rome. And they raised two wonderful children, Malcolm and Fiona.

But perhaps Bill and Jessica's broadest impact on our profession has been felt through their website for design, visual thinking, and cultural criticism, Design Observer. It started in 2003 as an experiment with two other friends. Ten years later, the site has hosted over 600 writers who have written 4,700 articles which have received 28,000 comments, with 92,000 Facebook subscribers, 575,000 Twitter followers, and over 175,000 unique monthly visitors.

It is through this project that I really got to know Bill and Jessica; with Rick Poynor, we were the site's four original founders. And it is through this experience that I learned the secret of how a designer can do whatever he or she wants to do. When they started Design Observer, Bill and Jessica didn't have a business plan. There were no agreements to sign, no contracts to send on to lawyers. There weren't any planning meetings with whiteboards and Post-it Notes. There was nothing more than a simple offer: let's do this, let's see what happens, and let's keep doing it as long as it's fun. "The minute it stops being fun, we'll just quit," Bill once said. It has been the simplest thing in

Michael Bierut, William Drenttel, Steven Heller, and DK Holland, *Looking Closer: Critical Writings on Graphic Design* (New York: Allworth, 1994); Michael Bierut, William Drenttel, Steven Heller, and DK Holland, *Looking Closer 2: Critical Writings on Graphic Design* (New York: Allworth, 1997); Michael Bierut, William Drenttel, Steven Heller, and DK Holland, *Looking Closer 3: Classic Writings on Graphic Design* (New York: Allworth, 1999); Michael Bierut, Jessica Helfand, Steven Heller, and Rick Poynor, *Looking Closer 4: Critical Writings on Graphic Design* (New York: Allworth, 2002); and Michael Bierut, William Drenttel, and Steven Heller, *Looking Closer 5: Critical Writings on Graphic Design* (New York: Allworth, 2007).

the world. I suspect everything they've done together — no matter how challenging — has seemed that way.

This is what Bill and Jessica have taught us. Their individual histories, so deep and expansive, have given them imagination. Their experiences in the world of culture and commerce, where they learned what they wanted to do and what they didn't want to do, have given them conviction. Their trust in their audiences, in their collaborators, and most of all, in each other, have given them optimism. All of these things have brought these two designers to a place in their lives where making great, important design can seem like the simplest thing in the world. And this is their lesson: you can just keep doing it as long as it's fun. And if you're lucky, it always will be.

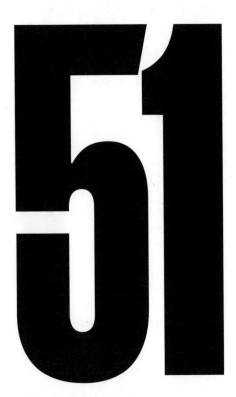

Not Diving but Swimming

1. Pharaoh's dance

When I was in junior high school, my favorite band was Chicago, the seven-piece horn band famous for "Make Me Smile" and "Saturday in the Park." While my hipper friends found them tame (if not lame), I genuinely liked their music, which I found catchy and inventive. But I suspect that I was just as attracted to the way they were packaged. Columbia Records art director John Berg had commissioned a lush calligraphic logo from Nick Fasciano, and that logo — the same size, the same position — was the only thing that appeared on the band's covers. With one trick. On each new record, Fasciano rendered the logo a different way: built from brushed stainless steel, carved into wood, sewn into a flag, modeled to resemble a candy bar, concealed in a vintage map, one variation after another, each one the same, but somehow different. To a thirteen-year-old who wouldn't have known the word "branding," this was a memorable demonstration of corporate identity in action. I loved Chicago.

     I was discussing my enthusiasm with a camp counselor one afternoon in the summer of 1971. He was baffled. "Chicago, they've got trumpets and stuff, right?

First appeared in Design Observer, March 1, 2016.

Like jazz rock?" Yes, I said, I guess you could call it that. "Oh," he said. "Then you should definitely check out Miles Davis. That's what real jazz rock sounds like." That weekend I went to the Parmatown Mall and bought *Bitches Brew*.

Interview with Marc Myers, "Designer Michael Bierut on Miles Davis," *Wall Street Journal*, February 16, 2016.

Marc Myers writes a column for the *Wall Street Journal* called Playlist where he asks people to name the one song that changed their life. Not their favorite song, which is a different question. But the song that fundamentally altered the way they think about the world. A few weeks ago, he put the question to me. I would have had trouble picking a favorite song. But I can pinpoint the moment my mind was changed about what music was and what music could be. It was when I heard the first song, disc one, side one, on *Bitches Brew*. "Pharaoh's Dance" didn't sound anything like Chicago. It didn't sound like anything. It didn't seem to have any structure — no verses, no bridges. I hated it. But I listened to it again, and then again. I started absorbing its dense, subterranean patterns. And I realized, for the first time, but not the last, that something truly new takes time to appreciate and understand.

Logos for the Metropolitan Museum of Art. Top, after Luca Pacioli, 1971. Bottom, Wolff Olins, 2016.

2. Does this logo make me look pathological and self-loathing?

We live at a moment that rewards snap judgments, ideally delivered in short, Twitter-ready bursts. As a fifty-something graphic designer, for decades I practiced my career in relative obscurity. For most of my life, people have reacted with mild bafflement as I tried to explain what I do for a living. No more. After thirty-five years, suddenly everybody is interested in what I do. I just tell them that I design logos.

Early in 2016, a new logo started appearing here and there. It was for New York's Metropolitan Museum of Art. Many new logos get criticized for being too simple and boring. The Met's logo is not that. It reduces the name to two red three-letter words — THE MET — and composes those six letters in a complex arrangement, connecting each to the next, merging the verticals in the HE and ME pairs, all in a font with exaggerated serifs that border on flamboyant. It is a nervy, bold design that begs for a strong reaction, and that's what it got.

Justin Davidson from New York fired the first salvo, calling it a "graphic misfire" that looked like "a red double-decker bus that has stopped short, shoving the passengers into each other's backs." Soon, others joined the chorus, including *Times* critic Michael Kimmelman ("pathological and self-loathing"), *Vanity Fair*'s Paul Goldberger ("the vibe of insecurity"), and Hyperallergic's Jennifer Bostic ("a really unfortunate mistake.")

The visceral reaction provoked by this peculiar combination of letterforms was further augmented by an onslaught of affection for the Met's previous logo. This was a constructed letter *M* in a circle, based on drawings by Franciscan friar Luca Pacioli first published in his book *De divina proportione*. People tend to prefer old logos to new ones. The Met M-in-circle had been in use since 1971; if that isn't old enough for you, Pacioli published his book in 1503. Abandoning five hundred years of tradition was too much for otherwise progressive designer Karim Rashid, who told the *New York Times*, "We're talking here about a museum that's all about history. So the best thing they could do is hang on to keeping their mark — or their logo — historic." Of course what Rashid is describing is not a museum, but a cemetery.

The quotes are from Justin Davidson, "The Metropolitan Museum of Art's New Logo is a Typographic Bus Crash," *New York*, February 17, 2016; tweet by Michael Kimmelman @kimmelman, February 18, 2016; tweet by Paul Goldberger @paulgoldberger, February 18, 2016; and Jennifer Bostic, "The Meh-tropolitan Museum of Art's Rebranding," Hyperallergic, February 23, 2016.

The Karim Rashid quote is from Robin Pogrebin, "The Met and a New Logo," *New York Times*, February 18, 2016.

3. The more you know

Okay: I admit it. I liked the new Met logo the first time I saw it, and the more I see it, the more I like it.

There are lots and lots of reasons that this is, if not a great logo, then certainly a better logo than the one it's replacing. The old symbol, that beloved (albeit to my eyes kind of generic and clip-artsy) Pacioli M, needed to be captioned with the full name of the institution: five words, ten syllables, twenty-six letters, all in poor old Trajan. This was cumbersome in every sense, particularly as the institution prepares to open in the former Whitney Museum building on Madison Avenue (to be renamed the Met Breuer after its architect). That new site, along with the less-visited but utterly lovely Cloisters, makes the Met a citywide complex that demands not a monolithic identity, but a way to connect up all the pieces. The new logo, a self-reading wordmark that acknowledges the institution's two-syllable colloquial name, will serve effectively as the hinge for the whole system.

The logo's multiple ligatures are no doubt the new identity's most polarizing element. As an experienced design pitchman, I knew immediately these were meant to signify "connections" well before its designers at Wolff Olins said as much. But more importantly, I'll bet you that I could find half a dozen precedent examples of the same typographic conceit on medieval manuscripts and classical inscriptions within a five-minute walk from the Met's front door. You want history? Here's history. The Met, perhaps the world's most overwhelmingly overstuffed encyclopedic museum, is nothing if not complex. The new logo's refreshingly idiosyncratic typography is a perfect analog for that complexity. And red is the perfect color. But all of these thoughts came later. The first thing I thought when I saw the new identity was quite simple: *If this thing were forty-five years old, it would be the most beloved logo in New York.*

4. The lure of preemptive cleverness

All the fuss that's made about logos camouflages an embarrassing secret: people are reluctant to admit how they actually work.

Imagine it's 1968 and you're the head of marketing for a midwestern department store called Target. You go to the country's most respected corporate identity consultants, Unimark International, and they give you a cleaned-up logo that's...well, a target: a red dot with a red circle around it. Blessedly, social media hasn't been invented yet, so you're spared the now-inevitable Twitterstorm ("How much did they pay for this?" and "This is the best they could come up with?" and the mandatory "My five-year-old..." et cetera). Nonetheless, there must have been some doubtful whispers in the corporate hallways.

What you couldn't have told anyone — what you couldn't have even guessed — was what would happen over the next five decades: that the blank simplicity of the mark would enable an astonishing range of creative uses. There are many examples of symbols that might have been dismissed as underwhelming at their birth, from Chanel to Nike. What they have in common is what Paul Rand called "the pleasure of recognition and the promise of meaning." What everyone gets confused about is the difference between meaning and the promise of it; like the "pursuit of happiness," what you're guaranteed is not success but its potential.

This quote is from the privately printed brochure that was used to introduce the proposed NeXT logo to Steve Jobs, written and designed by Paul Rand, "The Sign of the Next Generation of Computers...*for Education*," 1988.

How do you design for potential meaning? How do you convince a client to view a new identity not as a purchase, but as an investment?

When my team was working on a new logo for a major telecommunications company last year, I felt we had arrived at a solution that solved every problem but one: it didn't demonstrate how creative we were. After many attempts, I came to feel that all these gestures were self-

Now You See It

indulgent and, in fact, interfered with the communication of clarity and simplicity. We went with the simple solution and took the consequences.

Along the course of my career I became addicted to something I've come to think of as preemptive cleverness, delivering logo systems that appear to be fully articulated on day one. Like moving into a fully furnished house, this can be reassuring and convenient. But at the same time, it makes it much harder to make the place your own. Something more open-ended allows, and even invites, participation. I remain haunted by a great example — those Nick Fasciano logos for Chicago I loved when I was thirteen: one design, endlessly inventive variations.

5. Just wait

Most design disciplines think in the long term. Architects design buildings to last for generations; industrial designers create products that will withstand endless hours, if not years, of use.

Graphic designers, whether we admit it or not, are trained for the short term. Most of the things we design have to discharge their function immediately, whether it's a design for a book or a poster, a website or an infographic, a sign system or a business card. In school critiques, architecture and industrial design students produce models. Graphic designers produce finished prototypes. The idea that we create things that are unfinished, that can only accrue value over time, is foreign to us. It's so easy for us to visualize the future, and so hard to admit that we really can't. That's what we face every time we unveil a new logo.

And so every time a major identity is introduced today, it's subjected to immediate scrutiny. Why not? It's fun. It's risk free. Every client wants to have an audience "connect on an emotional level with their brand." And then when they do, it's not always what they hoped for. People love the Metropolitan Museum of Art. Naturally they take it personally when the Met decides to change its logo.

Whether we want to acknowledge it or not, anyone evaluating a brand-new logo at first glance is — to paraphrase my partner Paula Scher — reviewing a three-act play based on what they see the moment the curtain goes up. Or, to put it differently, they think they're judging a diving competition when in fact they're judging a swimming competition. The question isn't what kind of splash you make. It's how long you can keep your head above water.

The School of Massimo

52

First appeared as "Massimo Vignelli, 1931–2014" in Design Observer, May 27, 2014.

I learned how to design at design school. But I learned how to be a designer from Massimo Vignelli.

In June 1980 I graduated from the University of Cincinnati with a bachelor's degree in graphic design and moved to New York City to take a job at Vignelli Associates. I can barely picture the person I was thirty-four years ago. I was from Parma, Ohio (a middle-class suburb on the wrong side of Cleveland), the newly hired, lowest-ranked employee at Vignelli Associates.

The tasks I would be doing at my new job would be barely comprehensible to young graphic designers today: menial operations involving rubber cement thinner, X-ACTO knives, and photostat developer. I was a schlub, a peon, a punk. I knew nothing. Massimo and his wife, Lella, were to discover very quickly that Parma, Ohio, and Parma, Italy, had very little in common.

Today there is an entire building in Rochester, New York, dedicated to preserving the Vignelli legacy. But in those days, it seemed to me that the whole city of New York was a permanent Vignelli exhibition. To get to the office, I rode in a subway with Vignelli-designed signage, shared the sidewalk with people holding Vignelli-designed

Bloomingdale's shopping bags, walked by St. Peter's Church with its Vignelli-designed pipe organ visible through the window. At Vignelli Associates, at twenty-three years old, I felt I was at the center of the universe.

Massimo Vignelli, 2011.

I was already at my desk on my first day of work when Massimo arrived. As always, he filled the room with his oversized personality. Elegant, loquacious, gesticulating, brimming with enthusiasm. Massimo was like Zeus, impossibly wise, impossibly old. (He was, in fact, forty-nine.) My education was about to begin.

At Vignelli Associates, I was immersed in a world of unbelievable glamour. If you were a designer — even the lowest of the low, like me — Massimo treated you with a huge amount of respect. Everyone passed through that office. I met the best designers in the world there: Paul Rand, Leo Lionni, Josef Müller-Brockmann, Alan Fletcher. And not just designers. I remember one time Massimo was working on a book project with an editor from Doubleday, and he decided to give her a tour of the office. He brought her to my desk and introduced me. It was Jacqueline Kennedy Onassis. "Mrs. Onassis, this is one of our young designers, Michael Bierut," said Massimo. "It's an honor to meet you," said the former first lady. I think I just said, "Guh, guh, guh."

From Massimo, I learned that designing a book wasn't about coming up with a clever place for the page numbers. He taught me about typography, about scale, about pacing, about refinement. I learned to think of graphic design as a way to create an experience, an experience that was not limited to two dimensions or to a momentary impression. It was about creating something lasting, even timeless.

Most importantly, I learned about the world. From my hometown I knew only the Parmatown Mall, anchored with Higbee's and the May Company. Massimo taught me about the Galleria in Milano. I learned about architecture, fashion, food, literature, life. It was with Massimo that I had my first taste of steak tartare and my first taste of Stilton with port. Imagine, raw meat for dinner and cheese for dessert! For Massimo, design was life and life was design. Finally, from Massimo I learned never to give up. He was able to bring enthusiasm, joy, and intensity to the smallest design challenge. Even after fifty years, he could delight in designing something like a business card as if he had never done one before.

It was Massimo who taught me one of the simplest things in the world: that if you do good work, you get more good work to do, and conversely bad work brings more bad work. It sounds simple, but it's remarkable, over the course of a lifetime of pragmatism and compromise, how easy it is to forget: the only way to do good work is simply to do good work. Massimo did good work.

I intended to stay at Vignelli Associates for eighteen months and then find something new. Instead, I stayed there for ten years. I loved my job. But I had finally reached a point where I realized I had to move on. Quitting was the hardest thing I've ever had to do. I had a speech all prepared, and the night before, I was driving on Interstate 87 and rehearsing the speech in my head. Suddenly I saw the lights of a police car right behind me. I was pulled over. "Do you know how fast you were going?" "Um, sixty-five?" "Try eighty-five. You pulled up right behind our squad car" — it was a marked squad car, by the way — "passed us on the right, and then cut us off." They made me get out of the car, checked the trunk, and took me to the state trooper barracks for ninety minutes while they ascertained that I wasn't a drug addict or a terrorist. Massimo had that kind of effect on people.

The next day, when I told him I had decided to leave, Massimo was the same as he always was: warm, emotional, generous. He had had many other designers work for him before me and would have many others afterward. But for me, there would only be one: my teacher, my mentor, my boss, my hero, my friend, Massimo Vignelli.

I saw Massimo four days before he died on May 27, 2014. Up to the end, he was still curious, still generous, still excited about design. He left behind his wife, Lella; his children, Luca and Valentina; and generations of designers who, like me, are still learning from his example.

I'm with Her

November 2016

It was going to be the most thrilling night of my life. As I walked the darkening streets of midtown Manhattan toward the Jacob Javits Convention Center, from blocks away I could glimpse an enormous image on the JumboTron over its main entrance, a forward-pointing arrow superimposed on a letter *H*. After an endless series of queues and checkpoints, I found myself about fifty feet from the venue's main stage, VIP credentials dangling from my neck. I was surrounded by a happy throng of people who, like me, were there for one thing: to celebrate the election of the first woman president of the United States.

I had never been to a political victory party before. Like everyone else, I knew that nothing was a sure thing. Indeed, the previous weeks had brought more nail-biting revelations and abrupt reversals, capping off a grueling campaign that had been anything but easy. Yet the mood in the crowd was optimistic, even giddy. Everyone claimed to have inside information: exit poll results from contested demographics, early vote totals from swing states, all of it adding up to a Hillary Clinton landslide.

First appeared in Design Observer, March 28, 2017.

And everywhere I looked was that H logo: on badges, buttons, stickers, T-shirts, and tote bags; on directional signs and video monitors; and ablaze on a giant screen that hung above the stage. It was on that stage that we expected to see our candidate before the night was over, arms raised in victory beneath an emblem that I had designed.

The night ended sooner than I thought, and differently than everyone expected. Going home, with my necktie with its pattern of H logos loosened around my neck, embarrassed by my hubris and worried about the future of our nation, I tried to figure out what had gone wrong.

January 2015

Almost two years before, I was invited to volunteer my services on a secret project: the design of a logo for the possible presidential bid of the former first lady and secretary of state Hillary Rodham Clinton. I was excited. I had never met Secretary Clinton, but I liked her when she was my senator and I was impressed with her performance as secretary of state. I had assumed she'd be the candidate in 2004, until Barack Obama had come along. Eight years later she was even more qualified. This was a historic moment. I said yes immediately.

I put together a three-person team: me, designer Jesse Reed, and project manager Julia Lemle. We would work in secret for the next two months. Our first meeting with the Clinton team began with a simple statement: "Our candidate has 100 percent name recognition." There is a well-known marketing principle that is often credited to midcentury design legend Raymond Loewy. He felt that people were governed by two competing impulses: an attraction to the excitement of new things and a yearning for the comfort provided by what we already know. In response, Loewy had developed a reliable formula. If something was familiar, make it surprising. If something was surprising, make it familiar.

That same principle applies to political campaigns. In 2008 Sol Sender, Amanda Gentry, and Andy Keene were faced with the challenge of branding a candidate who had anything but name recognition. Barack Obama's design team responded with a quintessentially professional identity program, introducing — for the first time — the language of corporate branding to political marketing. Obama's persona — unfamiliar, untested, and potentially alarming to

Derek Thompson, "The Four-Letter Code to Selling Just about Anything," *Atlantic*, January/February 2017.

Scott Thomas, *Designing Obama* (Albany, California: Post, 2009).

much of the voting public — was given a polished logo and a perfectly executed, utterly consistent typographic system. In short, they made a surprising candidate seem familiar.

We faced the opposite problem. Our candidate was universally known. How could we make her image seem fresh and compelling?

Things had changed in the intervening years. For the Obama team, digital communications meant websites and email. Now the world was dominated by Facebook, Twitter, and Instagram. Voters had become accustomed to broadcasting their own voices and making direct connections. To work in this environment, whatever we designed would have to be concise and efficient, capable of standing out on a tablet, a phone, or a wristwatch.

One more thing was different now. In 2008 the Obama team had found themselves customizing their logo to appeal to different groups: veterans, teachers, the LGBT community. Looking back, some of these graphic adaptations seemed forced to me. With its concentric circles, its curves and gradations, the Obama mark was handsome but complex. It already looked finished. I began thinking about a logo that was the opposite: simple, open-ended, something that would invite participation.

The Clinton team shared our ambition to create something new and different, and in the weeks that followed, that's what we tried to develop. The candidate had used traditional serif typography in her previous campaigns. We all agreed on a clean, bold sans serif, which its designer, Lucas Sharp, agreed to customize and make available to the campaign for free. Barack Obama's favored all capitals. We recommended upper and lower case: friendlier, more conversational.

And although we explored dozens of symbols, the one everyone gravitated to was the simplest of all: a perfectly square H. But its simplicity was deceptive. What looked like an H was really a window, capable of endless transformations. It could contain pictures and colors, patterns and motifs. Because so much communication for the campaign would happen digitally, the logo could change at a moment's notice. It could be customized not just by various interest groups, but by individual supporters. It was the ultimate dynamic identity system. Still, we worried that the H alone, even as an ever-changing frame, was too static. We finally found what we thought was the right finishing touch, the simplest thing in the world: an arrow, emerging

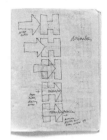

Early sketch for Hillary for America logo, Michael Bierut, 2015.

Love trumps hate.

Unity font, Lucas Sharp, 2015.

Hillary for America button, 2016.

John Podesta, "Re: Fwd: Visual Identity/ Design Rationale," email to Jennifer Palmieri, February 15, 2015, WikiLeaks.

naturally from the geometry of the letterform, pointing forward, toward the future.

It wasn't clever or artful. I didn't care about that. I wanted something that you didn't need a software tutorial to create, something as simple as a peace sign or a smiley face. I wanted a logo that a five-year-old could make with construction paper and kindergarten scissors. Finally, the time came to present the logo directly to Secretary Clinton.

I witnessed firsthand what so many called Hillary Clinton's greatest skill. She was one of the best listeners I've ever met. Walking into the meeting, I knew that a session with the logo designer had to be among the most trivial subjects on her schedule that day, or maybe that week. Yet she gave me her full attention, asked thoughtful questions, and — despite her claims that she wasn't "an art person" — spotted a few weak points in our presentation I'd hoped no one would notice. Even more surprising was the call I received the next day. Secretary Clinton thanked me warmly for our work, elaborated on a few points from the day before, and added some new thoughts. There was really no need for her to do this personally, but she did it. She was brilliant and genuine. I had never had the chance to evaluate a future president close-up. I was sure the country would be in good hands.

April 2015

On Sunday afternoon, April 13, 2015, Hillary Clinton officially announced her candidacy for president of the United States. It was an open secret by then that she was going to run. Every television news organization was standing by for the announcement.

I had not heard from the campaign in weeks. We had completed our work more than a month before. I knew there had been internal controversy about whether our direction was the best and that other firms had been invited to contribute ideas. At times I had reconciled myself to being dumped, despite the candidate's initial enthusiasm. (I would be disconcerted more than a year later when exchanges debating the merits of our work showed up, of all places, in the midst of the vast trove of emails published by WikiLeaks.)

The announcement came in the form of a two-minute video. It began with ordinary Americans talking about their plans, about making new starts. Then, wearing a red and blue suit, the candidate appeared and said she too was starting something: her campaign for president. Finally, at the end, there it was: a skillful animation, the H built from the faces from the video, the arrow entering from the left, resolving into a red-and-blue version of the never-before-seen Hillary for America logo. The colors, red and blue, matched the candidate's suit. Or perhaps it was the other way around. What we had been working on in secret was suddenly public. It was really happening.

The announcement video is on YouTube at https://youtu.be/N708P-A45D0.

Then, within minutes, the social media reviews started coming in. "So what lucky third grader won the Design the Hillary Clinton Campaign Logo contest?" "Hillary's logo was clearly designed in PowerPoint by a PowerPoint user." (This is a deep insult for a graphic designer, for reasons not worth explaining.) People said the logo reminded them of a sign for a hospital, or the Cuban flag, or, in more extreme cases, of swastikas or the destruction of the Twin Towers. The fact that the logo was really the only new thing of significance in the announcement video made it an irresistible target for pundits. The red arrow pointing right — what did that mean about the campaign's strategy? Then followed the think pieces. "The Internet Freaks Out over Hillary Clinton's Campaign Logo." "Design experts trash Hillary Clinton's new logo." "Why everyone went nuts over Hillary Clinton's new logo." It all reached a surreal peak when I got an email from a writer for a prominent magazine. "So I'm sure you've seen the Hillary logo hysteria," he wrote. "I think it's a case where — and you may disagree — the internet is kind of getting it right. I think it's a train wreck." I was then asked to participate in an invitation-only contest to redesign my own logo. I declined.

Mark Wilson, "The Internet Freaks Out over Hillary's Campaign Logo," Fast Company, April 13, 2015;

Darren Samuelsohn, "Design Experts Trash Hillary's New Logo," Politico, April 17, 2015;

Liz Stinson, "Why Everyone Went Nuts over Hillary Clinton's New Logo," Wired, April 13, 2015.

I had already designed several controversial projects in the age of instant Twitter reviews, but nothing prepared me for this. As New York magazine said, "Basically, Hillary secretly gave America a Rorschach test, and the results are terrifying." After consulting with the campaign, we agreed to adopt a no-comment policy about the logo. I held my tongue. The country had bigger issues to deal with. Nonetheless, perhaps because I was the only designer in the world who didn't seem to have a public opinion about it, its authorship soon became common knowledge.

Margaret Hartmann, "Everything That's Wrong With Hillary's New Logo, According to the Internet," New York, April 13, 2015.

It isn't pleasant to have talk-show hosts making fun of your work on national television. And there was something all so gleefully vicious about it. It was just some simple geometric shapes and a couple of primary colors, yet it seemed to drive so many people crazy. My wife, Dorothy, helped put things in perspective. "Maybe," she said, "this isn't really all about your little logo." Through it all, I was heartened by the resolve of the team at Clinton campaign headquarters. They were confident in the work and told me they had no intention of abandoning it. And we all knew something the world didn't know: that the red and blue logo was just the start.

The potential of the identity system wouldn't be revealed until a few weeks later, as the Supreme Court prepared to hear oral arguments in *Obergefell v. Hodges* to determine the legality of same-sex marriage. On April 28, the campaign changed the logo on all its digital platforms to the rainbow colors of the LGBT movement. As we'd hoped, the world noticed. This transformation opened the door to more and more versions of the H and arrow combination.

Domenico Montanaro, "Panned When It First Came Out, the Clinton Logo Is Saying Something Now," NPR Politics, April 28, 2015.

"It's kind of becoming the Empire State Building of presidential campaign logos," said a writer at NPR's website, "changing colors to celebrate any variety of milestones and holidays, from pink for breast cancer awareness to red, white and blue for Memorial Day to 'pastel fades' for Easter." A month and a half later, the idea of this dynamic symbol had taken hold. "It's official," declared Quartz. "Hillary's logo is actually perfect."

Annalisa Merelli, "It's Official: Hillary Clinton's Logo Is Actually Perfect," Quartz, June 10, 2015.

July 2016

The moment had come at last. At the Democratic National Convention in Philadelphia, Hillary Clinton was to become the first woman candidate for president of the United States. Much had happened since she had announced her candidacy fifteen months before, so little of it foreseen: an unexpectedly hard primary fight, the emergence of the unlikeliest of Republican opponents.

Jennifer Kinon had worked with me as a senior designer at Pentagram. She took a leave of absence from the firm she founded, the Original Champions of Design, to manage the Hillary for America design effort.

A former colleague, Jennifer Kinon, was appointed Hillary for America's full-time design director and built an extraordinary team that worked tirelessly to ensure that the campaign's message was being communicated consistently and creatively on every available channel: microsites, videos, GIFs, hashtags. The grassroots slogan #ImWithHer — with the now familiar logo serving as the H — was ubiquitous. And the design team's powers were on full display in Philadelphia, minute by minute, night after night. The H-plus-arrow logo was everywhere. Every sign in the convention hall bore the campaign's signature typeface, perfectly sized, perfectly spaced. As only an obsessive graphic designer would, I noted with satisfaction the placards that greeted Bernie Sanders in Philadelphia the night he rose to call for unity on behalf of the party's candidate. His graphics had been almost random during his grassroots campaign; that night, Sanders faced a sea of signs bearing his name, not in Clarendon, the closest thing to a standard his team had managed to achieve, but in Unity, the Clinton font. In a concession to his staying power, a silhouette of a bird topped the lowercase *i*. Like everything else, it was perfect.

As the campaign moved into its breathless final weeks, Hillary's supporters took her graphic identity as their own. The simple geometry of the H-plus-arrow was reproduced in thousands of forms: arrayed in patterns of seashells on the beach on Labor Day, carved into pumpkins on Halloween, stacked in beer kegs in Milwaukee, embedded in the state's name in Ohio. The underground army of supporters who called themselves Pantsuit Nation made the logo its own. Voters posted every possible rendition online: hand drawn, crocheted, scrapbooked, appliquéd. My favorites were the ones from kids. It turned out the critics were right: your five-year-old *could* do this logo.

Then there was Donald Trump. Bad typography; amateurish design; haphazard, inconsistent, downright ugly communications. When the Trump/Pence monogram was mocked for its how-did-they-miss-that salaciousness, their campaign team committed the ultimate act of weakness: they blinked and took it down without comment. The Republican convention was a gruesome and tawdry spectacle. And everything was topped off with nothing more than a red hat with a badly kerned, caps-locked slogan.

Later, filmmaker Michael Moore pointed out that where he came from, the industrial Midwest, people didn't care about polling data or carefully calibrated social media campaigns, but they did wear baseball caps. He saw it coming. I did not.

One supporter, Karen Todd, was particularly ingenious and posted a different interpretation of the logo on her Facebook page every day for months. They are preserved on the campaign's website: Brian McBride, "Check Out the Creative and Beautiful Versions of Hillary's Campaign Logo from One Super Fan," Hillary for America, November 3, 2016.

Hilary Lewis, "Michael Moore Explains Why Trump Won in 45-Minute Commercial-Free 'Morning Joe' Appearance," *Hollywood Reporter*, November 11, 2016.

January 2017

In many ways, going to design school is all about surrounding yourself with a beautifully crafted bubble. At least it was for me. Most normal people don't know or care about custom typography, the fine distinctions between nearly identical colors, dynamic graphic identity — any of that stuff. Growing up in the rust belt, just like Michael Moore, I certainly didn't. With each class assignment, with each studio critique, I became more skilled as a designer and I became further from normal. Moving to New York put me at the center of a highly specialized profession practicing what would have seemed to my old friends in Ohio like a hopelessly esoteric brand of black magic.

Teddy Goff,
The Design of Business/
The Business of Design
podcast interview,
January 10, 2017.

As we worked on the campaign, it never occurred to us to be anything less than perfect. (As our campaign contact Teddy Goff observed much later, to be imperfect would have been inauthentic to our detail-obsessed candidate.) During the height of the primary battle, Lindsay Ballant, a Bernie Sanders supporter, wrote a perceptive critique that compared the graphics of the two campaigns. "While Hillary's visual campaign is inarguably successful by all traditional design principles, it's also calculated, expected, and contrived," Ballant wrote. "It reinforces the perception of establishment status, which is one of the main criticisms of her as a candidate. One of the consequences of a campaign so tightly controlled is the campaign *feels* so tightly controlled." In contrast, the design of the Sanders campaign had the homespun charm one associates with do-it-yourself craft sites like Etsy. They looked and felt authentic. When I read this in the spring of 2016, I had to admit she was onto something.

Lindsay Ballant,
"Bernie, Hillary, and
the Authenticity Gap:
A Study in Campaign
Branding," Medium,
March 1, 2016.

On the other hand, Donald Trump's graphics were easy to dismiss. They combined the design sensibility of the Home Shopping Network with the tone of a Nigerian scam email. Like so many other complacent Democrats, my only question was: Why is this even close?

Armies of smart people generated oceans of words in the aftermath of the election trying to figure out what happened. Talented pundits and strategists and pollsters, all masters of their craft, were racked with self-doubt. I too wondered if the very thing I was so good at had somehow betrayed me. We had spent months developing a logo; Trump had spent years building a brand. Had Trump won not in spite of his terrible design work, but because of it?

See, among others,
Diana Budds,
"The Worst Design of
2016 Was Also the
Most Effective," *Fast
Company*, December
16, 2016.

The day of Donald Trump's inauguration, I was on an Amtrak train to Washington, DC. Dorothy had made plans to attend the Women's March as soon as she heard about it. The car we were in was almost all women. And everywhere we looked, we could see pink, the knitted hats with cat ears that would become the defining image of the march. The next day, we found ourselves in a crowd that seemed to stretch for miles in every direction. A forest of homemade signs became a display of wit, imagination, and passion that instantly went viral on social media. None of them matched, and all of them were beautiful. There was only one element of consistency. Those homemade pussyhats — which began as a three-woman project in a Los Angeles knitting class and became a national cottage industry that produced more than a hundred thousand hats in a matter of weeks — were so ubiquitous that they turned every photograph of the throng into a sea of pink. There was no guidelines manual, no design direction. Instead, here was something thrilling: individual creativity in the service of collective solidarity.

Rob Walker, "The D.I.Y. Revolutionaries of the Pussyhat Project," *New Yorker*, January 25, 2017.

I still believe in Hillary Clinton, and I am prouder than ever of the work we did for the campaign. In that vast crowd in Washington, I wore the same blue-on-blue H-plus-arrow button I did on election night. I knew how to do something, and I was good at it. But that day I realized I was just one voice among many. The future will not depend only on experts drawing the battle lines, but on the courage and enthusiasm that each of us can bring to the fight.

We are in uncharted territory now, and it is at once frightening and exhilarating. Frightening because we face extraordinary challenges. Exhilarating because I believe, more than ever, in the power of design. Design can provide comfort in the face of devastating change, and it can shake us out of our complacency when action is demanded. And now, more than ever, at the moment we need it most, it belongs to all of us.

Interview with Peter Merholz

Originally appeared as an interview with Peter Merholz in three parts on AdaptivePath in 2006. Part one was published on June 6, part two on June 26, and part three on July 31.

Peter Merholz One of the reasons we're excited to have you speak at our User Experience Week event is because you're willing to publicly challenge design orthodoxy. Two of your Design Observer posts stand out in this regard: "Innovation Is the New Black" and "The Obvious, Shunned by So Many, Is Successfully Avoided Once Again."

What has led you to take such stances that are not widely held? What experiences have shaped these design philosophies?

Michael Bierut If it's true, there may be several reasons. One is that my wife, Dorothy, isn't a designer, she's an MBA. We started dating when we were in high school in Ohio, and now we've been married for twenty-six years. Dorothy has always been the first to roll her eyes at some particularly choice design affectation, and she certainly won't let me get away with any herself. I often find myself wondering what a "normal" person would think about my work. By normal I usually mean Dorothy.

All that said, I don't really try to be argumentative or confrontational. I think there are a lot of ways to practice our craft, and almost all of them have some kind of merit. Some people have said that rather than challenging orthodoxy I'm more likely to be a defender of the status quo. It may be because, for designers at least, self-conscious difference for its own sake creates its own kind of orthodoxy.

PM You mention that your wife has an MBA. As I'm sure you're aware, there's a lot of activity in the "business and design" space. The [IIT] Institute of Design's Strategy Conference took place last week, AIGA's Gain conference is coming in October, *Businessweek* and Condé Nast are planning "design and business" publications, business schools are preaching "design thinking" as a new way of solving old problems, et cetera, et cetera.

In your practice, how do you bridge between "business" and "design"? In your client work, how do you demonstrate business impact?

MB Too many designers enter the field spouting design jargon and, predictably, meet resistance or indifference from their clients. So they switch to business jargon, which is usually worse. I did this for a while, got good at it, and then got disgusted with myself.

I've come to believe strongly that one of the roles of design is to bring humanity, intelligence, and beauty to the world of business, and indeed to everyday life. In my experience, good clients and good designers don't see this goal as being opposed to — or even separate from — achieving business goals, but rather an integral part of it. It's a dirty secret that much of what we admire in the design world is a byproduct not of "strategy" but of common sense, taste, and luck. Some clients are too unnerved by ambiguity to accept this and create gargantuan superstructures of bullshit to provide a sense of security. Not only do designers enthusiastically collude in this process, but many have found ways to bill for it.

I measure success the same way anyone does: increased sales, better response rates, higher profit margins. At the same time, I'm painfully aware that design — especially graphic design — can only make a partial contribution to these outcomes, even at its most effective. This, of course, is useful to remember when the numbers don't go your way.

PM I agree that we have a responsibility to bring "humanity, intelligence, and beauty" into these practices. But, and I'm going to beat this horse just a little bit longer, how do you hold yourself accountable? How do your clients hold you accountable? How do you justify (what I assume to be) your high rates? The top designers seem to command their position through the development of an aura of brilliance. Is cultivating an aura what it's about?

Before you answer, I want to posit an assertion: from what I see, graphic design is becoming something of a commodity practice. Adaptive Path doesn't promote graphic design services (though we offer them) because competing in that space means battling over ever-shrinking margins. Graphic design seems to have two huge forces working against its viability: an immense supply-side, with so many designers offering virtually indistinguishable services, and an almost allergic reaction to demonstrating explicit business value, so that pricing graphic design is something of a voodoo art.

MB Peter, it's funny when you talk about graphic design's commodity-based supply-side, with so many designers offering the same services: that's what many of my partners have said for years about web consulting.

Your questions combine issues that have to do with providing value to clients' businesses and running one's own successful design business. To address the first question about accountability, I'd like to know the answer to that one myself. Has anyone ever proven, really proven, a connection between good design and a client's business success? "Good design," first of all, is hard to define: for instance, I find most of the examples of work in *Design Management Journal* pretty mundane. Second, while I think you can argue that good design can make a good business even better, good design alone can't make a bad company good. IBM and Enron didn't succeed or fail because of their logos (both of which were designed by the same guy, by the way). So if a client asks me if I can prove that my work has had an effect on my clients' bottom lines, I have a short answer: no.

Instead, I tell them that the best thing design can do for a company is to express that company's personality accurately and compellingly, and in so doing permit that organization's inherent strengths to prevail. This can be through graphics, product, environments, or experiences. The way Pentagram is set up creates a bias for this answer, of course. We're owned by partners who are all working designers and whose practices span the disciplines I mentioned above. The clients who hire us work directly with those partners; we have no account executives or client handlers. Each partner has a pretty distinct point of view and doesn't attempt to conceal it. Our clients are people who want to work with smart, talented, committed designers whom they like spending time with. Clients who don't value that go elsewhere.

This is also a pretty efficient and stable model financially. Each partner runs a pretty small, autonomous team. The overhead is low. I write my own proposals and negotiate my own agreements. I can ask for whatever fees I want, but we basically try to cover our time and expenses plus a 20 percent profit margin. So much for the voodoo art of pricing.

So it's efficient and stable, yes. But I suspect it wouldn't be of much interest to, say, an ad agency holding company. They would look for growth, which we really don't care that much about. And they'd get exasperated by the idiosyncrasies of the designer/owners and try to replace them with people who could deliver a more reliable product with less muss and fuss. That's what you mean by a commodity, right? I think we might make more money this way, but we'd give up what is a pretty ideal life in design.

PM Okay, I'm going to pick up a different thread here, though I think it's related to your comment on an ideal life in design.

My colleague Dan Saffer has just finished writing a book on interaction design, and the last chapter of his book concerns ethics. Many of us at Adaptive Path are admirers of Tibor Kalman, as well as the book you helped put together about him. What is your sense of the role ethics played in Kalman's work? Was it explicit, or is it just that he couldn't imagine how to work any other way? How do ethics inform your design work?

MB One of the sad aspects of Tibor's early death is that it puts other people in the unhappy position of having to speak for him, which I really can't. Working on his book with him, I came to know Tibor as a person who, simply put, was uncomfortable being comfortable. His intuitive reaction to any status quo situation was first to disrupt it. This is an interesting characteristic to bring to the world of commercial graphic design, where you're constantly being asked to accommodate yourself to your clients' goals, very few of which will correspond perfectly to your own. Tibor's genius was that he didn't attempt to separate his work and his life, as working designers do. Ethics played a big part of that with Tibor, I guess, but it seemed to me to be a larger attempt to fully integrate your values as a person with your values as a designer. After his death, this has all boiled down to an image of "Saint Tibor" that I'm guessing he would have found pretty aggravating, to tell you the truth. He was more complicated, and more interesting, and just plain more fun than that.

I think that designers who are interested in ethics tend to focus on specific issues of dramatic conflict: Would you work for a cigarette company? is a favorite. That implies we can all pick and choose those special moments where we "have to be ethical." I also sometimes hear that, for instance, design and politics don't mix. Sure they mix. Everything mixes. The goal is to seek an integrated life, which is what I think Tibor did. You may be a designer with special expertise, and certainly that's why a client would retain your advice. But try not to answer as a designer. Try to answer as a citizen, as a human being, and as a designer.

It helps, of course, if you're in a situation where you think you have a sense of agency, where you think you can walk away from situations that you don't feel are right. And of course, you always do: the only question is what it takes for you to exercise it. My biggest failing as a designer is that I'm very polite, averse to conflict, and eager to please. As a result, as I've gotten older I've tried to get better at choosing my clients. I find that when I work for people whom I personally like and who are doing something that I admire or find interesting, I'm happier, the people I work with are happier, and we all do better work.

PM You mention the mix of design and politics. A colleague of mine pointed me to your contribution for Partisan Project. Apart from some ethical stands (which, as you so pointedly demonstrated, mostly relate to the type of clients we would not take), we at Adaptive Path have been careful not to get too political with our design work, mostly out of respect of the array of viewpoints/perspectives within our organization.

How political a designer are you? I'm only familiar with the Partisan work — are there other examples out there of your political design? Have your politics ever made it...awkward in your client work? Also, what politically oriented design work of late has most impressed you? What seems to be having an impact?

MB During the Republican convention, Pentagram New York hung a NO BUSH banner outside our building, so I guess we don't hesitate to take political positions as an office or as individuals.

The Partisan Project image was, in fact, an earlier design for the banner that was rejected by my partners for being "too subtle." Hmm!

I've found that any reluctance I've had to doing more of this "political design" has to do with my own fear that things like T-shirts and posters are usually feeble tools to address the enormous problems we face as a society today. Sometimes, of course, something really clicks, but in my own work I dread the sense that I'm using something bad in the world as an excuse to make a clever design. Often, it just makes more sense to me to simply support a candidate or donate money to a cause.

I've seen some propagandistic design work that I've liked — I'm thinking of the campaign that Emily Oberman did to launch Air America (I did a Design Observer post on this called "Catharsis and the Limits of Empire") — but what I really admire is clear information design. Nigel Holmes did a piece in *Harper's* several months ago (tragically unavailable online) on America's addiction to debt that was really amazing. Similarly, I admire the way that MGMT. translated Al Gore's PowerPoint show on global warming into the book that accompanies the movie *An Inconvenient Truth*.

Speaking of *Harper's*, Art Spiegelman also did a great article last month in which he analyzed — rated, really — the notorious Danish Mohammed cartoons. Absolutely fascinating. Not available online either!

PM Okay. I'm going to switch gears here. Another Adaptive Pather, Ryan Freitas, has mentioned you a couple times on his blog, and I wanted to follow up his thoughts. His first post came after your appearance at SFMOMA, where you spoke about Pentagram's work with United on developing the identity for Ted. He was struck by how effective the *Wall Street Journal* articles from the future were at communicating your vision.

His second post came a little later, prompted by your entry "Warning: May Contain Non-Design Content," and he quoted this passage: "Over the years, I came to realize that my best work has always involved subjects that interested me, or — even better — subjects about which I've become interested, and even passionate about, through the very process of doing design work. ...To me, the conclusion is inescapable: the more things you're interested in, the better your work will be."

What I was wondering, rereading Ryan's posts, was how these two notions might be connected. How your work for United was influenced by your multifarious passions. And, perhaps related (you tell me), how you hit upon the *Wall Street Journal* mockups as a tool to communicate your

In the presentation referred to here, I made realistic prototypes of imaginary *Wall Street Journal* articles reporting on possible decisions the client might make.

concept. Have you used such "tangible futures" in your work before?

MB Being able to make vivid counterfeits is one of the joys of being a graphic designer, and one that we don't take enough pleasure in. One of my partners in London once mocked up a whole issue of *Fortune* to help a client see his business differently.

One of the hard lessons I had to learn as a designer starting out was that good design is not a self-evident imperative for most people. I tell students that they are spending time and money in design school acquiring an abnormal sensitivity to design that most regular people should not be expected to share. Yet various groups of these "regular people" are usually the ones who initiate our work, fund and approve it, and ultimately are the audiences for it. So the biggest challenge we face is figuring out how to meet people on their terms, not ours.

I never talk about "educating the client." I hate that phrase. Almost always it's the designers who need the education, not the client, not the audience. Yet designers and clients both tend to recede into their areas of expertise, and it takes work for us to wrench each other out of it. Making prototypes that help people imagine the effects that design decisions will have in the real world can be a very potent tool. Those fake *Wall Street Journal* articles were supposed to do exactly that: remind a client who had spent six months showing themselves PowerPoint presentations that there was a real world out there filled with people who didn't share their fascination with their business strategy or, actually, care at all whether they succeeded. It's a good reality check, and it helps to shift the design work from an internal exercise that's done for management approval to work that's done because you're seeking results with real people in the real world.

So of course — to get to the other part of your question — dealing with the real world means being as interested as possible in stuff that's not about design. All of the work I've done that I'm proud of somehow emerged from the fact that I've gotten really interested in that other part: the subject matter of a book, the business of a client, the content of an exhibition. Luckily I can get interested in nearly anything. And I have learned the hard way that there are a few things I'm just not interested in and can't seem to do good design for: I avoid these projects now.

PM From 1998 to 2001 you were president of the American Institute of Graphic Arts (now known as "AIGA, the professional association for design"). As such, you had broad exposure to what was being done in graphic design. What did that role help you realize about the field and practice of design that you could not have found out any other way? What insight or wisdom did it provide that can aid others in their day-to-day practice of design?

MB I've been involved with AIGA for a long time. I did a mixtape for the very first event of the New York chapter back in the early '80s. I met my future partners at Pentagram — Paula Scher, Woody Pirtle, Colin Forbes — through AIGA. I met Bill Drenttel and Jessica Helfand through AIGA, and we announced the founding of our blog, Design Observer, at an AIGA conference. I've been inspired by countless other people I could have only known through AIGA. I always thought that AIGA was fantastic at this aspect of the profession.

On the other hand, when I was president of the organization, I always had the sense that people felt vaguely guilty about this social aspect of AIGA. I think the attitude tended to be "I don't need help making friends." Instead, what our members always wanted was something else: they wanted AIGA to increase the respect that design gets from the general public, especially from the business community. Now, this is really a challenge. The fantasy was that there could be a kind of invisible gas that could be discharged into the air of every boardroom in America, and all those clients out there would just somehow become mysteriously receptive to suggestions from designers, more inclined to obey us, and of course pay us more. It's a nice dream, but it's only a dream. There is no such invisible gas.

The only way design gets more respect is when an individual designer creates a great design for a single client. It's a war that's fought one little battle at a time, and with each victory, things get — in some ways at least — a little bit better. The best thing AIGA has done for me, then, is exposed me to people and ideas who have made me a better designer and a more effective fighter for design.

PM You mentioned Design Observer and being exposed to people and ideas. You've been writing for Design Observer for almost three years now. How has blogging affected the way you work? What effect has it had on how you approach design?

MB I've always liked writing, but I didn't take it seriously until we started Design Observer. There are many things I like about blogging. Selfishly, it gives me a way to think through issues with the discipline that happens when you put things in writing. To the extent that people read the pieces, particularly from outside the profession, I hope it gives them a little more insight into what the world of design is all about.

If you're reading a long comment thread, the really interesting contributions can seem few and far between. It's the offline contacts and conversations that have been more rewarding for me. A few times I've walked into a meeting, and I'll be surprised by someone who brings up something from the blog. More often than not, this person isn't even a designer. To me, this means that design is becoming something that normal people are getting more and more curious about.

Has writing a blog affected the way I work? At first I was going to say no, but when I think about it, I realize that it's helped me get more confident that the issues that we designers deal with are relevant in the outside world. This in turn has helped me think less as a designer faithfully sticking to the task I've been assigned, and more as a person who's willing and eager to broaden the context for the work. Like I've said before, this is the only way I know to make my work better.

PM Your statement about evolving into a "person who's willing and eager to broaden the context for the work" resonates very strongly with what we're trying to achieve with our User Experience Week event. In prior years, we focused on issues of web design; whereas this year, alongside our web design material are discussions of product strategy and design, design of services, cross-cultural research, mobile devices, museum design, comics, and information visualization.

So, I guess I'd like you to expand a bit on "the issues that we designers deal with [that] are relevant in the outside world." Is it that these designers' issues have actually always been relevant and the outside world only now realizes it? Or is it that designers are only now addressing these issues relevant in the outside world? Whichever, what has led to this change? Any examples from your work you could share?

MB Back in 1975 I was relatively precocious. I knew what graphic design was (most seventeen-year-olds didn't) and I entered a university program in graphic design that started teaching graphic design studio classes in its freshman year (many such courses didn't). I was really into graphic design, so I couldn't have been happier.

It took me a while to discover that graphic design was a fairly new profession and that many of the designers who did work that I admired had received a more general education than I was getting. This included not just early heroes of mine like Paul Rand, but mentors I'd meet later like Massimo Vignelli and Tibor Kalman. I got a great education in the skills a designer needs. But I slowly learned that mastering the skills of design was only one element to being successful and effective as a designer.

To this day, I'm not even sure it's the most important skill. I don't think I'm a great natural designer compared to most of my partners. I probably wasn't even the best designer in my class at school. But what I discovered was that design — and this is particularly true with graphic design — is a way to engage with real content, real experience. The key to the whole thing is your ability to learn about that stuff — what I called the "outside world" stuff — and if you can do that, your work will resonate in a way that it can't if your goal is simply resolving the formal "design" issues.

Making room for the real world is even harder today than it was thirty years ago. The amount of technical skills a young designer needs is vast, and the degree of professional specialization is staggering. All of this helps to foster an atmosphere that seems to reward tunnel vision. But in the end, the designers who are doing the most exciting work — and in some cases it coincidentally happens to be the most beautiful work — are the ones who don't hesitate to claim the whole world as their subject matter.

Now You See It

INDEX

Index

Index

CREDITS

Page 17:
Image reprinted with the permission of Polly Gnagy Seymour

Page 26:
Image reprinted with the written permission of the organization

Page 28:
© Google 2017

Page 36:
© Jeff Goldberg

Page 52:
© marish, Depositphotos

Page 59: © Charley Harper Art Studio

Page 62: Image reprinted with the permission of Jeremy M. Lange

Page 65–67:
Images reprinted with the permission of DDB North America, New York, NY

Page 69–72:
Mad Men excerpts reprinted with the permission of Lionsgate Television Inc., Santa Monica, CA

Page 75:
Reprinted with the permission of Pocket Books, a division of Simon & Schuster, Inc. All rights reserved.

Page 83:
Photo by CBS Photo Archive/Getty Images

Page 95:
Photo by Associated Press

Page 101:
© Yoshie Nishikawa/ www.yoshienishikawa. com

Page 122:
Image reprinted with the permission of Christopher Wilson

Page 126:
Image reprinted

with the permission of Experimental Jetset, Amsterdam, Netherlands

Page 132:
Image used with the written consent of the Brannock Device Co., Inc., Liverpool, NY

Page 147:
© New York City Transit Authority. Image reproduced with permission of Standards Manual, LLC.

Page 159:
Image used with the written consent of IOC, Lausanne, Switzerland

Page 170:
Images reprinted with the permission of University of California Office of the President, Oakland, CA

Page 188:
Image reprinted with the permission of Kalle Lasn

Page 204:
Images reprinted with the permission of the Metropolitan Museum of Art, New York, NY

Page 217:
Image reprinted with the permission of Karen Todd

This book was designed by Michael Bierut and Aron Fay and typeset in Schmalfette (Walter Haettenschweiler, 1954; digitized by Jeremy Mickel, 2014), Benton Modern (Tobias Frere-Jones, 1997), and Benton Sans (Tobias Frere-Jones, 1995).

Special thanks to Erica Olsen for proofreading; to Susan Clements for indexing; to Tess McCann for her tireless and ingenious research support; and, especially, to Sara Stemen for expertly editing this book from its earliest days to its final details.